Blade Runners
Lives in Football

Gary Armstrong

To Mum and Dad

blade
runners
LIVES IN FOOTBALL

Gary Armstrong

 The **Hallamshire** Press 1998

© 1998 **The Hallamshire Press**

Photographs:
Pages 44 and 248, courtesy of Denis Clarebrough.
Pages 92, 93, 106, 121, 169, 177, 182, 215, 227, 270, 283,
    294, 306 and 332, courtesy of Martyn Harrison.
Pages 111, 160, 172, 184, 189 and 225, courtesy of Matthew Bell.
Pages 140, 144 and 148, thanks to Bob Booker.
Page 291, thanks to Andy Daykin.
Cover photograph, thanks to Billy Whitehurst.
All other photographs courtesy of Sheffield Newspapers.

Published by **The Hallamshire Press**

The Hallamshire Press is an imprint of
Interleaf Productions Limited
Broom Hall, Sheffield S10 2DR

Typeset by Interleaf Productions Limited
Printed by The Cromwell Press, Trowbridge, Wiltshire.

British Library Cataloguing in Publication Data:
    A catalogue record for this book is available from the British Library

ISBN 1 874718 38 5

Contents

Acknowledgements

A variety of individuals, occasions and promptings assisted in the production of what follows. Nevertheless, I take full responsibility for what is written: all of it ultimately the end product of my curiosity, questioning and occasional feats of endurance.

Because all the lives featured herein were at one time involved with Sheffield United Football Club, I owe a big thank-you to the men who took me as an eight-year-old to watch the red and white wizards of Bramall Lane. The first to do so was the Reverend Tony Frain and the next was my dad. Without their kindness, tolerance of my silly questions and the sacrifice of their free time, this book would not have been written. Over the next 30 years I attended United matches with a variety of mates and acquaintances, the company and location in the ground changing with the season as life got a hold of us in various ways. You know who you are and my thanks go out to all of you.

All followers of Sheffield United contributed in some ways to this work. Over the decades your passions were infectious and your comments, be they of praise or abuse, towards the team and club were noted and often resurrected in interviews. Particular thanks, however, are due to a few individuals whose generosity and hospitality I cannot hope to return. Thus I am indebted to Denis Clarebrough, United's historian, whose wonderful archive collection and generosity with material and memories make him in my eyes a gentleman and a scholar. A similar debt is due to Matthew Bell, the editor of the United fanzine, *Flashing Blade*, both for access to his databases and personal memories and for the opportunity he provided to publish my early writings.

Conversations over beer or on telephone lines accompanied by many laughs with Pete Stone and Mick Rooker provided many other non-official, even scurrilous, accounts of life at a football club. The former, the secretary of the travel club, holds a football memory indicative of a form of autism or at least a sad life. The latter, the pools manager at

Bramall Lane, makes me ask: Has a more decent bloke ever been employed by United? Many of the interviews were facilitated by Mick and his one-time boss, Andy Daykin, to whom I also owe a big thank-you. Others were a product of the former United manager, Dave 'Harry' Bassett, who allowed me access to his squad and an insight into a football world that millions of fans and journalists would die for. A big thanks to the best manager Sheffield United has ever had.

For the ability to read my handwriting and decipher my corrections I am indebted, as I have been for ten years now, to Karen Kinnaird. For seven years' tolerance towards my affliction to Sheffield United I have to thank my wife, Hani, who, sensibly, when the subject is football, cannot see what all the fuss is about

That this book exists is down to the competence of the commissioning editors at the Hallamshire Press: in Pauline Climpson and Andrew Fyfe I found the quickest deal I have ever had in publishing and not a moment's problem in communication. For the excellent task in proofing and editing I am grateful to Dean Bargh.

Finally, sincere thanks are due to all the men profiled in this collection. I owe gratitude to you all for your time, memories and honesty. I thank you also for the part you all played in the making of 'my' team and club.

Gary Armstrong
September 1998

Prologue

The starting point for this book is envy. Why is it that some men can make a living out of doing things they loved doing as a child while the vast majority of us cannot? Running around half-dressed in the fresh air kicking a ball in a contrived theatre of emotions which does not last too long was always considered a good and healthy thing to do by elders and later in life provided for a lucky few the chance to be well paid and take the acclaim of partisan audiences. Unable to match them in footballing ability, I had to content myself with being a critical but loyal spectator of one team: Sheffield United. Too old now to play football of any decent standard, the only role that remains for me in the game is in describing people, places and events that I (and no doubt most readers) wished they had been part of in some way.

All the men who feature in what follows had a destiny in football—rarely was it totally of their own making. All of them experienced a degree of fame and celebrity status that for the most part left them when they left the game, but which they will always retain to some degree depending on their one-time footballing ability or notoriety. Some of the men I met had an ability for football that bordered on genius. Others could motivate in a way no textbook could ever capture. Others were not particularly good players, but tried their best. Eulogising the former is easy, but it takes a lot of hard work to portray mediocrity—and that is a quality that the fans of Sheffield United have had more than their share of over the past 50 years.

My main aim in this work is to attempt to provide accounts of lives in a way that seeks to explain, not criticise. If statues exist or portraits are hung on pub walls commemorating the critic, I have yet to see them. Besides which, like many of us in our lives, failure is something we have all endured in our pursuit of success. What is revealed in these lives is, at times, unremarkable; at other times it is tragic; some details just provoke anger. Professional football can be a wonderful occupation, but it is frequently cruel. If some accounts seem banal, remember that football provides a euphoric spectacle that provokes the euphoria in the event itself, rather than in anticipation or memory. My purpose is not to provide endless exposés, but to permit those involved in one football club over a period of around 45 years to explain how they came to be there and, once there, what their lives involved and what became of them when they left. With such a level of curiosity around these people, it surprises me no end to read the platitudes and banalities afforded by the plethora of football magazines and official club publications. Why there is no greater curiosity I cannot explain, but I am not complaining, as this gap in the market makes for what follows.

The reason why a subject area is selected, researched and ultimately published is always largely due to the biography of the researcher. I am a Sheffield United fan, which means I am, to borrow from the club's nickname, a Blade. I therefore still harbour an ambition to play for the team and, once in it, to humiliate city rivals Sheffield Wednesday in front of a worldwide audience of millions. Being a Blade means I cannot stand anything to do with the success of Sheffield Wednesday. That said, a reader must not get me wrong: some of my best friends in life have been supporters of the Owls, but I would not want one living next door or seeking the hand of my daughter in marriage. Furthermore, I was a parks footballer and played for years at 'pub football' level. Consequently, I am part of the millions of similar status who, by virtue of running about on a Sunday morning, become instant experts on the game up to its highest level for the rest of their life.

Football was the biggest 'thing' in my life until the age of 18. Then adulthood crept up, and with it other responsibilities and the pursuit of other recognitions and dramas. I hold no illusion about what I could have achieved in the game. I can categorically state that I had not the ability nor, more importantly, the 'heart' to become a professional player. Content to spectate, I now rejoice in my team in a more dispassionate way than in former days. Nonetheless, I was and remain fascinated by the occupational culture of the professional footballer and all the people who make a living tending to his needs.

My first knowledge of professional footballers came from an uncle who played for Sheffield United in the mid-1960s. Thus, as a child, I regularly saw a First Division player when he visited the family home. He was unlike any grown-up man I knew at the time, in that he was lithe, walked in a funny way, had a brand-new car and wore pastel-coloured V-neck sweaters. Between the ages of 8 and 14 I met other players via him at the other clubs he went to. Over the past 20 years, I have been in his company maybe three hours in total and have no idea when I will see him next. So there is no sentimental story of a much-loved uncle or mentor, just some oblique fascination with something that, in juvenile years, passed as exotic and status-enhancing in the eyes of my peers.

Since then I have met dozens, if not hundreds, of players. They are different to men the same age as them. Their pinched faces and healthy glow puts them in the category of the seriously fit. Most have the ability to talk to a wide variety of people, listen to their comments and, while staring into the distance, allow themselves a banal reply and smile which oscillates between patronising, loathing and affection. In a world of thousand well-wishers and back-slappers who become abusive and critical very quickly, maybe players need the ability to be dismissive or talk without listening and get away with it. But why is it that we as fans can then depart satisfied with our exchange and care little for what the player might be calling us in the company of fellow professionals?

One question that I cannot answer and which remains in the domains of, variously, philosophy, anthropology and maybe even psychiatry, is what a football club actually is. I know it's something to do with bricks and mortar, something to do with personalities and memories, and more to do with identity and urban living, but I'm stumped if I can articulate what it is that makes me follow and worry about 'Sheffield United FC'. In the absence of definitions, I find it easier to let those that made the club have their say.

Selected mainly by my personal choice, but occasionally by the promptings of Blades curious about particular individuals, what follows comprises the life stories of 25 men associated with Sheffield United FC in various ways over five decades. For some, their times at Bramall Lane were brief; others were around for decades. Some remember their days at Bramall Lane as their best; others remember the place with less treasured memories. The book aims to allow its subjects to provide their versions of history in their own words. In a world of competing truths, this collection presents 'truth' as told from the lips of those responding to my questions. Others aware of the facts of the same matter may well hold different versions of the truth. Hopefully, future publications will consider discrepancies or points of view.

My task, besides being the one who posed the questions, is to 'build' the character of those interviewed via archive and opinion. Each interview has a theme: some will be more explicit than others, but on each must hang an idea or epoch. Some conversations are presented in colloquial English—some people come across better in dialect than others; others have their conversations presented in a more formal manner; some interviews contain strong language, which I refuse to sanitise. All of these were my decisions, based on an attempt to convey character to a reader. The alternative to these approaches is an absence of mediation, which in my eyes is monotonous in style and too often simply public relations for those interviewed. Readers will thus have to permit me the conceit of commentary and attempts at analysis, which means judging both me and the interviewee. While you do, please recognise that my primary purpose is to describe and detail people and events that many of you were aware of when they occurred or know about in retrospect, but either way wish you had at least known about to a fuller extent.

The table of contents shows many absences. The most notable is that of women. In this decade, any book about football seemingly has to have a 'women's angle' to satisfy the metropolitan middle-class female, many of whom, discovering the game post-1990, think they have invented the wheel. Such people can rest assured that the day a woman plays for the first team or reserves or becomes a significant figure in the backroom staff or board of directors at Bramall Lane, I will be the first to ask for an interview. Other absences will be noted by Blades, many of whom will inevitably ask why wasn't *x* included? The answer is a combination of limited space and my personal discrimination.

Distance and death made for other absences. The death of the great Jimmy Hagan—probably the greatest post-war United player in his 20-year career—in January 1998 was preceded by many years of a degenerative illness. He was not capable of providing an interview and is the most notable omission. Another is the manager between 1981 and 1986, Ian Porterfield, whom I tracked down to Oman in the Middle East. His time in charge elicits very strong emotion in those connected with the club and I would have loved to meet him, but the distance made it impossible and I do not do interviews over the phone.

I chose people whom I felt had a story to tell. More famous players than some of those included do not always have such interesting careers or lives. Nonetheless, there is always the chance of them appearing, should readers consider a second volume worthwhile.

Introduction: Sheffield—United by Football?

Is it strange that desire should so many years outlive performance?

[William Shakespeare, *Henry IV, Part 2*, II.iv]

THE MOST APPROPRIATE PLACE for a book about footballing lives to be written is surely the city in which the game began—Sheffield. A variation of the game we know has been played in the Sheffield region since the late eighteenth century (cf. Young 1964); industrialised society simply changed the rules somewhat. Since its codification (in Sheffield) and popularisation nationally and internationally in the mid-nineteenth century, the game of association football, and the football ground, has been, and remains, alongside the public house, the male working-class leisure space *par excellence*.

The game has always provided degrees of identity. The football ground initially offered the late-nineteenth-century industrial workers a relief from drudgery, for, only a generation removed from their former village and farm-labouring existence, such people were suffering alienation from the impersonality of town living. Since then, generations of boys and men have organised informal but rule-controlled games, often in the streets or on wasteland or recreation grounds. In the decades from the mid-1960s to the mid-'90s, tens of thousands of men in the city between the ages of 16 and 30 participated in local league teams to various levels of competency. Consequently, the South Yorkshire region is well known for producing footballers, and, amid the plethora of competing leisure interests, both strenuous and sedentary, available by 1990, South Yorkshire still had over 500 amateur clubs in Saturday leagues, and nearly 1,200 teams playing on Sundays.

The game engendered a civic pride and a sense of membership for the industrial working class, as well as providing a topic all men could talk about. Watching promoted solidarity and sociability: it is still seen in the pursuit of passion in weekly scenarios where good friends and family are replaced by a plethora of acquaintances and a temporary escape from life's realities. The game can provoke moments of happiness and hope—hence its popularity to generations of the downtrodden and poor.

All Sheffield men will have played football at school: for decades this was the only organised winter sport. No other winter sport in Sheffield can compete with football, either for players or spectators. Options are available in greyhound racing, rugby league and motorcycle speedway, but the first and last have seen better days, while the rugby league team, after only a decade of existence, is still striving to attract more than a few thousand supporters. Meanwhile, modernity challenges these traditional sports and sporting venues via Americanisation and the transglobal diffusion of sport. This has brought to Sheffield, post-1990, the indoor spectacles of ice hockey and basketball, capable of attracting decent crowds. But nothing, as yet, can compete with the crowds that watch football.

Over a hundred-year period, professional football matches have provided (and still provide) gatherings that have no parallel in Sheffield. What else could regularly attract 50,000 to stand or sit for two hours in the open, frequently in winter? Seduced by an unscripted drama, every motion is open to question, to ridicule and is a vehicle for constant disappointment for the fans. It is an enchanting dramatic activity in which standards can never be hidden nor the customer be deceived. It is an arena in which spectators can shout, dance, gesture and abuse others—rights denied us for the most part elsewhere today. For decades, the match was regarded as a liminal zone, in which much male behaviour and opinion that is not permitted or articulated elsewhere was easily accepted. Fans attend to experience pain, envy, despair, euphoria, all wrapped up in two hours of love and hate mixed with sincerity, passion and humanity. The match permits 90 minutes of ridicule, rejoicing, indignation and a chance to suggest to very fit muscular men that their sexuality is unconventional, or that they are a disgrace to their trade. And all of this without the fear of them physically beating you by way of reply. Indeed, the game induces a kind of all-consuming, irrational and totally child-like happiness in adults and even a form of promiscuity, as an individual shares passion with, at times, total strangers.

The simplest way of expressing one's Sheffield United/Blade identity is to enter United's Bramall Lane ground. Football grounds—the icons to the community from which the club draws its followers—are revered emblems of local identity. They enjoy the personality of place, and have always been subject to social demarcation. Areas within the ground are self-selecting, with demarcations for decades dependent on price differentials. Today, these separations are mostly informal, with people choosing the space to suit their personal preferences.

Impressive in juvenile years, the football ground still inspires feeling in a devoted fan later in life. At one time, to an under-12, it was the wonderment of so many voices, the plumes of cigarette smoke rising from packed terraces, the twinkling of hundreds of matches and lighters igniting cigarettes in the darkness of night games. In adolescence, the ground permitted a growing social awareness. Thus, in the 1970s, from the middle of the Shoreham End looking towards the Bramall Lane End, one could see Sheffield old and new contrasted. To the left, in the 'gaps' between the ground's building structures, one could see the back-to-back buildings that had been there for a hundred years and housed the small workshops of the steel industry. In contrast, in the right-hand gap, one saw the vulgar modernism of three 15-storey tower blocks. Behind this lay the leafy south-western middle-class suburbs with two imposing hospital and university buildings dominating.

From the Bramall Lane End, visiting fans could see beyond one corner of the Shoreham End to the 'model' estate of Norfolk Park. In the 1970s, this was the Council's pride and joy, for it was modern, with plenty of greenery, and a symbol of the brave new world of Municipal Socialism. Since the mid-1970s, fans sitting beyond the halfway point to the rear of the South Stand could see the city-centre skyline across the roof of the John Street side. The once-dominant spires to the Glory of God have competed with, but now lost out to, the new god of money, and to the new cathedrals of corporate worship. Not all fans will notice this, but some do.

The Two Clubs: Two Reputations

Antagonisms and oppositions around football identities in Sheffield take many forms, but have always centred around the conflicting loyalties of Blades and Owls, the nicknames given to Sheffield United and Sheffield Wednesday and adopted by their fans. But many refer to their rivals by the mutual term of abuse: 'the Pigs'.[1] Hostilities take various forms: most blatantly, certainly, since the mid-1960s, Blades have always wanted the Wednesday team to lose. A United victory and Wednesday defeat achieved what the victorious factions term a 'Sheffield Double'. United fans generally enjoy a certain *Schadenfreude* at their rivals' misfortunes, be they at a club, player or fan level.

---

1. The term 'Pigs' as a form of mutual abuse began in the 1970s. United fans claim they invented the term as an insulting substitute for 'Owls'. The Wednesday fans claim they pioneered its use because United's kit of red and white stripes looked like rashers of bacon.

There have been various forms of hostile but non-violent opposition around the notion of football loyalties centred on identification with respective colours, fan numbers and football chants. Thousands of United fans (and Wednesday fans) have taken part in some or all of these oppositions. The association of club colours has always been taken seriously. From their beginnings, United have always worn a kit of red and white stripes, with Wednesday in a similar one of blue and white. Match days would always see colour-demarcated ground division, but colour rivalry also exists outside match day. Some United fans could never wear blue sweaters or jackets or paint their homes blue, and the opposite is true for Wednesday fans. Colour prejudice also affected smoking habits, with some Blades never purchasing the popular Embassy Regal cigarettes because of the blue and white packaging, preferring plain Embassy with its red and white packaging. Fans would argue heatedly about who had the biggest support or highest level of loyalty.

It cannot easily be argued that success in football competitions is the reason that large numbers of loyal fans flock to watch United and Wednesday. Historically, neither side has been superior to the other for very long; and neither has won an FA Cup or League Championship for over 50 years. Recently, Wednesday won the Coca-Cola Cup in 1991 and have been beaten finalists in that cup and the FA Cup in 1993. Overall, however, the city has not seen much silverware—United have not won a thing for 70 years. Considering this, the loyalty manifested in attendance figures is staggering and, from a population of half a million people, the clubs could attract a combined average of 50,000 per game when both were in the Premier League in 1990–94 and, needless to say, they could pack Wembley Stadium in 1993 for the United–Wednesday FA Cup semi-final.

There is no obvious social or historical reason why the United–Wednesday rivalry should be so strong. The bitterness often expressed from either side seems quite remarkable. One possible explanation comes from the Sheffield journalist, Jonathan Foster, who states:

> Sheffield is a uniquely insular city, the least cosmopolitan of all the large cities in Britain, with little apart from football in which jealousy or passion can be invested (*The Independent*, April 1993).

In a search for explanations, the history of the two clubs provides some clues as to some of the later rivalry (cf. Young 1964; Farnsworth 1982; Clarebrough 1989). The Wednesday team were founded in 1867 from a cricket club consisting of traders who had a day-off on a Wednesday.

The football team was established to keep members together through the winter. United were formed in 1889 from the Sheffield United Cricket Club when a member of the ground staff at Bramall Lane saw an FA Cup semi-final played there. The revenue it had grossed, added to the appeal the game held prompted him, with an eye to potential future profits, to suggest to the directors that another football club could be founded.[2] The owners of Bramall Lane formed a football team (Sheffield United) and advertised for players. Having advertised in Scotland, the club drew a large response, and in the first season the team consisted mainly of Scottish players! Regardless of the player's birthplace, the foundation of the new club caused tension. The first 'derby' match was in 1890. The following season the clubs met twice and supporters of both sides produced funeral cards announcing the death of the rival side. Local football archivist Farnsworth (1982: 33) notes:

> It is said that some families were so divided on this issue that fathers ceased to speak to sons and brothers fell out with brother.

Historian and club archivist Clarebrough (1989) tells of hostility between the two clubs founded on accusations that United were trying to poach Wednesday players. No doubt this was exacerbated when in 1890 United undercut Wednesday's admission charges and, at the same time, several Wednesday players joined United. Matches between the sides were violent occasions. One game in 1892 saw players leap into the crowd to fight spectators before 40 police restored order.[3]

---

2. United existed in name before the football team and United's Bramall Lane ground was originally used by Wednesday and other teams in the city. When Wednesday turned professional in 1877, their desire for the full receipts from admissions led them to move to a new ground. Initially, this was close to Bramall Lane, at Olive Grove. They were to play at four grounds before finding their home at Hillsborough.

3. Players crossing the city either way are remarkably few in number. The first was Bernard Oxley, sold in 1935 by United to Wednesday. Two years later, United took a player on a free transfer called George Cole. Not until 1948 did the next transaction occur, when Joe Cockcroft sign for United for a small fee. In 1952, United's reserve centre-half went to Wednesday, but never played in a first-team match. A gap of over 30 years passed before, in 1987, Jeff King signed for United on a free transfer. Since Terry Curran's move from Hillsborough in 1982 only Wilf Rostron has moved to United on a free transfer in 1989.

In origin, then, United fans were men who were not dyed-in-the-wool Wednesday fans, and were drawn from other declining clubs in the city, the local population around the Bramall Lane ground, or were those who wished to be part of a new ground and new team—perhaps even the city's social aspirants and *nouveau riche*. The Wednesday were the older, more traditional club, who, as a gathering of market traders, might be said to represent the local male *petit bourgeoisie*. The nicknames of each club that the supporters have adopted have a varied history. The term 'Blades' was a journalistic cliché attached to any team from Sheffield at one time (akin to speaking of the men from 'Steel City'). As such, no club can claim to have originated the term. Ironically, Wednesday were originally nicknamed 'the Blades' and United, founded later, were, like all teams from Sheffield at the time, referred to as 'The Cutlers'. When Wednesday moved from Olive Grove to a new ground at Owlerton (close to their present one at Hillsborough), they lost the nickname 'Blades' and became known as 'the Owls'. United then became known as 'the Blades'.

Divisions of football loyalty are today not perceived to have any origins in class, race or geography. There is no marked difference in the localities from which the supporters come. Unsurprisingly, there is a certain clustering of support in the districts surrounding the grounds of each club—Wednesday to the north, United to the south-east. Otherwise, each team draws support from every part of Sheffield and the surrounding villages and districts. There is no correlation here between football support and religious or political identity.

One aspect of the rivalry is found in the relative status of the two clubs. When the Football League doubled in size in 1882, the 14 founder members permitted two more teams to join Division One. In a ballot, Wednesday were admitted to Division One, United to Division Two. Because of this, Wednesday have ever since been seen as the city's premier club, giving the United fans a chip on their shoulders and an inferiority complex in respect of their more famous neighbours. Such a status is visibly evident. At Wednesday's Hillsborough ground, a magnificent cantilever stand was built in the early 1960s to host the 1966 World Cup preliminary rounds. It was only a matter of time before United had a similar stand in an attempt to compete for similar international status. Completed in 1975, it crippled United financially for the next 20 years.

Status (and prejudice) is more than structural, however, and many Unitedites believe the local powers-that-be are against their club. As many a Unitedite will tell you, 'They are all Pigs.' Thus, the elected members of Sheffield Council have been dismissed since the 1970s (bar a few honourable exceptions) as consisting of an unofficial branch of Wednesday's Supporters' Club. However, the evidence was not overwhelming, although to Unitedites the Council's anti-United bias was typified by their refusal of the United chairman's development plans in 1983 for Bramall Lane, and this opinion is probably not just uninformed prejudice. If publicity was anything to go by, there were more councillors who watched Wednesday than United throughout the 1980s, though what this actually meant was difficult to argue.

United fans, however, had their own litany of mistreatment. In 1984, with Wednesday winning promotion to Division One, a civic reception at the Town Hall was given for the team. Then, as United were surprisingly promoted to Division Two a few weeks later, they too were given a reception. Of course, to the United fans, this only came about because the Council had been compelled to appear impartial. Later, in 1990, with United promoted to Division One, Blades awaited a similar treatment to that which the Council had afforded Wednesday in 1984—an open-top bus ride around the city. They are still waiting.

The link between Council and Wednesday has a long history and, as Fishwick (1989: 30) notes, Wednesday, as the older club, always had closer links with the local élite than United. Furthermore, Unitedites believed that the local evening paper, *The Star*, had, and still has, a Wednesday bias. Older United fans have still not forgiven its 1973–74 'Save Our Owls' campaign, as Wednesday struggled at the bottom of Division Two. This campaign consisted of *The Star* producing and distributing thousands of stickers, posters and badges, and advertising discount admission prices. The 'Save Our Owls' logo adorned the top of the sports page for two weeks. The campaign was futile, however, for Wednesday failed to win any of their last 17 games and were relegated. In 1980–81, United were able to fall all the way to Division Four without even the hint of a similar campaign and, in their opinion, received fewer 'photo specials' in the paper after a big match and had fewer slogans comparable to the 'Good Luck to the Owls' printed on the sports sheet before big games. Many United fans despise this apparent bias, but have to buy the newspaper because there is no other source of local football news.

Football Support: Duty and Devotion

The experience of attending a match is not defined by any formal structure: the essence of support is its essential anti-structure. How, we might ask, is this devotion and duty to a football club learned? The answer, to a large degree, is that fans are 'autodidacts', i.e. self-taught with self-agreed knowledge. In part, this is learned through their own oral community, and in part from regular attendance. Although at times moral to the point of piety and self-righteous to a level that provokes ridicule, they are also passionate with an envy and spite that reveals them to be completely hypocritical. This is the appeal of it all!

Some would postulate that love of football is not due merely to its practice or spectacle but, in Bromberger *et al*.'s (1993: 117) argument, to its 'dramatic qualities', which they equate with the 'genres of theatrical production' providing a unity of time, space and action which favours the communion between players and spectators. Whatever the reason, 'fandom' produces people who are neither rational in their thinking nor polite. What this means is that they do not sit on the fence, for fans do not seek the approval of other men.

Fandom is also sentimental. Fans' collective memories generate affection and romance and help make sense of the world. We talk of our teams and our experiences of being a fan. There are varying self-delusions, ways of remembering, nostalgias and narratives. For some, football support can be a rock of stability in an uncertain world. For others, the game offers a surrogate community for the lonely. Football can also provide a leisure focus for those who belong by deepening integration; exposure to football can lead to knowledge of other topics. It is all things to everybody. In a complex, industrial and allegedly rational world, football actually seems somewhat anomalous.

Without doubt, there is a quasi-religious aspect to support: loyalty is a form of faith, an element of existence never fully explicable. You either have it or you do not, and, for those with it, football (like religion) gives 'meaning' to life. Like religion, football is a ritual with cultural constructs that generates symbolic communication with performance elements. It 'says' and 'does' and has meaning and value for the participants by allowing for various emotions. Like religion and religious ceremonies, the match provokes emotions that allow for a view of the world that reflects social relations and various other phenomena: the comic, the tragic and the manifestations of attitudes that the converted and devoted presume to be 'correct'. We construct ideas of the 'virtuous' and the 'bad' and, like a Greek tragedy, allow the game to articulate theatrical conventions. The plot and ideology are constant, the actors change, but support continues despite the personalities of the players. Fandom introduces ideas of Fate and Fortune, and achievement, whether as player or spectator, is rarely seen to be the provenance of merit or grace alone. The game, both for players and spectators, is a source of massive contradiction, for it aims to reward the best, yet really enhances the role of luck. And, if this is assisted by cheating, then so be it. Fans soon learn that the best and fairest do not always win, and that status is precarious. Fame is a fickle mistress and you are only as good as your last performance. Indeed, football is beyond your control as a fan—and sometimes as a player—for it is plain unfair.

Missionary Positions?

The fan, however, is an illusory participant; managers, players and, in particular, the chairmen are the real power-holders. But that does not stop thousands from enjoying the feeling that they are important. In this sense, the game could be seen from a Marxist perspective as a form of false consciousness: a way of keeping down the 'dangerous class' under Industrial Capitalism and thus promoted by middle-class teachers and clerics who promulgated a game they had learned at public school. One could argue that this was the reason the Sheffield and Hallamshire Football Association was founded. Its aims were missionary: to make the game and people who played it 'respectable'. Its officials were mainly middle class, but the teams' players and their spectators were working class (Fishwick 1986: 10), originating in pubs, factories, shops and even churches. In fact, the local Bible Class League was, until its demise in 1991, renowned for taking Muscular Christianity to extreme levels!

The game could always provoke rowdy behaviour, both at the grounds and in the streets. (In 1908, Sheffield Wednesday had their ground closed because of the rowdy behaviour of spectators.) Fishwick (1989) cites letters from 'Ratepayers' to the Sheffield press in the 1920s and '30s complaining about noise, swearing, rowdiness and betting, consequent to the football, which disturbed their Saturday afternoons. Because of this, the provision of football pitches for native young men was not a priority of the Socialist City Council, and, in the inter-war years, they even banned collections for junior football club funds. Sheffield magistrates discovered they had been sending youths to prison for playing football in the streets in 1928. Unknown to them, the exact nature of the 'crime' had been changed in the prosecution evidence to a charge of 'disorderly behaviour'! (Cf. Jones 1988: 137.)

Despite this, and rather contrarily, football was encouraged by industrialists in times of social worry. In 1912, pit managers organised teams and competitions for striking miners, reportedly to keep the men from trade union activity (Fishwick 1986: 19, 27). Whether this worked is not known. Similarly, the city's one-time largest employer, steel magnate Sir Robert Hadfield, promoted the game with the intention of combating industrial unrest and post-First World War fears of Bolshevism, as well as to increase fitness and productivity (Fishwick 1989: 13).

Later, the game was seen as a way of absorbing the monotony of unemployment (Fishwick 1986: 44). In the 1930s, unemployed leagues were organised by the local FA with the support of the local press and City Council, but hand in hand with property-owners. Private pitches were made available, producing, in Fishwick's words, a paternalism from those with power and money to those with neither (1989: 13-16). Nevertheless, this did not stop a 6,000-strong riot in 1935, or the barracking of police football teams by unemployed spectators.

Perhaps significantly, shortly after the General Strike, with Wednesday having won promotion to Division One, 40,000 people, including civic dignitaries, employers and employees, watched a Sheffield derby. As Fishwick noted, this was not a city on the brink of social revolution; on the contrary, 'football seemed to represent a spirit of solidarity and continuity' (1989: 138). To assist this, in 1932 and 1934 Sheffield United even attempted to reduce admission for the unemployed; but the Football League Management Committee refused them permission! (Mason 1980: 170.) And, in response to rumours that the unemployed would storm the gates at the next home game, hundreds of police surrounded the ground. It was not until Christmas 1992 (i.e. 60 years later) that a scheme was proposed whereby the unemployed and full-time students could gain reduced admission.

Sport is always influenced by the resources people have or can acquire. Hence, sport in Britain has always had a class dimension. To some extent, then, contest between classes is the norm, although various authors who address this issue disagree on the nature of the contest and the effects. The local industrial, working-class culture that grew in the South Yorkshire region was built around collective planning and the discipline of labour, both of which exhibited pride in masculine strength and self-reliance. There are plenty of skilled, working-class men to be found in this milieu and toughness abounds, but these same men have placed and still place great prestige in an industrial skill (and not just brawn) that always involved considerable care in order to escape injury or death.

Like such denizens of the factories or coal mines, footballers are appreciated for the variety of their diverse abilities. One would presumably analyse the male, working-class culture of Sheffield, look at both the skilled steel-making artisan's independence and then analyse those whose occupation produced a proletarian, collectivist experience in steel and coal production. Maybe we could then deploy words such as 'tough', 'grafters', 'skilled', 'teamwork', 'craftsmen', and presume a correlate. This would be very pragmatic. The Italian sociologist, Portelli (1993: 91), seeks parallels between the masculine style of a city and its team's style of play. But could we presume any simple connection between the performances of the local football teams and the industrial performance of the workers? For me, the game does not simply reflect society or culture, but rather as Archetti and Romero (1994) postulate, the game

> is part of a general process of the way society models some of its central existential, moral and political issues.

Significant here are the words of Harry Pearson (1994: 111), whose brilliant study of north-eastern football culture reflects on this issue:

> Men who during working hours proved beyond doubt their durability had no need to use a game to advertise their toughness. Instead football was a means to show they were capable of more than their jobs allowed; of brilliance and creativity.

Holt (1986: 165) similarly addresses this when arguing:

> The plain truth is that we do not know how football was culturally related to work. The game has no agreed 'essence', no single or uncontested meaning which can be explained in terms of work.

There was, however, a decade-old belief that, in seeking a good strong footballer, one had only to whistle down a pit shaft. Coal mining communities made sport a central part of their lives and contributed throughout this century to sporting achievement in rugby, cricket and particularly football.

Playing with Style

It is not possible to argue for a 'Sheffield style' of playing the game, for its manifestation at a professional level has not been consistent. Changing with the team selections and player purchases of the managers of the two clubs, any discernible style could not be said to have a local origin, as, for one thing, no United manager has ever hailed from the city (until 1998 when Steve Thompson was caretaker-manager for three months).

Nevertheless, players and spectators expect from their clubs something unquantifiable and vague. This is 'commitment', and it operates on two levels. One is embodied by the supporters standing by the team through thick and thin; the other is embodied in performance on the pitch. Fans want to see a player 'active' and 'involved', and matches at the city's two professional team grounds reverberate to shouts encouraging players to 'get stuck in'. Spectators require a level of masculinity that will not shy from physical challenges, and above all these players must not act as the masculine antithesis that would see them classified as: 'bloody fairies', 'gret puffs' or 'nesh bastards'. The ideal player 'gets a good one in early doors', i.e. strongly challenges an opponent at the first opportunity to imply there is more where that came from. This is a form of intimidation that is intrinsically part of the nature of a game where physicality is respected.

At both junior and adult level, the game is played to a series of clichés full of masculine double-talk and metaphor, which players adopt to construct a seriousness and commitment out of nothing. The game permits various antagonisms to present themselves. Thus parks and recreation grounds resound to cries of criticism, praise and frustration from team-mates and those whose skills lie in 'management': 'you're watchin''; 'peddle'; 'build it'; 'get a foot on it'; 'get a grip'; 'calm it darn'; 'jockey [harass] 'im'; 'in 'im'; 'on 'im'; 'get a man!'; 'let's have a jump'; 'put 'im under'; 'up 'is arse'; ''it 'im hard'; 'and again'; 'don't wanna know'; 'get interested'; 'quality, son'; 'bottle's gone'; 'playin' like bloody women'; 'come and stand wi' me'; 'let 'im know you're there'. Injured players are treated to a variety of helpful suggestions: 'get t'spray'; 'bucket o' watter'll sort it'; 'run it off'; and the comforting 'tha'll be oreyt'. All of this is in pursuit of some vague idea of glory best encapsulated by the words of the Italian footballing genius, Roberto Baggio, who states: 'There's no achievement more beautiful than the one you achieved by sweat' (*The Guardian*, 18 May 1998).

Drawing on this legacy, the ideal team, for generations of United supporters, would contain a backbone of muscle and brawn colloquially described as three 'big hard bastards' who would 'battle' in a 'team full o' triers', and who would 'die for t'Blades', and, when necessary, 'dish out some clog'. That said, all football teams, while containing 'stoppers' and 'kickers and cloggers' will have alongside them 'nippy wingers' and 'midfield maestros', as well as those seen as idle but indispensable: the 'goal-hangers' and 'shit-liners', who seem to do nothing but do score goals. These, too, are appreciated, for football is not a non-competitive pastime based on word recognition. It is often war which, even if normally without the casualties, produces an *esprit de corps* and the type of player who will be known as a 'man's man'.

The Making of Football Men

The obvious element in all of this is that it is synonymous with men. Without a doubt, the game provides access to male credibility. As the anthropologist, Lever (1984: 155), reminds us, 'virtually all male socialisation, not just sport, teaches boys to be competitive'. Explaining why football is so popular is difficult. The historian Holt (1986) relates the game to Geertz's (1973) idea of 'deep play', arguing that football is like a mirror for its spectators. It is, he tells us,

> [a] celebration of intensely male values...where skill and cunning were valued, but hardness, stamina, courage, and loyalty were even more important. Fairness and good manners were not held in high regard (Holt 1989: 173).

A consequence of this is violence, because as various commentators have argued, sport provokes a desire to 'do violence to others' and likewise to be attacked and suffer. Suffering is common in local adult leagues, which for a minority provide the occasion to express a very high level of footballing ability. For the majority, the 11 am Sunday-morning kick-off is the theatre of the 'pub player': the moment when the Tap-Room Twelve become athletic heroes. For some, the amateur game is an uncomfortable occasion when the previous evening's alcoholic activities have to be run off in sub-zero temperatures. And, for others, there is the growing realisation that, for those in their early 30s, someone young enough to be their son can run rings around them.

For those under 16, suffering is usually postponed until the Sunday-afternoon match. Subjective experience suggests these afternoons are usually very cold and wet, with the only accompaniment to break the quiet of these moments coming from the ice-cream vans' chimes. To make things worse, opponents are usually bigger, the pitch is too hard or too wet, and the ball is too heavy. This is not everyone's idea of fun.

It is popularly believed that the concept of emotion and irrationality is a female trait, but when we look at football playing and spectating we can see how it allows men to express these qualities. Even though, a century ago, women were observed at Bramall Lane in numbers (Mason 1980: 171), cultural mores say that football is a 'man's game'. Women played organised games of football in the city during and after the First World War (Fishwick 1986: 26). In 1992, a junior girls' football league was established in the city with ten teams. Women were always part of the city's two supporters' clubs, but, as Fishwick documents (1989: 38, 57-58), the local press and male supporters did not have much regard for their football opinions.

Boys were and still are taken to watch 'the lads' at the match by their fathers, grandfathers or other male adults. Later, their attendance with male peers in what was a significant life-stage is taken further when allowed by guardians to go to away games. Certainly, in the period 1960–90, women supporters were a 10% minority at Bramall Lane.[4] Football in the region is the activity that allows men to hold opinions on everything, enact various levels of emotional turmoil and shout at the TV with mates. Of course, women can do all these things, but their opinions and emotions will never be considered by such male fans as significant and meaningful.

The common-sense opinion is that out of sport comes truth, respect and fun. To an extent, this may be so, but out of sport comes exclusion and a variety of reputations. Historically, one aspect of football's

---

4. I dispute figures provided by the Carling Report commissioned by the Football Association in 1994 and produced by the Leicester University Centre for Football Research, which states that the Bramall Lane audience was 21% female, for this figure was arrived at by a methodology that was flawed and produced a wildly inaccurate result. A self-selecting sample of 1,600 in a crowd of over 16,000 brought responses to the questionnaire handed out at the turnstile. Anyone who had attended between 1975 and 1995 would dispute their claim that 1 in 5 fans at Bramall Lane was female.

masculine-enhancing qualities between 1900 and 1940 has been identified by Fishwick as follows:

> There was thus a subculture of football, reinforced by other working
> class institutions and meeting places. Not to have a view on the local
> team, or to have been to the most recent local derby, would often
> have marked a man out at some of these institutions (1989: 55-56).

At one time, not to attend the match was the obvious marker of the
outsider. A more recent marker has been missing a game on TV. And,
though some consider that only by attendance can a 'true fan' be known,
millions more are informed and opinionated via television. With 'Match
of the Day' beginning on BBC in 1964 and ITV replying to this with
Sunday-afternoon regional highlights in 1968, children in the 1960s had
two opportunities for forming their footballing opinions. And, though
a male elder might take the young aspirant to the real thing, parents
were not needed for televised highlights. Indeed, they could ruin the
pursuit of credibility with your peers if they refused to allow you to
stay up beyond 10 pm to watch the Saturday-night programme; similarly, Sunday lunch where the TV was prohibited could ruin the 1 pm
highlights. Later, the 'Sportsnight' post-10 pm coverage of midweek
games' highlights beginning in the 1970s presented further dilemmas.
How could a 13- or 14-year-old tell his mates he was not allowed to
stay up that late?

Football, therefore, provoked anxiety, and reputations were precarious.
The legacy of televised football lives on today. In times of joviality, the
informal boys' match on the rec would resound to recitals of the famous
'Match of the Day' theme tune. And, though grown men no longer
sing this while running after a ball, the sound of it on the TV set in the
pub will produce a quieter bar and all eyes on the screen. The ability
to play was also a source of credibility and popularity perhaps not generated by other facets of character. Thus the game could be enabling.

The game could make or break credibility in other ways. Collecting
football memorabilia and tokens could afford kudos to the collector.
One adolescent fad was to collect cards showing the head and shoulders of the stars, which came free with bubblegum, or were distributed
with petrol station coupons. And, though all boys chewed, not all could
afford to chew enough to obtain a full set, and not all parents had cars.
Thus the quest for credibility could highlight family status and poverty.

Of course, competence in playing the game was the most obvious
source of male credibility. The best juvenile footballers were not nec-

essarily those that sported the latest kit or the most recently advertised football boot. And, in this sense, their poverty did not affect the triumph of substance over style. Finally, there was a linguistic competency gained from reading and taking in information from the football annuals and magazines; and many became a walking encyclopaedia of specialised trivia.

For the male generations that grew up in the 1960s and '70s, part of the process of becoming a fan was learning to speak in football tongues. As a sixties child, along with millions of other young men, I learned to read and speak football clichés. Thus, players that were big, clumsy (and usually ugly) were 'uncompromising'; midfielders 'probed'; wingers and small players were 'tricky'; full-backs were 'overlapping'; goalkeepers were 'dependable' or 'agile'. Managers were 'disciplinarians' or 'track-suit' and injuries had to be 'shrugged off'. Awaiting the 'full, classified results' on the TV, we all became versed in the televised pantomime of wrestling which invariably preceded (I can still reel off 15 names of various 'stars' of the ring) and knew of every small town in Scotland via the Scottish Second Division. We all knew that the bounce of the ball was 'wicked', fouls were 'blatant', getting sent off was 'marching orders', dubious goals and penalties were 'disputed', crossbars were 'rattled' some goals were scored with something called 'aplomb', late goals were 'last-gasp', and offsides were 'suspicious'. We learned by imitating the commentators' style of speech how the match could be narrated and the post-match interview handled: 'credit' must go to 'the lads'; the team are 'quietly confident'; we all 'took each game as it came'; and 'hoped to be up there at the end'. We all knew the correct ways of appealing to the crowd, how to plead when fouled, of indicating pain to fellow players and showing disgust and indignation in a variety of situations.

Later in life, the game also provided for various male metaphors and flippant remarks relating to sexuality and fighting. Using commentator-inspired clichés, men can boast about, or be ridiculed in, their attempts at seducing women: 'nice approach work'; 'good build-up'; 'jinking into the box'. Attaining sexual intercourse is celebrated, as in football, with boasts of having 'scored', 'slid one in' or 'rammed one home'. Admonition when socialising with a female partner is 'getting t'red card', i.e. reprimanded for some form of foul play.

Away from sexuality, football can provide further clichés that most men will understand. Thus, impending trouble with a potentially violent opponent provokes questions as to whether the situation will 'kick off'. An individual considered to show low intelligence and general stupidity is sometimes dismissed with the footballing metaphor of being a 'head the ball'—following the common belief that too much use of heading kills brain cells, and hence the low intelligence accorded to footballers in the position of centre-half. Not all men use these phrases, but their availability means many choose an oral vocabulary that has football as an inspiration, and which will not need explaining in the local culture. And this, together with the experience of playing the game, produces what Archetti and Romero (1994) call a 'privileged male participation'.

Knowing the Score?

In its 109-year history, Sheffield United FC has never set the footballing world alight, but has retained a reputation for providing decent teams every now and then. Between 1893 and 1934, the club was a permanent fixture in Division One. Since then, they have frequently alternated between the top two divisions, bar a disastrous time between 1979 and 1989 when they were twice relegated to Division Three and once had a season in Division Four. The club's status was altered structurally in the 1970s when the club decided to get rid of county cricket. Until 1973, Bramall Lane hosted cricket matches for Yorkshire, and so the football ground had three sides and a cricket pitch. Two years' building saw the South Stand open in August 1975. Holding 8,000 seated spectators, the cost of the scheme was beyond the gates the club pulled and the success needed both to fill it and pay for it was beyond the ambition of the club. It therefore became a financial albatross around the club's neck for the next 20 years.

Drawing players locally and from the footballing hotbed of talent—the north-east—served United well for around 90 years. While never having a Sheffield-born manager until a few months ago, they had in their line-up and boardroom sufficient local men for the club to make the fans feel part of a local identity. Attempts to change this parochialism occurred in the late 1970s when Harry Haslam was manager and bought players from the Netherlands, Portugal and Argentina. One player the club watched and attempted to sign was an 18-year-old by the name of Diego Maradona. As the price was £200,000 more than the £450,000 offered, the United board vetoed the plan. The rest is history. Maradona went to Barcelona and World Cup victories; United went to Division Four.

The club has managed to appoint some very good managers since the war, and at one time such men would hold the position for a significant period. The 20-year (1933–52) reign of Teddy Davison was succeeded by three years of Reg Freeman whose death brought in Joe Mercer. His three years brought in John Harris, who, between 1959 and 1974, managed the team bar one season in 1968–69 where the task was given to Arthur Rowley while Harris went upstairs to the role of general manager. The two years (1973–75) of Ken Furphy brought the club to sixth in Division One, but Jimmy Sirrel, his successor, stayed only two years before Harry Haslam had his two years as the club found themselves in the Third Division. The six-month reign of Martin Peters ended in 1980 with United in Division Four. Six years later, Ian Porter-field left the manager's job with the club back in Division Two, only to drop another division two years later as the two-year reign of Billy McEwan gave way to Dave Bassett. In eight years, Bassett took the club back to Division One (subsequently to become the Premier League); after three seasons they were relegated and two years later he left the club by mutual agreement. Since then, United has remained in the new Division One, twice making the play-offs, once under Howard Kendall, who stayed two years, and once under the temporary manager, Steve Thompson. As I write, United have recently made Steve Bruce the club's third team manager of 1998! At boardroom level, however, the club has not seen so many successes. While for a hundred years the men with the money caused few ripples, the situation post-1989 has made United the laughing stock of British football. In a situation that is still not resolved nearly a decade later, the ownership of the club has changed hands a few times and in that time five men have held the title of chairman.

Fans the world over expect bad service, know the directors are often corrupt and know that, when a higher bid comes along, those players they adore will leave. Blades are no different. Such football support requires a daily reading of the back pages of various newspapers. Fact and opinion, in a local sense, comes from the letters page of the *Green 'Un*, considered the only 'real' way of expressing a printed opinion for the ordinary fan in South Yorkshire.

Saturday evenings in Sheffield in the decades 1920–1990 were char-acterised by groups of men, who from 5.00–8.30 pm waited outside newsagents, stand in city-centre meeting places and sit in pubs. The focus of their attention was the evening sports special, the *Green 'Un* news-paper, established in 1910. While I never saw men reading it over their dancing partners' shoulders, as mythology would have it, the *Green 'Un* is sold in pubs and working men's clubs and has been a vital part of fans' existence. The selection of fans' letters criticising or praising the team, the players and the management allows what Fishwick calls 'scrutiny and criticism that the journalist might be reluctant to do' (1989: 100). However, the proliferation this decade of other news sources has lessened the urgency of acquiring this printed medium.

A similar role has been provided in recent times by local radio phone-ins, the most famous since the mid-1980s being the Saturday 5 pm BBC Radio Sheffield 'Praise and Grumble' session. Fans phone in their opinions on their team's performance or express their elation or dejection.

But the club and its players have tended to speak to those considered 'reliable' in the media. Such a favoured status has produced for decades banal commentary and unchallenging questions to those employed at the club. This book aims for a greater objectivity. That, however, leaves what follows open to criticism: namely, how did I know the people with whom I spoke? How was a relationship formed that enabled a conversation to ensue? And, if research depended on what had previously been written, am I not repeating old news and previous mistakes?

My answer is that all the interviews were conducted after extensive research, both of archives and by talking to people who knew the person concerned. Conducted in a variety of circumstances, but always of the choice of the interviewee, such occasions averaged three hours' duration. Some individuals I subsequently phoned to check facts or press further on an issue. Some I met on a number of occasions, over either years or weeks. There was no template for each meeting and no two interviews were similar. I hope the information elicited and gleaned in this way is not a recycling of old news, and I hope the questions asked and the way they were phrased did not pull punches. Only the reader can judge if this technique was effective.

References

Archetti, E.P., and A. Romero (1994) 'Death and Violence in Argentinian Football', in R. Giulianotti, N. Bonney and M. Hepworth (eds.). *Football, Violence, and Social Identity* (London: Routledge).

Bromberger, C., A. Hayot and J.M. Mariottini (1993) 'Fireworks and the Ass', in S. Redhead (ed.), *The Passion and the Fashion* (Aldershot: Avebury).

Clarebrough, D. (1989) *Sheffield United: The First 100 Years* (Sheffield: Sheffield United Publications).

Farnsworth, K. (1982) *Wednesday!* (Sheffield: Sheffield City Libraries).

Fishwick, N. (1986) *From Clegg to Clegg House: The Official Centenary of the Sheffield and Hallamshire County Football Association 1886–1986* (Sheffield: The Sheffield and Hallamshire County Football Association).

Fishwick, N. (1989) *English Football and Society 1910–50* (Manchester: Manchester University Press).

Geertz, C. (1973) *The Interpretation of Cultures* (New York: Basic Books).

Holt, R. (1986) *Sport and the British* (Oxford: Oxford University Press).

Jones, S. (1988) *Sport, Politics and the Working Class: Organised Labour and Sport in Inter-War Britain* (Manchester: Manchester University Press).

Lever, J. (1984) *Soccer Madness* (Chicago: University of Chicago Press).

Mason, T. (1980) *Association Football and English Society: 1863–1915* (Brighton: The Harvester Press).

Pearson, H. (1994) *The Far Corner: A Mazy Dribble through North East Football* (London: Little, Brown & Co.).

Portelli, A. (1993) 'The Rich and Poor in the Culture of Football', in S. Redhead (ed.), *The Passion and the Fashion: Football Fandom in the New Europe* (Aldershot: Avebury).

Young, P.M. (1964) *Football in Sheffield* (London: The Sportsman's Book Club).

Club Servants

. . . and one rotten day the player discovers he has bet his life on a single card and his money is gone and so is his fame. Fame, that fleeting lady, didn't even leave him a farewell note.

(Eduardo Galeano, *Football in Sun and Shadow* [London: Fourth Estate, 1997]: 3)

Special Reserve...
Roy Ridge

One of the great mysteries of football support is why anybody attends reserve team games. Truth is, no one really supports them, or watches them away from home, or would be too bothered if they were relegated or went out of existence tomorrow. But most of us, at some time, have gone to such games and some go weekly. Why? Leaving that question aside for a moment, let's have a brief history lesson.

Maybe indicative of their status, United's original second XI were called Sheffield Strollers: the title 'reserves' did not appear until the mid-1890s. A nomadic existence in various local leagues was halted by the creation of the Central League for northern and midlands clubs' reserves in 1921. Since then, the championship has come to Bramall Lane just twice: in 1922 and 1966. For those that were interested, between 1921 and 1984 the reserves could always be found at the Lane when the first team was away; in the mid-1980s, fixtures became midweek. Then, 1994 saw a break with the past hundred years, when the team played midweek games 14 miles away in Chesterfield in a two-tier league named after a holiday camp. Who knows what the logic was behind this move, and who considered the fans' opinion? Maybe the club reflected the status of the reservers with such a move.

No one becomes a footballer to play in the reserves. On the other hand, no one really knows what motivates a man to aspire to be a pro.

Partly, it must be a technical thing—pursuing athletic perfection and performing a craft few can manage. Maybe linked with this is the desire to be an athletic hero to thousands of admirers. Then, of course, there is fame as the spur: footballers can be the epitome of the local boys made good and can often be counted on to be the regular guy with a nice line in clichés and pullovers. Is there anything better than pretending not to be noticed by admiring fans when out shopping or stood with a lager in Josephine's?[5] It can be glamorous, but few attain this status.

One man on the verge of this possible glory between 1950 and 1964 was Roy Ridge. He never opened a garden party or presented trophies in pubs, mainly because he spent the whole of his 14-year United career bar three months in the reserves. A footballing nearly-man, certainly, but one who was happy—and that's important, because as in life so in football: on the road to glory or heaven, many get the calling but few are chosen.

Born in 1934 in the village of Ecclesfield, then north of the city boundary, he was the younger of two boys to a father who worked in the steel industry. The old man supported United and wasn't a bad player, turning out regularly for the well-known local side, Red Rose. One day, while Roy was larking in the park with mates, one of their dads decided to organise these juvenile energy particles into a Saturday-afternoon team. Soon Ecclesfield Boys Club FC was founded with immediate success: two finals in their first two seasons. When playing the top local under-16 side, a Shiregreen outfit called Oaksfold, who were also United's nursery team, Roy impressed a watching scout. He was asked to start training twice a week at Bramall Lane. This was 1949 and thus began an involvement with United that lasted until 1964.

As part of the deal, he had to play for Oaksfold. Players got to wear United's old first-team strip: faded it might have been and two sizes too big, but when you trotted out so attired you felt six feet tall and barrel-chested. Originally a centre-half by virtue of his standing 5'7" at the age of 15, he was, a year later, a full-back: 'I didn't grow up anymore, I just thickened.' Capable of playing either flank, he was to play left-back for the first team and right-back for the reserves. He was fast, a strong tackler, comfortable on the ball and had average distribution. His skills were sufficient to get him signed on as a professional, but this was a gradual process with a few unusual turns.

---

5. Since it opened in the late 1970s, 'Sheffield's Ultimate Nitespot' has been a favoured watering hole for Sheffield-based footballers.

Like thousands of his peers, young Roy wanted to be a footballer. All the same, he didn't attend that many matches and never had a footballing hero. Roy was actually rather studious: he was a grammar school boy and, aged 16, had to make a decision whether to carry on into the sixth form or get a job. The latter option did not, for the time being, include becoming a professional footballer. Instead, he had to get a proper job. It was easy in those days: following the six weeks' school holiday, he walked along Brightside Lane into the offices of English Steel Corporation, told them he wanted to be a draughtsman and they replied, 'Start Monday.' Two years in training school resulted in his becoming a turner and entering the production shop. A future of skilled work and shifts lay ahead. Then United stepped in.

Thanks to United, for 12 years Roy had a job in Sheffield that did not require waking early and lifting heavy things all day. It took a few years to acquire such a comfort, mind you. In November 1951, he signed for United on a status that no longer exists: part-time professional. Soon after he got a game in the reserves and made the first team at 19. He learned of his selection in a roundabout way. The side was always chosen at Thursday evening board meetings. Roy, meanwhile, took his place on the 10–6 night shift. That night, a local press reporter phoned the works to interview him and tell him he'd be playing at Old Trafford in 36 hours. It was now the middle of the night and a kindly foreman, seeing the conflict of interests, let him go home early. Kindness extended its arm when the same man moved him onto permanent day shifts to help his football career.

Following the Manchester United match, Roy played the next ten first-team games. Aged 20, he signed professional forms, again in unusual circumstances. At work the foreman told him he was back on nights the following week, so Roy immediately went to see the United manager, Reg Freeman, who simply offered him full-time status. Now a fully fledged footballer, Roy left the factory, although the financial incentives were not what they would be today. As a part-time pro along with the factory wage he was on £10 a week. A full-time footballer got £12 a week and first-teamers pulled £14. They were then, as now, men who worked the least and dressed the best.

Attaining the status of professional and first-teamer was, and is, arduous. Quite a few young men in those days thought they were special—until they went training at Bramall Lane. They then found they were just one of 50 others each Tuesday and Thursday. They called it training, but it wasn't very scientific.

> It was a slog around the pitch, then stamina running, then sprinting
> up and down the back of the stand.

Disheartened, he missed a Tuesday, then both nights. Returning a week later nobody said anything. It took a three-week absence before the scout knocked at the door.

> I told him no one knows whether I'm there or not there. He said they
> do because they've told him I wasn't there!

Resuming training, he was picked for the 'B' team but, just Roy's luck, the opposition didn't show up. It was also the last match of the season! Fortune shone next season: two 'B' games lead to an 'A' game, which produced a call-up to the reserves. He was 18 and the big time was waiting, surely?

It all started so promisingly: a debut at Old Trafford at 19, then a sequence of games including playing against Wednesday. But he lost his place following a defeat at Hillsborough.

> I marked Alan Finney that day. He didn't do me any favours. We lost,
> I got the blame and I was out.

That was February. His next match was a County Cup fixture in April, but he was obviously well considered because he was part of the squad that toured Germany in the close season. However, the next season he got only one first-team game and, incredibly, did not play a first-team game for the next six years. Then, after one game, was never picked again. So after 11 outings in his first three months he got only two call-ups in the following 11 years.

Most of the problem was that, for seven years, United's defence picked itself. The two full-backs were Cec Coldwell and Graham Shaw who had both played for England, and when they were unavailable there was competition from Jeff Smith and Cliff Mason; the latter, Roy admits, was 'the bane of my life!' It was futile to crowd around the notice board on Friday mornings to look at the first-team choice the trainer pinned up.

> It was virtually cut and dried. Some who thought different would walk
> away grumbling but not me.

Then a first-team meeting would follow and one for the reserves. Roy knew the latter scenario off by heart.

The first team would play the reserves in practice matches. There was no animosity: they were all 'a good bunch of blokes' and the man who kept him out, Graham Shaw, was a mate. Similar to the first team, the reserves had a core who remained constant for seven years: Roy, Dennis Shields, Harry Orr, and Dennis Finnegan.

Contrary to popular prejudices, the reserves were never known as 'the stiffs' to those in football, only to outsiders, particularly football writers. Matches were always competitive—after all, there was a financial incentive: a £2 bonus and the chance of impressing the manager who occasionally turned up to see who was pushing or promising. There were also punters to entertain. Games at Manchester United and Everton could attract crowds of 10,000; Bramall Lane saw a regular 2,000–3,000—and more when the opponents were Wednesday. In all, Roy played around 400 such games, but no one match stands out and only one opponent, Barnsley's Gavin Smith, was feared: 'He usually gave me the run-around.'

On and off, Roy captained the team for ten years and they twice finished in the top four. Another bonus was playing with aspiring talent before they became public knowledge. Two such players stand out in Roy's memory: a young goalkeeper in the United side called Alan Hodgkinson and a combative midfielder for Manchester United called Nobby Stiles.

When playing away, the team received treatment on a par with the full team; they travelled comfortably and ate well. In fact the only bad thing was, occasionally, the crowd.

> You can hear every word at reserve games. I was fortunate, but towards the end of my career I got a few comments!

Remember that when next shouting 'advice' to ageing players or budding youngsters!

After such a good start in football, we have to seek an answer to the question: what stopped the progress? The main reason, probably, was the Army: national service interrupted his early career. Allowed to delay because of his work in the steel industry, he had to 'get some in' aged 21. During these two years, the man who signed him on as a pro died and was succeeded by Joe Mercer. Stationed in Kent, he would return whenever he could to get a reserve team run-out, but he was not to be one of Mercer's men. In fact, Mercer offered him to Bournemouth, but Roy wouldn't go, even though the journey there from Kent was easier than to Sheffield. The only other club that showed interest was

Brentford in 1960. This deal fell through when United's manager, John Harris, refused their request to take Roy on loan before making the deal permanent. So, for all those years, he remained in the reserves.

There was little incentive to seek a move elsewhere.

> There weren't a lot of difference in money between reserves and first-teams. They got maybe £20 a week; I got £17 in the reserves.

Nonetheless, footballing life was precarious.

> Like everyone else I got a one-year renewable contract. Each year the registered envelope came . . .

Look at it another way: even if he didn't get the glory, he was fit, worked a few hours a day, was doing what he enjoyed and, as captain, wasn't taking orders off too many people. What more could a man want? More than anything, he was happy. Sure, he could have handled more first-team football and fame but, when it didn't come, he didn't smoulder with resentment.

> I might have been better off going to Bournemouth but I didn't. I was a Sheffield lad: there was no incentive to go away. I was content; that was my downfall perhaps . . .

He was friends with everyone at the club; if he made an enemy, he was unaware of him and he left on good terms. He was never sent off or booked; if he scored a goal he cannot remember the occasion, and the pinnacle of his limited career was finishing third in the Central League in 1960.

His departure in 1964 was a pleasant occasion. Over a lunch he signed for Fourth Division Rochdale with the stipulation that he did not have to move from his Sheffield home. Without drama, he packed his bag and left.

> I shook hands with the lads, the management and the directors who were around. They told me I was always welcome back.

Interestingly, he has never once claimed a free ticket from the club he served for 14 years. Today, if watching United, he pays at the turnstile.

Anyway, aged 30, he entered the portals of Rochdale FC's Spotland ground. He had never been there before and it was, well, 'a bit of a surprise'. The wages, however, were comparable and, ever the contented, Roy found the set-up was 'a nice crowd with some good players'.

As a first-team regular for two years he just missed promotion. Deciding to rebuild, the club unloaded all its older players and Roy learned of his departure from a fan in the street—a fact confirmed hours later by the Rochdale manager, Tony Collins, the first black manager in British football and an ex-Owl.

A free transfer did not bring clubs flocking. Meanwhile, there was work to be done. Football had not provided him with a fortune: at that time, testimonials were rare, but he did get a loyalty bonus of £500 every five years. Fortunately, after Rochdale, a mate in Sammy Fox's steelworks put a word in and Roy got an office job for the next 21 years. Then, following redundancy, came eight months' unemployment followed by a new job which began seven years ago.

When I met him in 1996, he was 63 and worked five nights a week as a steel forge worker in Specialist Steels. His one brief flirtation with football since Rochdale came in 1966 when the Worksop Town manager knocked on the door, offering a tenner a week. A season begun in the first team ended with the youngsters in the County Senior League and no further contract. Since then, he has never played the game nor trained nor coached. One of his two sons had trials at Lincoln, but never made the grade, and his only football connection today is occasionally watching United.

So back to the initial question of why people attend reserve games. One reason is: it's cheap to enter, In the 1970s, it was 5p; then for a time it was free; now it's £1. For many a young Blade, it was the first affordable taste of professional football. Others, both in the past and today, might go to watch the potential ability of trialists and youngsters—but who are they to spot budding talent? Besides, few ever make it into the first team. Others probably attend out of boredom: after all, the hardest part of living in a city is finding something to do and people to hang out with in free time.

In the decades up to the 1970s, however, one of the main reasons for attending was the difficulty of following the first team. Before the days of motorways, good rail connections and cheap transport, many fans, while following the team in their hearts, wanted to be in the company of Blades who were thinking similarly and the reserves offered a place to gather. The one-page team line-up sheet contained an alphabetical list of matches corresponding to a board in the ground where the results were displayed—the 'A' was always the first team. A man would appear to present the quarter-hour progress. Fans reckoned they knew the outcome by the way he walked. Still, sometimes he tormented, picking up a zero instead of a one or making the mistake of broadcasting United 1–0 down instead of 1–0 up. He would change it and acknowledge the cheers.

From the 1970s, the advent of personal radio and now the full-match radio commentary made the man and his scoreboard redundant. A match from elsewhere would now crackle around the ground and the crowd would groan in disappointment for events miles away. The men on the pitch must have been disheartened to hear cheers as they lined up for a corner! If video killed the radio star, then radio killed the stars of the reserve team.

Nobody will ever play 400 reserve team games for one club again or have a similar story to Roy's. His legacy from United thankfully isn't a limp or arthritis: instead, it's the walls inside which he lives. His Stannington home was once owned by United, and he moved there in 1958 as a newly-wed. Following his transfer in 1964, they let him buy it off them. The only other artefact gained from his United days is a 1953 County Cup Winners' medal—not much for his years with them, but Roy describes it as 'lovely'. This is a content man who you sense holds no bitterness to football and enjoyed the limited chances that came his way. His isn't a sad story; he did what many only dreamed of doing, i.e. playing for United, and he once marked Stanley Matthews. Happy in his job, he acquired what many do not and will not have: good memories. He could have got a first-team game at maybe 50 other clubs but, like a good supporter, he stuck it out with the club he supported amid people he liked in a city he loved. You can't knock that.

One could say his waiting for the big chance was a triumph of hope over experience. That would be a bit rich coming from Blades, who spend good money watching a club that hasn't won a thing for over 70 years. Like Roy, such fans live in hope and enjoy any subsequent bits of glory and deplore those who latch onto success. A club cannot have 20 star players; like industry or business, a football club needs fellows who accept their limitations but who are proud of what they can achieve. As the poet Milton stated in attempting to overcome the disability of his blindness, 'They also serve who only stand and wait.' If everyone was hopelessly ambitious there would be turmoil and nothing would get done amid bitterness and rancour. Somehow, we fail to reward with adequate appreciation those players who display loyalty as staunch as that displayed by the fans. In Roy Ridge, United had a good club man: he 'belonged'. Aware of his ability, he did his best. He should be remembered for that.

Still Serving...
Graham Shaw

After 12 years, the fish-fryer left the job. She's virtually irreplaceable. The same day, somebody broke into his car. Thus, as we meet in September 1995, three months after retiring as a pub landlord, Graham finds himself in his chip shop working a full day with the fat and filling in forms for the Force.

It wasn't always like this. Thirty years ago, he was playing for England at Wembley and for United in Division One. I suppose crowds still flock to see him, but for fishcakes rather than football finesse. While a few, older men would recognise the man sweating amid the deep-fry in white overalls as a footballing hero, the younger clientele has no recollection nor interest: they just want decent chips.

Now aged 60, this local-boy-made-good lives a life of contrasts. When not feeding the five thousand in the fish market in the poorer end of the city centre, he might be found out on the west side on the greens or nineteenth hole of the Dore and Totley Golf Club with its dress code and 'Members Only' command over the entrance. An excellent golfer (learned in his footballing days), he was club captain and president in the 1980s. But, whether in the market or up-market, he's one of the most popular fellows in the city. Modest and measured, he belongs to another era.

Do you remember those days? I don't. Graham retired when I was six. Looking at old photos, I see players, all of indeterminate age, muscular, and with side-partings. A football world wherein managers wore shirt, tie and V-neck jumper; where trainers wore fleece-cotton tracksuits and physiotherapists white coats; where red and white striped shirts meant Sheffield United and white railings meant Bramall Lane. Nowadays, the latter are concealed by ads for private health schemes, the club has half a dozen kits, and chairmen are arrestable on sight. Gone are the days when young boys had their own turnstiles and the club badge extolled the virtues of the city and its steel-making heritage unaccompanied by marketing clichés about the family or the caring club.

All right, so the earth doesn't stand still and it's a commercial world, you'll say and, besides, what's so sacred about tradition? Call me confused, but I sense things were simpler then and there were reassuring notions of *certainty*. But the question is: Were those days any better for professional footballers? And, if born later, would Graham have fared any better?

Born in the Pitsmoor district of Sheffield, his family moved in the early 1940s to the super new council estate of Parson Cross. Young Graham's dad, a foundry worker and 'mad Wednesdayite' (is there any other kind?), while a gifted player, never made it as a professional but encouraged his eldest son of three in various sports. The end result is, by the age of 14, he was on United's books and learning to be a signwriter in a firm owned by a United director. But he had some decisions to make. At 16, he'd represented Yorkshire schools at cricket and been invited for trials at Headingley and had been a national finalist at boxing. He plumped for football and Sheffield United. Offered the chance to train at both Hillsborough and Bramall Lane, he turned the former down; he favoured United's training methods and, via this, grew to be a Blade. Years of being dragged to watch Wednesday counted for nothing!

Want to know how to terrify a 17-year-old Blade? Easy: take him to Hillsborough on Saturday afternoon. This is precisely what happened on Graham's debut in 1952. After only six Central League games, he turned up (by bus) for his seventh against Wednesday at Bramall Lane. Over the other side of the City someone failed a fitness test before the real thing. Next thing, Graham was being driven to Hillsborough at 1.30 and, 90 minutes later, out he trotted to a record post-war Sheffield attendance of 65,000. Has anyone in the history of the British game ever made a debut in front of such a massive crowd? I don't think so. He ran into 'a wall of faces, very steep . . . very frightening', and running at him with the ball was Derek Dooley. He'll never forget that day.

So began a long journey which ended 17 years later in 1967 after 478 League and Cup appearances. No Sheffield-born player will ever better this for United: Graham is unique; he is history. The defence he was part of played together for almost seven years: Hodgkinson, Coldwell, Shaw (G.), Shaw (J.), Richardson and Summers. Of these men, Graham is the classy right-footed left-back, the one comfortable on the ball and a good distributor. In the middle, Richardson clogged and clattered; Joe Shaw anticipated and stole the ball. Then, aware of their deficiencies, they would roll it out to Graham who could pass it upfield, accurately.

What the thinking man's full-back lacked in pace he made up with guile: greyhounds ran past him but usually to oblivion—he'd got it covered in other ways. While not an attacking full-back, he scored a fair number of goals. Some are described as 40–50-yarders, but this is not Hot-Shot Hamish. No, it was his job to take free-kicks around the halfway line. His orders were to punt it between the posts towards the back. Sometimes both United forward and opposing 'keeper missed it. Goal to Graham. Other goals came via penalties: his 75% success rate was due to a consistent method—low, hard and hit the stanchion.

Such consistency and overall ability was recognised at international level. He represented the national Under-23 side three times in 1955–56 (selected the day he began national service) and the England 'B' side three times. Five times between 1958 and 1964 he made the full England team and was never on the losing side. These occasions provide for amazing memories! He toured the USA and South America with the England squad, and his first international at Wembley against the USSR was 'a dream' and his most memorable match. Other unforgettable matches took place at Hillsborough, Manchester and Newcastle: he loved a big crowd. For some reason, he disliked games at Birmingham and Villa—'we always seemed to struggle there'. Only two opponents are particularly remembered as difficult: Francis Lee of Bolton Wanderers (later Manchester City) and Terry Paine of Southampton. Both were 'hard . . . sometimes nasty', the former in particular provided 'a few ding-dongs'. Read into that what you want, but throughout his career he was never booked nor sent off.

There were some occasions he would like to forget. One such involves a certain Stanley Matthews. Altogether, he marked the wizard nine times and, to be honest, he never found him a handful—except for Derek Dooley's testimonial at Hillsborough in 1955. That day he ran him ragged: 'I didn't know what day it was.' There was a huge crowd and many, seeing Graham in the streets for weeks after, reminded him. But it was all a set-up. The players were instructed not to go in hard and let the man with the ball play it. The truth is, Graham, under restrictions, made him look good!

Another match to be forgotten was the FA Cup semi-final (third replay) against Leicester in 1961, United, 2–0 down, won a penalty; Graham placed it wide; United lost. He's never forgotten that miss and doesn't thank me for reminding him. When watching World Cup penalty shoot-outs, his heart aches every time for the player that misses.

In and out of the England side and a regular in a United team that yo-yo'd between Division One and Two, Graham never asked for a transfer. However, one of his four managers, the late Joe Mercer, tried to sell him. The man who was to become famous for his 1970s Manchester City side and later managed England began his managerial career at Bramall Lane in 1956. He had recently retired, aged 40, as captain of Arsenal (and at one time England). Beloved in the marble foyers of Highbury and football's higher echelons, Mercer was to find a contrast in Bramall Lane, as Graham recalls.

> He was famous in London and he'd achieved a lot as a player, but he didn't get adoration in Sheffield. It wasn't big money and glamour here and a man had to win the respect of Sheffield people.

Football's favourite uncle went about it the wrong way. After only seven months in charge, he tried to sell Graham—recently the captain of England Under-23s—to Stoke City. Why? 'He said I couldn't tackle . . . and I lacked the killer instinct.' The move offered no financial gain but, more importantly, Graham turned it down because 'I was a Sheffield lad and a Unitedite. I didn't want to play for anyone else.' How many players wearing United's kit will ever say those words again? Did he whinge and see his agent? Did he hell. 'I rolled me sleeves up, played a few reserve games and got me place back.' In fact, it was all good character-building stuff: '. . . made me realise I couldn't take anything for granted. His words smartened me up—we all need it now and then.' Mr Mercer apologised for his remarks and Graham was an automatic choice for the next seven years for Mercer and his successor John Harris.

Graham is far right on the back row
in this 1964–65 team line-up.

In December 1956, Mercer made Graham right-winger for a match at Liverpool. The reserve full-back was the left-winger and regular centre-half played centre-forward! United lost 5–1. Two weeks later, Rotherham won 7–2 at the Lane. There were no chants for the manager's head, no demos outside, just mutterings into the winter night. There was no dressing-room revolt, no teacups thrown. Sarcastic comments were made out of the manager's earshot by men who had lost their place to those playing out of position. The latter were thankful for a game, but bewildered. The manager ruled by fear.

> You'd never swear at the manager. You respected him. You had to: you were frightened of getting the sack.

His next manager, John Harris, was equally distant. He, too, did not tolerate opinion or argument. Sunday-morning running around the pitch followed bad Saturday performances and the traditional Monday day-off was occasionally cancelled. The only nights out with the manager were to the London Palladium on the eve of games in the capital. Then, as now, the directors were at a remove. A couple would occasionally enter the dressing room and trot out the unoriginal 'Let's have a good win lads', then return to the bar. In the hotel, directors drank separately from players. One such man on the team coach to London demanded the pop music radio station be switched to the news. The squad sat through four hours of Radio 4. How can we account for this? Graham explains: 'There was a distance; but we respected each other.'

Throughout his career, Graham does not remember any dressing-room cliques or tensions. The only demarcation was between those who went drinking after matches and those who were teetotallers. Granted, words were exchanged after bad tackles in training, but such stand-tos were quickly forgotten. Maybe this had much to do with the fact that, at one time, 12 of the 24 professionals at Bramall Lane were from Sheffield or roundabout. Many knew one another from childhood. Over at Hillsborough there were also a lot of Sheffield lads. Matches were occasionally 'blood baths', but they were all mates in the bar afterwards.

After 11 seasons as an automatic choice, Graham faced two seasons in and out of the reserves. It was hard to be bitter: wearing his first-team shirt was his ten-years-younger brother, Bernard. His final game took place in 1967, aged 33. A testimonial the same year against Wednesday attracted 6,000. So, was he to retire wealthy and with good memories? The answer is, no. Things were so very different then. What might astonish a reader is that, throughout his 17 years, he never got more than a one-year contract. Thus, as the 1966–67 season ended, he heard rumours that the contract was not being renewed. The end was inevitable and, ideally, he should take it all in good part. But it doesn't work like that; he had been around the club so long he never thought it could come to an end.

It ended by post. A letter arrived; he already knew its contents. He was thanked for his services and wished well for the future. He told me reluctantly that he cried, and then experienced various emotions of rage and bitterness. There was no one to talk to: younger players didn't want to know what was coming to them; older players had the same problem. Thankfully, he had his wife and childhood sweetheart, Beryl, and the kids. He left them to enter Bramall Lane to empty his locker, and no one noticed his arrival or departure. His United career was over. He then found a pub and got pissed.

After 20 years as junior and pro, no one wants to shake your hand or ask what the future holds. Maybe miners and steelworkers know the feeling, but they had comrades from their shifts to talk it through with. How hard was it? 'It put ten years on me shoulders.' Next day Graham woke up as an ex-United player. Now what?

Initially it was Division Four and Doncaster: 'like going from Cole Brothers to a swap-shop'. In Alex Jeffrey there was an old chum from England Under-23 days and Graham's cousin was the trainer. After a season, he got the offer of a player-manager job at an up-and-coming outfit called Scarborough in the Northern Premier League. He took it, but lasted less than a year: the results weren't good and he rowed with the chairman. Disenchanted with the game, he sought alternative employment and bought a café in Castle Market with money from the testimonial. This was a success. Three years later he bought another and, years later, a chip shop.

For 16 years he ran three premises and employed 20 people. He worked 7 am–5 pm six days a week and, just as important, he was happy. He also took his FA coaching badge and trained schools, pubs and cub teams. After 15 years, he sold two cafés and took a break by running a pub! Not any old pub, but The Sportsman, 200 yards from Bramall Lane, packed on match days and home every night of the week to United's largest supporters' club. Why this pub? An unconscious desire to return to what he knew? No, it was simply the first pub available!

He resumed a role at Bramall Lane in the early 1980s. For five years, he was chairman of the Future Players Fund. The committee of ten organised various functions but never raised large sums of money and eventually the fund folded. Thus, as we speak in 1995, his only connection to United is watching them whenever he can. He occasionally sees former colleagues. But, with seven grandchildren, he has plenty of company. Only two months out of the pub, his biggest problem is coming to terms with unoccupied evenings in his new home. He has time to reflect on his days at Bramall Lane; he has a million memories, nearly all of them good; and he wishes he could play today in a game that is undoubtedly faster 'but not more ruthless' than it was in his day.

He did all the things good footballers do: opened garden fêtes, made hospital visits, presented trophies and took public admiration in his stride. He never made a fortune out of the game. While wages were good compared to mates working 40-hour weeks and shifts, they were only a bit above what men in other, industrial jobs were taking home. Even when the maximum wage was abolished in 1961, United, like most clubs, had a team wage structure. Sure, the players received more than they had previously, but the players agreed on a standard for the team. Thus, with one-year contracts and not much to rely on, the footballer's life was one of worry.

> You fear getting injured, being dropped or reaching 29. You worry about how much longer you've got and you rely on managers' training methods to bring the best out of you.

That sums it up: always at the hands and whims of a boss and knowing the next tackle could be the end. Fortunately, Graham only had one bad injury, sustained ironically while playing in a testimonial. A tackle from behind tore knee ligaments. It was 1964, he had just got back into the England team and he was out for six months. Moody, he snapped at the family until the day came when he could make his first tackle. But there were no more England caps, which was tragic. Two years later, when they won the World Cup, it could have been Graham at full-back.

A footballer's life is a strange one. They are different to you and me by virtue of their physical ability. Then they hit an age and become all too human. Then we look for their replacement to cheer. Had he played today things might be different. An agent might have provoked him to think big and the percentage of a transfer fee would appeal, but the past is another country: they did things differently there. Of course, he can fantasise about what could have been, and daily he has a reminder of his playing days. This comes in the form of arthritis. Some days he can hardly walk. This is the other side of football.

> We were pushed to play. Many games I shouldn't have played, I know that. Not because I was frightened of losing my place, but because I was Unitedite and we had a job to do.

He did that job very well and without complaint. He gave everything and expected little in return. We will not see his like at Bramall Lane again.

★   ★   ★

Graham continued to serve until February 1998. Feeling unwell, he took a few days off before visiting the doctor, who diagnosed advanced stages of cancer. He died ten weeks later. The funeral was attended by dozens of ex-players and the congregation of mourners so vast that traffic had to be diverted. My thanks are due to Graham's widow, Beryl, and their children Richard, Paul, Kathryn and Susan for permission to publish this interview posthumously.

The Handyman...
Alan Hodgkinson

That a man born in 1936 to a coal miner in a South Yorkshire pit village should similarly spend his life working with his hands should not
surprise anyone. Such working-class communities passed manual work
through the generations like a cultural legacy. Few, however, would
face retirement having spent close to 50 years catching or teaching others
how to catch a football. A one-club career produced an appearance record
bettered by only one man in the history of Sheffield United. The club's
most famous goalie had neither the discipline of the factory system nor
the demands of piecework to keep his performances under control.
Instead, he had a self-imposed regime which won him, both as a teenager
and when in his sixties, the admiration of British football's big names. Seen
recently sitting next to the manager of the Scotland team during the
France '98 World Cup, the man known as 'Hodgy' played with then
coached them all. Had his father had his way, however, his hands would
have been put to better use as a concert pianist. Shot-stopping is incompatible with Schubert's sonatas, but at one time it was a close call.

On leaving their piano lesson, Alan and his elder brother would go to the local recreation ground to play football. Duetting on the ivories, they played to audiences of 400 at Butlin's talent shows. Their songster dad could play a bit and encouraged their participation in the Sunday school choir.

But it all ended when he realised that football had taken a greater hold than the keyboard. An uncle had taken Alan to his first United match and, aged 13, truanting from school, he saw a childhood hero: Burt Williams, the Wolves and England goalkeeper. What impressed him? 'He wasn't the tallest, but he was brave and agile.' Those who remember Hodgy can recognise the similarities.

Playing in the net for his school brought a selection for the local best XI of Rother Valley Boys, which then led to Worksop Town Juniors. An invitation to train with the then-big Huddersfield Town proved a bit awesome for a 15-year-old, so he contented himself in the Yorkshire and Midland League with Worksop Town playing against many ex-professionals. Soon he was in the company of current professionals when a scout invited him to train twice a week with United. By 17, he was playing for the United team in the Yorkshire League and the same year signed professional forms. With no apprentice professional status at the time, the signing was a recognition of a precocious talent.

His status was hard-earned. For the previous two years, he worked six days a week on the butcher's counter of the local Co-op store. An understanding manager allowed him to work a 5 am–midday Saturday shift so he could play for United in the afternoon. Solitary training on an area of Bramall Lane known as the Bowling Green adjacent to the old cricket pavilion would see him repeatedly throwing balls at the cricket pitch roller. The unpredictable return path assisted his catching and reflexes. For signing professional he got a £50 fee and a £7 weekly wage reduced to £5 in summer months; Worksop apparently received £250. At 18, he made his debut in the reserves. By the time he retired, he had made 652 first-team appearances.

Compared to later decades, the coaching methods of the early 1950s were elementary. Most teams practised the 'W–M' formation. and training involved a lot of running and jumping.[6] Apparently, there was an underlying logic.

---

6. The W–M system was used to describe the tactical playing-shape format, and is associated with the innovative coaching methods of Herbert Chapman, the Arsenal manager of the 1930s.

> . . . idea was that if you ran all week and didn't have a ball you'd be eager for it on a Saturday.

Thursday morning saw the first team play the reserves and a strange scenario would ensue.

> Jimmy Hagan played . . . no one would tackle him! This was his big day 'cause the other days he trained on his own. He'd score sometimes six goals and off he'd go and do his own thing. I was in awe of such people; I was 17, a local lad, but I was doing what I always wanted to do.

At 5'9" he was not big for a goalie, but, as he explains: 'If you were good enough, you were big enough.' He trained hard to develop upper body strength and agility. There were no special training regimes for the goalkeeper. Ahead of him in the United net was Ted Burgin who played for the England 'B' team and made the 1954 World Cup squad. Spectacular in his saves and popular with the crowd, he was going to be a hard act to follow.

Aged 17, Alan accompanied the first team on a tour of Germany while Ted Burgin was on England duty. Two consecutive defeats early in the new 1954–55 season saw ten goals conceded and bottom-of-the-League United set to face top-of-the-League Newcastle the next Saturday. Told the day before that he was playing, a worried young Alan travelled with the team on the Friday and endured a night out at the Newcastle Empire watching American crooner Guy Mitchell. Against all logic, the visitors pulled off a victory next day. After only 13 full League appearances, Alan made his England Under-23 debut, but national service slowed the phenomenal rise.

Between 1955 and 1957, his duty to Queen and country saw him progress from wireless operator to regimental police. Playing with the British Army team, which included Duncan Edwards and Jimmy Armfield, he lined up against a Football Association Select. The Forces side won and Alan had a magic game. United's new manager, Joe Mercer, watched the match and afterwards told him that he was in the first team as soon as duty allowed it. Leaving the Army in February 1957, months later he was playing for England against Scotland at Wembley.

He was chosen for England after only 28 first-team appearances. While winning only five full caps (and never on the losing side), he was on the bench as part of the squad about 40 times. He went to Chile for the 1962 World Cup and, four years earlier, was a member of the 'shadow

Sweet sixteen: a very young-looking overcoated Hodgkinson lines up in 1953 with such luminaries as Fred Furniss (back, far left) and Jimmy Hagan (front, far left).

squad' for the World Cup in Sweden. Such recognition was the be-all and end-all of a footballing career.

The set-up compared to recent times was very different. For a start, England always played on a Saturday afternoon and the squad would rendezvous in a north London hotel. Aged 18, he was in the same room as heroes such as Billy Wright and Tom Finney and his first time in the communal bath at Highbury after a practice match was courtesy of an invitation from Stanley Matthews who found the young goalkeeper's deference charming after he had asked England manager Walter Winterbottom to get him Stan's autograph because he was too shy to approach the legend himself!

Playing for United until 1972 meant Alan saw three decades of change in both tactics and management. He faced opponents in men as diverse as Stanley Matthews and George Best. Alongside the United squad, he watched England humiliated 6–3 at Wembley by the Hungarians in 1953. Previously unbeaten at home, the defeat changed the face of English football and made a lasting impression.

> I still use that game when one of my sides gets beat. From that day, I decided, if I ever got into coaching, technique would be the most important part of the game.

For 14 years, Hodgy was a Lane favourite in his trademark green shirt, black shorts and white socks. Gloves and kitbag placed in the right-hand side of the net, the performance would begin. Quick to the ball, agile, good at anticipating the intention of forwards, he was considered a safe pair of hands. Ahead of him Joe Shaw played nominally as centre-half, but, in Alan's words: '. . . probably the first sweeper in English football without realising it'. What he developed with Joe Shaw he calls 'telepathy'. The other regulars, Summers, Graham Shaw and Richardson, played together for almost seven years and remained mates who met regularly 30 years later.

Strong shoulders and arms produced a very brave 'keeper who had remarkably few injuries, missing only a dozen or so games in all that time—and half of them were due to bouts of 'flu. Always conceding fewer goals than games played in a season was his yardstick of success. A Boy's Own last-minute penalty save from Bobby Charlton in front of the Stretford End stands out in his memory. Boy's Own clatterings came from Spurs' Bobby Smith and Cardiff's Alan Warboys, the latter leaving him aching for three days.

The manager who signed him was Reg Freeman, for whom he has only praise.

> . . . wonderful guy, wonderfully humanitarian. A gentlemen who'd be interested in everything you did.

His successor, Joe Mercer, was the first training-pitch manager at Bramall Lane who would be standing in the middle of practice matches and would bawl players out after games, but forget everything by Monday morning. He was succeeded by the single-minded John Harris, a serious teetotal, church-going bachelor Scot, who was very professional and keen on economics. Requests for pay increases were met by a response that the FA would not allow a raise! Players never questioned this dubious wisdom. The same man provided Alan with his most unusual fitness test. Before a match at Fulham, he informed his manager at a London hotel that he was not up to it due to a strained back. Taking Alan into an empty room, Harris found somebody's briefcase. Seizing it he repeatedly threw it at Alan over a green baize table with the instruction that he was to dive and catch it. He was still unable to play, United lost 6–0 and Harris did not speak to Alan for a month!

Never having more than a two-year contract, the close season saw the arrival of the dreaded telegram informing players whether they had been retained. Alan always was, but he remembers the precariousness of football.

> . . . 1953, the captain at the time was Harold Brook who was the leading goalscorer. I was there with him the morning the letter came telling him he was released. His wife had given birth at 5 am that morning.

At the time of his final games as a United first-team player in 1972, he was part of a Division One team with big crowds, but was paid £45 a week. There were win bonuses and 'crowd money' when gates were above a threshold. But there was an egalitarian idea throughout his career which today's professional would not understand: 'It was a team game so nobody got more money than their team-mates.'

Promoted to Division One in 1961, he was given a £30 a week basic. So young and with such huge potential, his captain told him he was daft to sign for United when bigger clubs would inevitably be sniffing around. So why did he stay a one-club man?

> I was loyal and I wanted to play for United . . . which in the long run probably cost me a fortune.

Promoted again to Division One in 1966 and reaching the semi-final of the FA Cup saw the players handsomely rewarded by the club directors with identical inscribed barometers and £5 raincoats.

Like so many men who have passed through Bramall Lane, the respect he earned from the supporters is not echoed in the player's sentiments to those who directly employed him. In all innocence, I asked about his 1968 testimonial match against Wednesday in front of over 15,000 and received a reply that he had barely told anyone in 30 years:

> . . . there was torrential rain that night. It affected the gate, because they were expecting 30,000. They said there were 15,000 or more there, but the Spion Kop was full and afterwards they gave me what they said were the gate receipts . . . it was £4,000. I questioned what the crowd was and the man who gave it to me said all the money from the Kop turnstiles had gone missing. No explanation was given then or later. It's something that's stuck in my memory. I'm not a vindictive individual, but that upset me after what I'd done and achieved for United.

He continued to play for another four years at the club that deprived him of what was rightfully his.

Possibly by way of recompense or out of guilt, United looked after him for a few more years after he stopped playing. Ever dignified, his departure was always going to be considered and adhered to.

> I was only 34 and could have played another few years, but decided enough was enough. When I was a young international, I remember watching the United team in the Yorkshire League. An old Scottish international was playing for Goole Town. He had been a great player and he had his entourage on the touchline. He was a sad reflection of what he was, but his friends were all there saying he should be playing professional—but he was a shadow.

After his final match, he never played in goal again, even for a charity game. Offered the chance of a comeback by John Harris when the man bought to replace him, John Hope, hit a bad time, he refused. He had new ideas and a new future mapped out in coaching.

Having taken his coaching badge at Lilleshall, United offered him the chance to run the reserves for the next three seasons. Under what proved to be difficult circumstances he did quite well.

> It weren't the best job at a football club. You'd have seniors who thought they should be in the first team and kids who were learning. You had to try to marry them together.

In his first season, the team finished runners-up. I regularly watched that side and always remember an incident that saw Alan leave his dugout in front of the John Street terrace and, using what Sheffield men of his age call 'Latin', tell a vociferous bloke behind me to shut up or face the consequences. He remembers it.

> . . . you get involved with young players. I wanted them to get the same chance as me. Sometimes comments would upset me. I was never an aggressive type of guy, though.

His manner and ability produced a decent reserve team. At the same time, he studied for a football management course run by the FA. Then, promotion of a sort came his way when his old team-mate and buddy on the FA course, Gerry Summers, became manager at Gillingham and invited him to become assistant manager/coach. He jumped at the chance, even though the newly appointed United manager, Jimmy Sirrel, wanted to retain him. A 22-year involvement with United ended in November 1975. The departure was amicable, but provoked reflection.

> I left as a friend of the club, albeit the testimonial incident stuck in my mind. I'd never questioned anything in my time at United . . . maybe I should have.

The six years at the Kent club saw Alan's career develop well when he began goalkeeper-coaching for the FA at the request of the head of coaching, Charles Hughes. Later he was to coach the England Under-18 goalkeepers and was goalkeeping coach to Graham Taylor's England set-up. Failure to gain promotion at Gillingham saw him and Gerry dismissed in 1982, but Alan can take some satisfaction in that the week I met him coincided with the appointment of Steve Bruce as the new Sheffield United manager. Bruce began his career at Gillingham and Alan was the one who brought him into football, having spotted him at a youth club tournament in Aldershot.

Out of work, he took a gamble with the idea of offering himself to clubs as a goalkeeping consultant. Inundated with offers, he realised the remoteness of Kent was a hindrance and moved to where the first job offer came from—Coventry City, under Dave Sexton. The midlands has been his home now for 16 years, and proved an ideal base for later employment at a dozen clubs, which have included Manchester United, Everton and Sheffield Wednesday. The United manager, Harry Bassett, offered him work, but he was too busy at the time.

A coaching job today at Glasgow Rangers means he works a five-day week at Ibrox. International recognition has once again come his way and, for 12 years now, he has been part of the Scottish national-side coaching team. Over the years, he has become guru to David Seaman and spotted a talented 'keeper whom he recommended to Alex Ferguson. His name was Peter Schmeichel. His work has resulted in incongruous situations, not least working at Hillsborough under Trevor Francis.

> It was strange, yes . . . but my allegiance is to goalkeepers, not the club. When Man United played Wednesday at Wembley, I was goalkeeping coach to both teams, the same as when Man United played Everton.

The travelling and multi-job scenario took its toll, however, when four years ago a heart condition required a quadruple bypass. A month after the operation, he was back coaching. Now lecturing at FIFA and UEFA courses, he is simply delighted still to be involved in the game and at such a high level, but his joy is tinged with reflection of times past.

> I'm delighted I played football when it was a sport for everybody—players and the working man. Now it's business at all levels; everything revolves around money. It's no longer the game I played in.

Sitting in his modest detached home on a modern housing estate, he is comfortable and content. He still plays the piano, but is surreptitious about his performances: 'If I'm in a hotel and I find a piano and the room's empty, I have a little go.' His two daughters are nearby, his glass cabinet is full of football mementos and he has a match programme for every game he ever played. It seems strange, but in physical appearance he's hardly changed since his days as United's goalie: anyone would recognise him. Both United and the game had a great servant in Alan, a self-confessed nice-guy who, in later decades, would have made a fortune, but who is happy to be able to offer younger players something he learned in return for involvement in the only job he knows.

Faithful Departed...
Cecil Coldwell

It's hard to believe in this day and age, I know, but there was a chap who played and trained at Bramall Lane for 33 years. Departing in 1983, he holds the distinction of serving the club for over one-third of its existence. As if having played 461 first-team games, being captain for nine seasons and then being coach for 15 years was not service enough, he was also called upon twice to be caretaker-manager. Often spoken of as 'Mr Sheffield United' and as the best manager United never appointed, Cecil Coldwell carries with him many stories but reveals little.

Now years into retirement, a modest abode in Cheshire is what he has to show for his dedication to one football club. The man who celebrated goals in the long-forgotten manner of a smile and handshake and who played on muddy pitches and ran out as team captain to strains of 'Ilkley Moor', both from communal singing and later from Tannoy systems, spent half his life at Bramall Lane. How does a man live, having departed from such a lengthy involvement in football?

Born in 1929 to a dad who drove a steamroller and a mum who had a full-time job bringing up five kids, the teenage Cecil would leave the house in the Stannington district just north of the city boundary and watch United and Wednesday on alternate Saturdays. While Mr Coldwell Senior liked football, he was keener on cross-country running. A happy childhood and an untroubled schooling career saw Cecil become a brick-maker in Marshall Refractories aged 15.

Bradford City expressed an interest in the 17-year-old factory player, but two years' national service put paid to that. Returning from the Army, he played in the Yorkshire League for Norton Woodseats, the City's best amateur team of the time. Scouts from professional clubs regularly watched their games. One from United saw something in Cecil and, in 1951, United gave Norton Woodseats £50 for his signature with a promise of a future £50 if he ever made the first team. After a year on part-time status, the United manager, Teddy Davison, signed him on professional terms and, at the age of 21, gave Cecil his first-team debut at Southampton.

His first-team appearances would have come more quickly and more regularly had it not been for the capable Fred Furniss holding the full-back position. When he did break into the first team, he remained there for ten years, becoming part of the famous defensive line-up alongside Joe Shaw, Graham Shaw, Gerry Summers and Alan Hodgkinson. Alternating as a youth between centre-half and full-back, he was to decide on the latter as his ideal role and became, in the memory of those who watched him, an intelligent, reliable and steady player, capable in the tackle and cool under pressure. Not particularly physically imposing nor naturally fast, his game, by his own admission, was based on anticipation rather than speed.

The late Jimmy Hagan and one-time team-mate once commented that no player worked harder than Cecil to make himself a class player. Was this true?

> I trained hard, yes . . . I suppose it paid off. I was an excellent tackler, if I say so myself. I watched the ball rather than the players' feet. I read the game.

Never booked nor sent off, Cecil was considered by all as sporting, helpful and an essentially decent man, both on and off the pitch. While he was reading the game, others were watching with interest, albeit too late in the day.

> I was told by one of the Directors of the FA when I was 34 that I was the best full-back in England but that they couldn't select me because of my age. It was nice to know that, however.

Various managers recognised a quality in Cecil. It was Davison's successor, Reg Freeman, who picked him regularly for the first team. His successor, Joe Mercer, made him team and club captain—a role he performed between 1959 and 1968. Despite his elevated status and being an ever-present in the first team, Cecil never saw anything greater as a player than a one-year contract. Renewed annually following a chat in the manager's office, the financial rewards would make today's footballers laugh. A win bonus was £4 and a draw saw £2 added to the basic. Not far removed financially from the fans who watched them, the players of this era were also physically near the fans to the extent that they would arrive for games on buses and trains with them as they walked through the town centre having lunched at Davey's Corner-House before home games.

Considering the number of games he played, his goal-scoring record is poor. I had it down as two; Cecil tells me it was four. None of them was memorable. The reason it was so low was that he did not have to push up to help the forward-line because they did a good enough job without him! In his time as a player, United alternated between Division One and Two and consequently Cecil marked the great wingers of the era: two that stand out in his memory being Preston's Tom Finney and Wolves' Jimmy Mullen. Offered the chance to join Aston Villa, he turned it down.

> I was local and I didn't think I'd be gaining too much . . . and I knew I had a chance to stay on at Bramall Lane with the coaching staff.

As captain between 1959 and 1968, Cecil had plenty of responsibility, but carried out his role in a typically unassuming manner. How come he got the job?

> Joe Mercer gave it to me first then the other managers kept me in the role. They must have seen in me an attitude, a dedication and a

> will to win. My job was to gee others up when things weren't going too well, you know . . . [he claps his hands then clenches his left fist and shakes it].

Simple tactics from a quiet leader. Did he never have to bawl players out?

> No. I might say 'I can't see you down there' if they weren't pulling their weight, but the players were a good bunch and didn't need me to tell them.

Off the pitch, the captain had duties both to fans and managers. The former role required him to attend youth clubs and supporters' club presentation nights. The latter saw him as the link between players and manager, to whom he would occasionally convey what he calls:

> team matters . . . if they thought they were being trained too hard or they were getting the wrong type of training.

First-team appearances began to fizzle out in late 1966. A few games followed when first-teamers were injured, but Cecil occupied himself as player-coach of the reserves and, in 1966, the team won the Central League Championship. The same year saw a testimonial game against an All-Star XI and an appreciative crowd of 15,000. It was a good payday, much appreciated, but 'not enough to buy a small business' because the admission costs were reduced for such games. Just as well, really, that Cecil had another job to do at United.

In 1968, he accepted the offer of a job as first-team coach from manager John Harris. Having realised that, as the game was becoming more professional and demanding he needed badges and certificates, he qualified as an FA coach. A few years later he was coach to a United side storming Division One. In what was a happy set-up, Cecil speaks warmly of the manager.

> John was a very friendly man. He was someone you could always talk to. Quiet in many ways, he knew what he wanted.

In what he describes as a 'good team to work with' was a precocious 18-year-old called Tony Currie who was almost beyond coaching, but not the occasional admonishment.

> You'd just have to give him the freedom of the park and let him do his own thing. One day John gave him a roasting, telling him that he wasn't

giving his best. It was the only time I ever saw John really open up. I think it knocked Tony over. Just before the players went back out I had a chat with him and tried to lift him. It worked: he played a different game second half.

Nice words and a cuddle were not always Cecil's style. Another precocious young talent by the name of Keith Edwards received the full force of Cecil's right boot up his backside one training session. Why?

He wasn't training like the rest of the lads. I kicked him because I knew he'd accept it. Then I brought him back for training in the afternoon to make him run round the track.

As a model professional himself, he could not countenance laziness. His dedication paid off and eight managers retained him as either a player or a coach. The club directors recognised something as well and twice made him caretaker-manager. One stretch in 1976 after the departure of Ken Furphy and before the arrival of Jimmy Sirrel saw Cecil hold the fort for a month. Then, in 1978, when the Sirrel left, Cecil took charge for 13 games, losing only a few before Harry Haslam took over. This tremendous achievement was recognised by many Blades at the

Len Badger inspects the damage on then-captain
Cec's right eye as Joe Shaw (far left) and Alan Hodgkinson look on.

time who believed Cecil should have been made manager. Today, people speak of him as the best manager the club never had. Reliable, and red and white through and through, why wasn't he offered the job?

> I think they wanted to get away from putting local men in charge. I don't know why. I wasn't even interviewed. I was told I wouldn't get the job by the chairman. I felt I could have done the job, but you've got to accept what the board decides. It does knock you back a bit, though.

With Ken Furphy's managerial style, Cecil became a coach alongside a manager who is on the training field himself daily. Jimmy Sirrel was the same and, when Harry Haslam came with his assistant Danny Bergara, the three of them coached until Haslam became too ill to do so. This trio was obviously considered by those in charge at the time to be up to the job: all were given five-year contracts.

The financial security this contract offered was some recompense from a chairman who had not exactly been sweetness and light to Cecil. Presumably annoyed by the public support Cecil had in 1978 for the vacant manager's job, which occasionally manifested itself in the local press, the chairman told him he was not to talk to journalists and to forget about the job—he would never be manager. Aware that some of his fellow-directors were impressed by Cecil's achievements, he then banned him from entering the boardroom after games, thereby preventing the admirers from chatting with him. Surviving that chairman, who departed in 1981, Cecil had another battle on his hands later that same year when Ian Porterfield took over as manager and brought in his own coaches. Cecil, however, still had three years left of his contract and was not going anywhere. What followed is difficult for Cecil to recall. Somewhat reluctantly, he provides snippets of information which in their brevity and sincerity are all the more real.

Not part of the new man's plans, Cecil suffered what he calls 'terrible times'. While never clashing with Porterfield, whom he suspects respected him deep down, those who arrived with the manager had their own way of suggesting where his future lay.

> It was often little things like, when it was pre-season club photos, one of 'em would say in front of everybody else, 'Get in quick, 'cause it might be your last time'.

When on pre-season tours, he was treated differently and told by the manager to go socialising with the players while the 'in-crowd' went their own way. At times, they would dine on one table as Cecil sat elsewhere. When it came to coaching, his experience counted for little.

> I'd be given the juniors to train. Then, in the summer when we had schoolboy trialists and part-time coaches, they would be given tasks and then they would pretend to try and find something for me to do.

It was no way to treat a man who had coached players longer than any of them, and played under more managers than they had. Believing now like he believed then that he had much to offer in terms of innovative coaching, he was in effect ridiculed and it had an effect. The recollection isn't something he wants to dwell on, but he tells me anyway.

> It drove me to drink for the first time in my life. I drank on my own at home. It was painful.

He was not the only one at the club who drank in those days, but he at least had a supportive wife and two lads to go home to. The inevitable departure in April 1983 was a relief, albeit a sad occasion and one that required some self-evaluation.

> I was sensible enough to realise that at my age it would be difficult to get a job in football . . . or at least one that I wanted.

But you cannot leave a job after 33 years without some emotion, surely?

> I felt awful that day. It was a sad day. It'd been made pretty obvious for about 12 months by the manager and his assistant that I wouldn't be staying.

Departure day produced a 'strange, empty' feeling, but the man of the old school took the initiative when those above him probably felt too ashamed or embarrassed. 'I found the manager and his staff and shook their hands and wished them all the best.' Without any grand farewell, this man left with no idea of what to do next day.

He returned soon after for a second testimonial game, thereby becoming the only man in the club's history to have two. Played against Wednesday in May 1983, the game drew a crowd of 9,500. Was it a good payday?

> I think it happened because certain people felt bad about what they'd done, and what I read into it was that, by having a match and giving me some of the income, they saved themselves a payoff which would be calculated on years of service. It wasn't so much a gesture of goodwill as a way of reducing what they would have to pay.

SOUVENIR **6**D. PROGRAMME

CEC COLDWELL

TESTIMONIAL MATCH

SHEFFIELD UNITED
VERSUS
ALL STAR XI

ON MONDAY, 31st OCTOBER, 1966. KICK-OFF 7.30 p.m.

BRAMALL LANE GROUND, SHEFFIELD

He didn't get a big payday from this game either. 'They had to take out costs of policing the match.'

A few months' reflection led to his owning a newsagent on a massive council estate in Sheffield which required 12-hour shifts.

> It was different, to be sure! I had to adapt. I missed the players, but the way I'd been treated changed my attitude towards the game.

Turning down the chance to coach Sheffield FC because of the demands of the shop, the same demands meant he no longer turned up at Bramall Lane, even as a spectator. While still a Unitedite, he rarely attends a game, but has bred a Blade son who goes everywhere. A period as a newsagent in one of the posh parts of Cheshire between 1987 and 1995 was followed by a useful retirement that involves Cecil in crown-green bowling and voluntary work with the disabled via the local church.

As I sit in the home of a man who gave almost half his life to Sheffield United, I notice not a single item by way of memorabilia of those days. I try to find a deeper significance in such an absence, but there's not much he wants to reveal.

> We never won much for me to collect! I've one or two scrapbooks, but we were limited in what we all got in them days.

Retaining the dignity and calmness that he displayed on the pitch, he gives fans cause to reflect on what might have been if his abilities had been appreciated by those in power.

> They've never been a club forthcoming in inviting people back. You were never really made to feel welcome. I speak for a lot of players when I say that.

One gets the impression that, even after 33 years, he left the club too quickly and certainly too quietly.

Sheffield Lads

A reporter once asked the German theologian, Dorothee Sölee: 'How would you explain to a child what happiness is?' 'I wouldn't explain it,' she answered. 'I'd toss him a ball and let him play.'

(Eduardo Galeano, *Football in Sun and Shadow*: 204)

The Home Front...
Fred Furniss

Had it happened today, the studio panel would have had a field day. Uncontrollable young; break-up of the family; lack of discipline; too much money; disgrace to their country. We would hear of sinister right-wing elements and one man, probably called 'The General', would be believed to be behind the mayhem. There would be calls for conscription, for a new pride in the country and a return to 'family values'.

But at that time amid high-velocity political rhetoric came high-velocity bombs, dropped by the Luftwaffe's Heinkels onto innocent civilians. At times, they killed thousands and destroyed acres; and one man, a Nazi by the name of Göring, was giving the orders.

Yet one game played in 1941 wasn't postponed. While anti-aircraft guns blazed, the sides played on. No one left the ground, and by half-time the sirens were silenced and the air raid was over. And the media did not make hysterical headlines over the event.

For an 18-year-old, this was his United debut. The venue was Goodison Park, Everton; the game ended a 3–3 draw; but the attendance was only 2,100 and gate receipts were a miserly £94.

Such behaviour was ruining the game.

It takes more than the Third Reich to upset a lad from Darnall. Born in 1922, Fred was to know the hardship and struggle that grew out of the Great Depression of the late 1920s and early '30s. There were plenty of stories about violence in those days: crowds fought police evicting families unable to pay rent; men fought each other for work at the labour exchange; and, in the mid-1930s, men of the National Unemployed Workers' Movement watched and barracked police football teams. Elsewhere the city's 'gang wars' claimed lives and left scars.

Football helped matters. United even attempted to reduce admission prices for the unemployed in 1932 and 1934. But there were always those who would criminalise anything and, should youths seek to relieve boredom by street football, some found themselves arrested and imprisoned on charges of disorderly behaviour. Some consolation came with the creation of unemployed leagues organised by the local FA with the support of the local press and city council, hand in hand with property-owners, some of whom made land available for pitches. It wasn't just philanthropy: the authorities feared Bolshevism and knew Sheffield was receptive to events in the Soviet Union. Materially, there wasn't much available in this city and there was little hope of change, but there was always football to forge a spirit of unity and the two teams could provide their fans with something to look forward to.

As the oldest of seven children, little Fred helped his old man (a collier) coal picking on local slag heaps. He mined it, and should have had all he wanted when times were hard, but people don't all think that way. So the family were forced to go scavenging for coal to cook, to eat and to stay warm when the mines were on a three-day week.

This happy lad loved his football at Phillimore Road School and, at 14, got picked to represent Sheffield Boys. Weeks later, he left school and enjoyed a few weeks' holiday, which was then the transition from boy to man. Out of the blue a man called to the family door, a shop-floor gaffer no less at the nearby Hampton's factory. He came offering an apprenticeship—so long as Fred would play for the works team. The gaffer had spotted Fred months earlier in the park, and saw one for the future. Months later, Fred was taking home 30 bob a week and, at the factory, even the higher echelons have a word with him—Charlie Hampton was a director at Bramall Lane. A few people were showing interest; it was now up to Fred to prove them right.

Aged 14, he played as a winger against grown men. He learned quick—he had to. A few of the city's better amateur clubs then started watching. First, Woodbourne FC asked him to play. He accepted. Sometimes, he played three games a week.

> I had a one-track mind . . . football. I weren't a bad scholar, but all I wanted to do was play with a ball. My dad was pleased as punch when I played wi' Sheffield boys.

The big time came when an ex–Hampton's player tipped off Fulwood Amateurs. They were United's nursery team and they sent him a post-card inviting him to play. He accepted the offer and, a few months later, got another postcard—this time from the manager of United, Teddy Davison, telling him to report for training. He enjoyed this.

> I'd done a lot of fitness training at Hampton's. They had a hut on their sports field. Sometimes after training we'd have pea and pies and a darts match. Some would get in the car and drive to the off-licence at Handsworth for beer, but I didn't drink.

Bottles of warm Whitbread delivered by a bone-shaking Trojan, last orders at ten o'clock and the coolest dudes with Homburgs on their bay rum-anointed heads—and all this in a wooden hut behind a slag heap at Handsworth. Ladies, what were you missing? Well, for one thing, a reluctant star in the making. However, he missed out training at the Lane due to the exhaustion of 12-hour shifts and disillusionment.

> I got browned off. Nobody was interested in me. We got 7/6 a week expenses which weren't bad . . . but I left.

An ex-Fulwood player persuaded him to return, and soon after came another postcard: the manager wanted him to report to Bramall Lane to play at Everton. The war was in its second year.

You might well ask why was football being played at such a time and why were fit young men indulging themselves in such a way? I'll answer the first question first.

Whether people should play or watch the game in such difficult times was debated at the highest levels. The previous war had seen heated debate between the clergy and politicians over this issue. Then, believing it would be over quickly, the League and FA Cup competitions continued—United won the latter in 1915. A sort of compromise was reached later: no FA Cup, but leagues could operate on regional terms. Second time round, football stopped for a few weeks when war began as clubs cancelled all fixtures. Then various clubs got permission to play from their Regional War Committees. Soon a two-league system, North and South, was established, each containing 22 teams.

As for the other question: how come there were fit young men available? Well, it was all down to Sheffield's industrial heritage. Living in the Steel City between 1939 and 1942, had its good and bad points. The latter was that the enemy sought to flatten the steelworks that provided the Allies' munitions. The former was that United had a decent team; the two circumstances were linked. At the beginning of the war. United had just been promoted to Division One, and the German invasion of Poland was, to a good Blade, bloody irritating—they'd waited five years to get into the top flight. Now, some silly bugger wanted to ruin the season with talk of world domination and the master race. Instead of glory games, Blades got their ground bombed in 1940. Then United won the League as the war ended. I'll explain the correlation.

If you were a fit, working-class young man, you joined the Forces and went to war. The exception to this rule was whether you worked in a reserved occupation such as steel and coal production. So, while a few first-teamers cleared off to fight in foreign lands, many remained to work in trades learned before they became pro footballers. At United, this extended to the manager, who worked at the Town Hall, and the trainer/coach, who worked in steel production at Firth Vickers. All over the country in similar circumstances were ex-pros looking for a game; thus was born the status of 'guest player'—basically, a player who was available to turn out for his local team even though before the war he was registered with someone else. Because of the availability of so much local talent, United never used this facility much.

It was these circumstances that permitted Fred to play for United throughout the war. Furthermore, if Blades can thank the Germans for one thing, it was sorting out the pitch. Before a cluster bomb landed on it, there was regularly six inches of sludge in front of the Kop. The bomb churned the area up and United saw the opportunity to stick some drains in. All the players got a shovel and helped with the digging.

Nonetheless, Fred tried to combine military service with his duty to United. When the war began, he applied to join the ground crew of a local RAF base, reasoning he could get Saturdays off to swap the blue serge for red and white. But, threatened with five weeks of schooling, he lost interest and, instead, became a Bevin boy. The Minister for Manufacture and Industry, after whom these young men were named, deemed that those in coal production could work the seams in place of military call-up. Around the country, thousands of young men went down the mines. They were not all local lads, some were middle class and a lot of colliers resented them. But, being a local lad and fit and a footballer, Fred was liked.

He spent 18 months working shifts in Orgreave Colliery until, one day, a runaway coal tub nearly killed him. Seeing it coming he crouched in a two-foot wide gap; he lost the skin off both knees and refused to go down below again. His offer to do any job on the surface was considered insubordinate. They sacked him.

Two months later, he got a letter telling him to report for Army training at Lincoln. Fortunately, the war in Europe had ended. While he did not see active service, he saw action via sport representing the Army at running, boxing and football. He played for the Army against an FA XI and, when he could, he played for United.

The war years saw some strange proceedings. In the beginning, the crowds were very low: in December 1939, only 5,000 watched a Sheffield derby. By Christmas Day 1940, 15,000 turned out for the same fixture; it could have been higher, but that was the maximum crowd allowed by the Government Commissioner. Fearing an air raid during a match, this number was reckoned to be the maximum for a rapid exit. Despite this, the same man wanted both Sheffield clubs to play at Abbeydale Park to avoid this scenario altogether. As the war progressed, crowds picked up, people got used to war conditions and, after 1942, the chances of a daytime raid in the city were so slim that people felt safe. By 1944, a match at Bramall Lane pulled 48,000. Mind you, the opposition varied in quality: no one knew for certain who would be playing and there was always the odd stranger on the pitch—one game saw a team from the Polish RAF.

It's hard for us to picture what match day meant in those days. Due to rationing, the best refreshment you could hope for was a cup of Bovril. Should you wish to read about it, all that was available was a two-page supplement in a late edition of *The Star*. Depending on the time of year, kick-off was 2.15 or 3.00. The crowd always contained a fair sprinkling of various military forage caps as the lads came home on leave and, to make things better, there were a few chants to join in with. So let's hear it for '2–4–6–8—who do we appreciate . . . ? U–ni–ted!' A more elaborate rendition was drawn from a 1935 anti-Mussolini war song; the words were slightly changed:

> Roll along Sheff United, roll along
> Put the ball in the net where it belongs
> If Rickett gets the ball
> It's sure to be a goal
> Roll along Sheff United, roll along.

Others shook air raid precaution rattles bought from shops and painted red and white—they made a hell of a racket. Quaint, eh? Interestingly, on a city level, the one product not rationed was beer. Imagine it yourself. There's a war on, relatives missing, the chance of being bombed and no end in sight. A gallon of Ward's and a Blade victory then, as now, would always make the world seem a better place.

The club had a good manager at the time in Teddy Davison. He had the foresight to realise that the war would end one day and normality would resume. For this reason, he nurtured many young players. It paid dividends. United won the Northern League in 1945–46 with a team consisting of nine Sheffielders, the biggest part of whom had received a signing-on fee of only £10. The following year the full League and FA Cup were restarted and the club finished sixth in Division One and made the quarter-final of the Cup. Huge crowds flocked to football. A County Cup game against Wednesday in 1949 saw 50,000. Then, in January 1952, 65,000 watched the same fixture in a League match at Hillsborough. Fred played that game.

There were 'gifts' of a kind in those days in football too, but hardly worthy of an FA inquiry.

> When we played at Grimsby, we always got a box of kippers. When we were at Portsmouth, the director, Arnold Laver, had a farm down there and he'd call in and get us all a chicken . . . thought he was givin' us the world, he did. At one time, Teddy Davison loaned me to Youlgrave FC in Derbyshire for a bit of experience. They were a village team, so I always brought him back a sack of vegetables. We had a good thing goin'!

Mind you, it wasn't all innocent by the sound of things. Players moved from club to club and a nod was as good as a wink to some.

> There were bungs in them days. They kept it all quiet . . . some got more money on our team than others; we didn't know for sure, but we knew it wo' goin' on. Nobody said owt.

Also, journalists then, as now, were not regarded as the source of all wisdom. In those days Fred Walters of *The Star* travelled with the team, but sometimes made himself absent during the match.

> Some thought he was in the pub biggest part o' afternoon!

To say the game has changed in the past 50 years would be trite. But it is worth describing what the footballer's lot was in those days.

Let's start with home games. The usual rendezvous was Davey's Corner-House on the Haymarket at 11.30 am. A choice of fish or chicken (fol-

A 1952 line-up with Fred second from left in the back
row, standing behind the legendary Jimmy Hagan.

lowed by rice pudding) led to a game of snooker on Cambridge Street
and a saunter to the ground. The kit and boots were laid out by the
'odd-jobman' and the tidying-up was done by the two charladies. The
only other people who entered the dressing room were the directors.

> Mr Lawrence, Mr Graham and Blancow Yeats . . . Mind you, they only
> wanted to talk to Jimmy Hagan, not the rest of us.

By his own admission 'not a socialising man' and, until he married
at 29, living at home with mum and dad, he was and remains a tee-
totaller. Amiable rather than gregarious, he was pleasant to all his colleagues without socialising with them. Some were notorious drinkers
in pubs around the ground. Others were forever on the pull in the 1940s
version of Josephine's; it was called the City Hall and featured the band
sounds of Carl Gibson, Harry Roy and Joe Loss. While Fred slept, his
playboy colleagues attempted seduction over bottles of stout and gin.
More private dates saw young couples listening to Sheffield's 'Mr Organ'
himself, Reginald Dixon, at the Gaumont. Fred attended the annual
club 'Tour Dance' at the Cutlers' Hall. Top prize was a trip on Sheffield
United Tours; the drawback was having to sit through the top of the
bill—a 20-year-old named Max Bygraves.

On away matches players were permitted to take a male guest with
them. Fred took his dad, who found himself popular with workmates
wanting match tickets. The pair saw a world they had never known:
eight-hour journeys to London, dinner in the Adelphi Hotel in Liver-

pool, the chance to see Tommy Trinder at the Palladium. Some places he visited were part of training techniques: there were 'brine baths' at Droitwich Spa and Buxton. Football helped to augment his wardrobe: the team were issued with club blazers in 1950. Nothing was too much bother: by 1951, United even appointed a club secretary to look after things. Football took him abroad shortly after the war: he went to Germany and remembers Stuttgart.

> We were treated very well. Mind you, it wo' strange to see kids beggin' for scraps as you left the restaurant.

Three times he played for a Sheffield and Hallamshire FA Select on tour of Holland and played twice in the Isle of Man against Sheffield Wednesday in what was an annual exhibition match. The world was becoming a smaller place and technology was changing the football world. He sat out the first floodlight match at Bramall Lane in 1954, but played in the second, a special game against Hibernian of Edinburgh. He wasn't too impressed.

> The lights weren't very good. We got them second-hand; there were a lot of shadows. They were cheap, to be honest. Even with big gates, United were always arguing poverty, even then.

Some things never change.

He was a good club servant: by his reckoning, the score should read '485 first-team games and 20 in t'reserves'. He was a regular in a defence of White, Burgin and Cox. For years, they were automatic choices. He was never dropped and the maximum injury sideline he suffered was seven weeks. Following his debut in May 1941, he signed pro in January 1943 and played his last game for United in February 1955. A full-back all his career, he had a few games at centre-half and outside-right, usually when the team was injury-hit. Very strong and very fast, he was years ahead of his time in being an overlapping full-back. A tremendous crosser of the ball and able to be back in position in seconds, he, unlike many of his team-mates, would have been a great player in later decades. His competitive edge extended to penalty-taking: he missed only 2 out of 20. Contemporaries talk of him as the best uncapped full-back of the time. He agrees.

> It wo' all about who you know. Players chosen were mostly from down south. It wo' just one of those things. I wo' quite happy wi' my own form. I did me stuff week in and week out.

If he had a bad game, he can't remember it, but remembers difficult opponents in Liverpool's Billy Liddell and Jimmy Delaney of Manchester United. Another memorable opponent was a stocky black fellow at Doncaster, renowned for clogging people. His name was Charlie Williams—wonder what happened to him?

He signed a contract annually until, one day, the letter came telling him he was being released. It was in May 1955; prospective buyers were told he would cost £1,000, which he thought a bit steep, but there was more to it than that.

> They'd decided on that 'cause I was due a second loyalty bonus. What they reckoned on was if someone paid that I'd get me £750 and the Club would get a nice £250 windfall. Well, I went to the players' union and they had words and United had to pay me the money and let me go free. What got me though was that Harold Brookes and me had just got United back into t'First Division. Our reward was a transfer.

He left earning £16 a week with a £2 bonus when the average skilled worker in the city was on about £5. Mind you, in the beginning, he started on 6/4. Even so, it was top money for a man his age and his first home was in the des. res. district near Ecclesall Road.

He joined Chesterfield in August 1955. Teddy Davison was now manager there and Fred got the job of coaching the juniors. It didn't work out and, after three years, he played a season at Worksop. Then he moved into local league football, played competitively until aged 55, and played exhibition games till 64. He then took up refereeing; he still does games today.

Other sporting successes came his way in these years. At one time, he was among the top ten snooker players in the city—a product of unoccupied afternoons as a footballer. While colleagues sank a few in The Railway, he sank reds and blues on one of the tables above the Boot's store in Attercliffe and celebrated with a glass of sarsaparilla. In more recent times, he made the last eight of the national Flat Green Bowls Championships. A life of moderation and keep-fit ensures that he can swim daily and dance in the evenings. If there's a fitter 75-year-old bloke in Sheffield today, let him come forward.

Obviously, he had to make some money after the end of his footballing career. This led him into a variety of circumstances. Initially, he ran a drapery shop, then a couple of grocers'. Tiring of long hours for little money, he joined the gas board in the 1960s, working shifts as a gateman until made redundant eight years later. Then he returned to where it all started—Hampton's, by now renamed Record Ridgeway. For ten years he worked as a machinist, then came redundancy again. Since retiring, he's got better things to do than lament the vagaries of industrial production. He had to keep busy to overcome bereavements, and he's out seven days a week and every Saturday either at Hillsborough or Bramall Lane.

It's hard to imagine those days of crowds of 60,000 at Bramall Lane, some watching games standing on the cricket pitch, rattles waving. It all happened in another world, one lost today; all that remains is photos and names. When will Blades ever have a team line-up containing blokes called Harry, Aleck, Jack, Walter, Albert, or even Fred? In photos, they stand there seemingly a happy bunch beside the charabanc they're about to board on their travels. With long coats and derbies covering their centre-partings, they resemble a cross between George Raft's gangster movies and a convention of George Formby lookalikes. Maybe the low divorce rates can be explained by their appearance: having pulled once, they knew they might not be so lucky again! Such solid people. They worked long hours and never got rich, but loved their football. They, and the game, kept tens of thousands happy in a collective experience without parallel then and today. They wanted for a brave new world

A convention of George Formby lookalikes?
A United party arrives at Blackpool in 1946; Fred is third from right.

and were told by the politicians in the 1950s they'd never had it so good. Then the same politicians blamed their offspring for the so-called decline of society in the 1960s, while their successors closed the coal mines and steelworks that helped win the war.

The Big Man...
Derek Dooley

For over 25 years now, a big man has been nearly a daily presence at Bramall Lane. Now approaching 70, but looking younger, his big frame and upright stature carries a man who can watch all the games he wants, but can only dream of what he could have achieved himself. A limp gives an indication of past trauma; a broad Sheffield accent reveals his local roots; and intelligent eyes and a willingness to smile reveal to those who are unaware of history that a sharp mind and humble nature lurk. Born in poor times, enduring a war and coming to terms with one of the biggest personal tragedies in British football history would be enough for most people's memoirs. But add to this an ignominious dismissal as a footballing manager and being at the centre of one of the most ridiculous boardroom sagas in recent times and you have a man to whom the phrase 'seen it all' is an understatement.

He saw a fair amount as a child, much of it pleasant but also at a time of world war. Born in the Pitsmoor district of Sheffield in 1929, the youngest of two brothers to a mum who did not work and to a dad who was a file cutter at the vast Firth Vickers factory, football ability ran in the family. Invited for trials at the then-mighty Bradford City, Mr Dooley Senior dismissed the approach on realising that the steelworks paid him better than football clubs! Fondly remembered as the biggest influence on his son's subsequent footballing career, the old fellow was able both to 'keep my feet on the floor' and provide a stable home environment.

> He was strict; we were brought up right. While we were not rich, we always had a holiday . . . usually in Blackpool.

The local Catholic school of St Catherine's with its goalposts chalked on walls provided Derek's first footballing experience: '20-a-side games played with a tennis ball'. All in all, childhood was a happy, if somewhat turbulent, affair.

You see, while the grown-ups in his immediate environment were responsible people, many adults in the world at the time were involved in escapades never to be forgotten. Consequently, Derek celebrated his eleventh birthday sitting in an Anderson air-raid shelter avoiding the Sheffield blitz. For three years, his schooling was conducted in various front rooms of houses via a system known as Home Service Schooling. Three days after the family moved home, their former abode suffered a direct hit from a massive bomb. The new occupants lost all their earthly possessions, but fortunately not their lives. During these dark years, there was no local league football and few pairs of football boots to be had. There were football matches to watch at Bramall Lane and Hillsborough (see the Fred Furniss section) and young Derek watched Wednesday play various Army teams. He followed the Owls for years after, home and away.

Aged 12, his footballing ability stood out when a teacher took the lads from his school to the grammar school at Firth Park, which kindly lent them a pitch to play on. The teacher allowed the budding talent to do his own talking.

> I picked meself at centre-forward . . . that was how it all started! A few
> weeks later, I got picked for the school second XI and in the first year
> of big school got picked for the first XI. I was 12; they were 16.

Leaving school at 14, he continued to play while he earned money. Fortunately, the football club, run from the YMCA, and his place of work were nearby and the job wasn't particularly arduous.

> I made hearing aids! It was a clean job: me dad told I wasn't gonna
> work in the steel.

The YMCA, then located in Fargate, had the most number of teams in the local leagues and had good equipment and coaches. Playing for them, he attracted attention. Aged 15, he received a telegram from Lincoln City asking him to report to the Denaby United ground in Rotherham next Saturday to play for the visitors. Two trams and a trolleybus later, he was playing in the Midlands League against grown-up men, many returning from military duty hoping to resume their interrupted playing careers. As footballing beginnings go, it could have been better.

> They gave me a red and white striped shirt . . . which I weren't happy
> about wearing, and we lost 6–1.

He did, however, score the consolation goal and got half-a-crown to cover his travelling costs. Unfortunately, the match was played in a thick fog so 'nobody could see if I were any good'. It took three weeks for a letter to arrive inviting him to train with Lincoln at Sincil Bank. When he finally went, they signed him and, aged 16, he was playing first-team football in the Third Division (North) League. In three games, he scored three goals and was chosen for a Sheffield and Hallamshire Under-18 Select against Doncaster and scored four in a 6–1 victory. A chap who was the trainer of Wednesday asked him afterwards if he was interested in meeting Eric Taylor, the general manager of Wednesday, and the man who picked the Wednesday team.

Around the same time, an administrative error on the part of Lincoln found Derek out of contract and both Wolves and Nottingham Forest sniffing. Meeting Eric Taylor at his beloved Hillsborough was enough to make him sign part-time professional under the eye of coach Alan Brown. The deal was £3 a week with a £2 win bonus, £1 for a draw. In return, he trained twice a week, played for the reserves, then made the first team.

After only a couple of games, he scored two goals in front of the Kop in the 2–1 victory over Barnsley. People started talking about him as the next big thing in English football. Big he certainly was at 6' 2¼" and weighing in at 13 st. 10 lb.—and don't forget, he was just 17. He had one hell of a shot on him and was a Yorkshire sprinting champion, which made him one of the ten fastest men in Britain at the time. Just as important, he had an indefinable asset known in football as 'attitude'.

> I feared nobody. I couldn't be intimated. I'd been cock o't'school as a kid and I fancied me chances at boxing.

National service in the Air Force saw him stationed in Scotland. He managed a few games for the nearby Dundee United then, when moved to west London, he got a couple of stripes on his tunic in return for remaining in the Force an three extra months to enable him to turn out for the RAF team! Demobbed, he returned home, got married and played for Wednesday as a full-time professional after a procedure unlikely to be re-enacted in this day and age.

> I was wondering what Wednesday were doing, so I saw Eric Taylor and said I'd like to sign professional . . . so he signed me!

Turning out for Wednesday teams in the Hatchard and Yorkshire League produced bags of goals—he scored eight in one game. The inevitable first-team debut occurred in 1949, ironically against Preston, the team that saw his last-ever game. Now earning £6 a week, he was dropped after failing to score in his first two outings and then came a realisation in a Probables *v* Possibles practice match that there were 44 men in kit watching or playing. Arranging a meeting to find out what future there was for him at Hillsborough, Derek prepared to meet Eric Taylor.

> I rehearsed me speech with me dad! I went into his office and remember everyone was fearful of the manager. Anyway, I said to him 'I don't think you're being fair with me!' He looked at me . . . and he agreed! That Saturday, I got a game for the reserves, scored two and kept me place. Then I got a first-team call-up and scored 16 goals in nine games and never looked back.

The jealousy of fellow-professionals was not just down to his ability. National service duties cost many players years of earnings as full-time professionals. So, when he was 22 and in the first team, most of the others on the pitch were five or more years older, a fact not lost on many older heads.

> They'd verbally taunt me! But Alan Brown would warn me of opponents and tell me what to do. He never stopped me playing my natural game or challenging goalies!

In those days, you could kill a goalkeeper and the referee wouldn't blow. One such challenge brought him his one and only booking in football, which he learned about in unusual circumstances.

> It was me who was knocked out cold. I come round and the ref's stood over me as I'm lying there asking me what my name was.

He faced some difficult opponents, but in his first-team career there were only five games in which he did not score, and when forced to retire he had scored 64 goals in 63 games for Lincoln and Wednesday. At one time the First Division's second-highest goalscorer, he was close to being called up for England duty when disaster struck.

A February Saturday at Deepdale, Preston, in 1953 witnessed a tragedy forever etched in the footballing memory of the Sheffield public. An icy pitch was protected by a layer of straw and fertiliser. The first half saw Derek sustain a cut leg; in the second half it was broken in a collision with the Preston goalie. Gas gangrene from the fertiliser entered the cut ('a lot of men in the war died this way') and, with no antibiotics at the time, Derek's footballing career died. In traction in hospital on Saturday night, he noticed 24 hours later an absence of sensation in his toes. The following day (St Valentine's), his leg was amputated to his upper thigh. The surgeon was Mr Garden, whose son achieved TV fame in the early 1970s as one of 'The Goodies'. For the next nine weeks, Derek was prostrate in hospital.

He tells me all this slowly and matter-of-fact without apparent emotion. I scribble away, hoping he won't notice my eyes getting a bit watery. Does he remember it all?

> Oh yes. Preston played the offside game a lot. I was quick and we decided to break their trap. I chased a ball, the goalie hesitated then came out outside the box with his foot up and went into me leg and broke it a yard outside the box. This was 13 stone 10 pounds at full speed!

What did the goalie do subsequently?

> He wo' scared to come to see me at the hospital. It wasn't his fault . . . it was an accident. Tommy Docherty and Tom Finney [both at Preston at the time] came every week to see us.

Do you blame anyone?

> . . . No . . . What if it had been me that broke the leg? And it could have been because I was a robust player. I'm not sure I could have carried on playing if I'd have done it.

Did this generation have no time for self-pity? I find the memory harder to discuss than him, and now he's happy to tell me more and to consider those whose lives are changed as a consequence.

> It was difficult when I woke up and realised my leg was off. I'd only got married eight months earlier. We were living with my mum and dad. So I'd no home, no job, no trade and a 20-year-old wife. I'd lay there at night thinking 'what am I gonna do!?'

Football tried to help. The Professional Footballers' Association donated £200 and a testimonial match at Hillsborough saw a Sheffield XI play an international XI in front of a staggering 58,000 in what was the first game under floodlights played there. He received £7,000 from the gate receipts and sacks full of mail.

> I realised then what an impact I'd made all over England. I thought, Christ! Fancy putting pen to paper for me!

Strangers sent him money and the total proceeds of all this sympathy helped him buy a house for cash. He's lived there ever since. But, the applause over, Derek had to adjust to life as a different person. It wasn't easy.

> People don't realise what you go through . . . even crossing the road. I thought when me false leg was fitted I'd be able to run! They brought me home in an ambulance and dropped me off and I tried to walk, but I fell over. I started crying thinking 'how's my wife going to look at me?' I'm insecure now because I can't provide . . . but I've got no choice but to learn to live with it.

While rehabilitating, he went to watch Wednesday. What was that like? '. . . Hard . . . I even went to watch 'em training. I wanted to stay in football.' Football offered a job in the shape of the tabloid *Daily Mirror*.

The task was simple enough: watch a match and phone the reports in on Sunday morning. In return, they paid him what he was getting at Wednesday when his career was finished—£14 a week. He did this for two years and got his life together. A Sheffield brewery offered a job but, being teetotal at the time, he thought such an occupation futile! In the end, he went once again to see Eric Taylor when his sense of morality was conflicting with the demands of tabloid journalism. As he explains:

> I could get into dressing rooms, but I wouldn't turn confidences told me into scoops. I couldn't betray people for a story.

A Wednesday director at the time was a Mr Gunstone who owned a bakery. Employed as a telephonist/receptionist at £8 a week, he remained at the firm for eight years, rising to the position of assistant sales manager. At the same time, he was employed as coach to Wednesday's juniors for £2.50 a week, and spotted ability in aspiring youngsters who went on to star as professionals: Pete Eustace, David Ford and John Hickton.

His commercial abilities eventually overtook his abilities in football coaching, but here stands a famous story in Sheffield folklore. With the growth of commercialisation and revenue being sought beyond the turnstile, clubs in the early 1960s were experimenting with something called Development Funds. Initially, Eric Taylor asked Derek to flog tickets to the Gunstone's workforce. He sold dozens, and offered to run the scheme. Appointed pools manager in 1962 on £20 a week, he no longer coached the juniors as Saturday was his busiest day.

Nine years later, he was manager of a different sort at Hillsborough—of the first team—in what must be the only example in British football of the pools manager converting to team manager. It happened the following way:

> One Friday, I was sat on me own in the office when Eric Taylor told me to come up and see him. Him and Sir Andrew Stephen [the chairman] were sat there. The team manager was Danny Williams. I'd got a good relationship with him; we even went to games together. Anyway, Eric Taylor says to me: 'If we offer you the job of manager, what would you say?' I were flabbergasted. I said 'What about Danny?' They said, 'Don't worry about him.' They'd decided to sack him the night before so my decision had no bearing on that. I said I'd discuss it with my wife. On the Sunday, we met Andrew Stephen and the vice-chair

Derek as manager at Hillsborough.

and they grilled me about what I'd do as manager. After all that, I asked them what would happen if it didn't work out. The chairman said, 'Derek, don't worry we'll always find you a job at Wednesday.'

The job was a dream come true for Derek and one welcomed by all those connected with the club.

I was popular with the Wednesday fans: after all, I'd played for them. As pools manager, I'd made the club a lot of money which went towards building the gym and Leppings Lane End.

Assuming control when the team were lying eighteenth in the then Second Division, they were in virtually the same position when he was sacked nearly two years later. His first season saw the club finish fourteenth. A decent start to the second campaign ended with a month of bad results due, in Derek's opinion, to a mystery virus that infected the entire first team.

We got the health people in; they sprayed the dressing rooms and closed the ground for a week. We never found out what it was, but some first-teamers didn't kick a ball for three months. I was so low on players I had kids in some weeks: one time I had to select a school-teacher and a goalie from a working men's club team.

In 135 games as manager, Wednesday won 43 and lost 57. Just when performances were improving and players were recovering, he was sacked. Any regrets?

None whatsoever. I enjoyed being manager: it's the next best thing to playing. The crowd weren't happy, but they had a go at the board and not me.

His final day in charge was memorable. Believing that people would be too busy with festivities to notice what the Wednesday chairman was up to, Matt Shepherd sacked him on the morning of Christmas Eve. The staff of *The Star* were all in the pub. Printers had to rush back to get the special edition out. After 20 years of service, Derek left Hillsborough in tears.

I was . . . full up. I offered him the complimentary car keys and he said, 'Don't be daft, how are you gonna get home?' I went downstairs to see the players, but after two sentences broke down and left the room. Tommy Craig was captain; he had a chat and I talked him out of asking for a transfer.

Wednesday honoured his contract for the remainder of the five months. But the promise of employment made by the previous chairman was not quite what he expected. Returning to the ground a month after his dismissal, he asked about the promise and was offered a job selling match-day tickets. Disgusted, he walked out and did not return until 20 years later in his role as a director of Sheffield United.

This capable and industrious man was never short of work. Weeks after Hillsborough, he became a sales rep for Stylo Matchmaker football boots. He lasted nine months, then gave it up to become in 1974 commercial director of his beloved Wednesday's rivals and, over the next 20 years, held just about every job there is at boardroom level. That he should consider taking a job with United was down to the kindness of John Hassall, the United chairman at the time.

After the sacking, he sent me two tickets for the directors' box and a car parking space. It was nice but strange, 'cause the only time I'd ever been to Bramall Lane before was when trying to sell football boots. John Hassall told me to come down and I took a bag of boots and started on the sales pitch. He looked at me and said, 'You can throw them away . . . we're offering you a job.' I told him, 'I don't like you lot!' The vice-chair who was with him said, 'You'll get to like us!' I discussed it at home with Sylvia and accepted it days later.

He soon made his mark. He turned the pools system around and only Liverpool beat United in being the first club to carry an advert on the team shirt. The programme was revamped and the first match ever sponsored at Bramall Lane (1975 *v* Derby County) was down to him.

His rise from commercial director was tied up with the appointment of Reg Brealey as United chairman in 1981. Wanting his football experience on the board, he made Derek an associate director. For the first time ever, clubs were permitted to have one paid director: Derek became United's in 1985, and got a vote with it. Three years later, he became managing director, with a hand in everything from mediating between manager and chairman to sorting out ground improvements. The eight-year reign of Harry Bassett as manager provided Derek with his happiest times in the game, and Harry remains a good mate. Not all managers were mates: he's too discrete to tell me, but there was an infamous sce-

On speaking terms again after 20 years:
Derek Dooley and Sheffield Wednesday.

nario of him and Ian Porterfield having a mutual finger-stabbing-in-the-chest duel in the Bramall Lane car park!

As Derek got older, the United boardroom got dafter. Taking what he calls 'early retirement' in 1992, he thought his days of footballing drama were over. Soon after, he was asked to be chief executive, and then found himself as acting chairman while two men who had previously held that title, Reg Brealey and Paul Woolhouse, fought it out in the High Court as to who owes what to whom (see the Reg Brealey section). This undignified spectacle was a world away from the football world he had known in his youth. His willingness to speak out in the 1993 ownership sagas didn't do him any favours.

> Paul [Woolhouse] was doing things he shouldn't have been. I told him he couldn't do certain things. He'd tell me he was chair and he'd do what he wanted. I'd argue against him and I'd be the only one, but I saw it as my job to look after the interests of the club. I opposed contract changes to the catering and a lot of other things which I won't go into.

So how did it all end?

> He kept offering me a new contract which I'd refuse to sign! In the end, he says I'll put £35,000 in a pension scheme as well. But if I'd signed, I'd have got the sack in a few months.

Banned by the new chairman from travelling on the team coach to away games like he had done for decades, he was then criticised by the same man for drinking with the team manager while on a pre-season tour. Derek received a written ultimatum: resign and accept compensation or face dismissal without recompense. The letter also contained a variety of libellous allegations. At the next board meeting, the issue was not mentioned. Derek's folder of evidence against the chairman was not needed because he disappeared soon after along with thousands of pounds of ticket money.

For nine months, Derek was out of the game, then, with Woolhouse's disappearing act, the remaining board members recalled him to become chairman. In doing so, he became the first former professional footballer to become a club chairman. Leaving the board (by choice) in 1996, Derek was given the honorary appointment of vice-president of the club. His main task today is to mix with the directors of other clubs and run a few committees.

One decision he made in 1993 had taken him 20 years to reach. This was when he returned to Hillsborough. A change of personnel at board level, allied with good relations between the boards of the two clubs—a product of travelling together to London to discuss the establishment of the Premier League—led to a dinner invitation before a Wednesday *v* United fixture in 1993. He thought long and hard about it and decided to go. On alighting from his car, he was hugged by an old Wednesday steward, which made him cry. Over dinner, he was told by the Wednesday chairman to prepare himself to be presented to the capacity crowd before the match. Out he walked to an ovation from 40,000. He could not talk; he just wept. It was big of the Wednesday chairman to do this and a fitting tribute to a man who does not bear grudges. Today, the office complex at Hillsborough hosts a restaurant which is full on match days, and available for private hire. Its name is 'Dooley's'.

Football can be such a cruel world. The game took his leg and his livelihood and at the same time gave him various lifelines and looked after him. In turn, he made it his job to look after the younger and less fortunate. His All-Stars team of ex-pros played various Select XIs and made thousands for various charities. In the 1970s and '80s, he coached Sunday teams with some success. In 1993, he was made Freeman of the City by the Council—the only sportsman in the city's history to receive the accolade.

This unassuming man refers to past events as 'pitfalls'; most of us would call them calamities. Fortunately, he was never alone: in Sylvia his wife of 46 years he has a remarkable woman whose hospitality towards the various strangers who find themselves in the United boardroom is legendary. One day, maybe Derek will write his memoirs and be explicit about what went on in his time at the Lane. Such reading would be dynamite. One gets the impression, however, that to reveal too much would be against his nature. Maybe what he has been through personally makes him see the boardroom tangos as little more than amusing details—the tribulations of men far smaller than himself.

Red Mist...
Len Badger

Pride of place above the mantelpiece on the living room wall is a fiftieth birthday present from four people, one of whom signs himself as 'T.C.'. The initials stand for Tony Currie, a former team-mate of the recipient and now just mate, and the birthday gift is a frame containing illustrations and photographs of United players of the past hundred years. Entitled 'Portrait of Legends', it contains all the names who matter and the centre figure is obviously T.C. To the left is the face of a full-back in a mode known to all who watched him—an intense stare lurks below a fringe accompanied by two thick sideburns that belong to the early 1970s.

The man who greets me on a summer Sunday morning in 1998 is now white of hair and ample of girth and looks every inch the jovial publican that he now is. A beautiful pub in its own acres of land on the top of a hill in Derbyshire is an idyllic setting in which to reminisce on the career of a right-back who achieved international honours and who, 30 years after leaving Bramall Lane, remains a fanatical fan and retains the common touch that made him so popular with Blades fans. In conversation, he still refers to city rivals as 'the Pigs'.

Born shortly before the Second World War ended meant a childhood of post-war austerity made more difficult by the death of his father when he was ten. Employed in the nearby pit, which closed in the early 1950s, Dad then had to find employment, which he did in the Hadfield's steelworks, where the Meadowhall shopping complex stands today. An upbringing among the factory grime and noise of Tinsley Park produced a happy brother and sister and a remarkable mum who, to keep bread on the table, worked from dawn until late afternoon cooking for the privileged students at Sheffield Collegiate College. Both mum and dad came from United families and, having recounted stories about Jimmy Hagan, father took son on the train to Bramall Lane and they stood on the terraces to watch their mutual hero. Little Len also had a soft spot for a good-looking and stylish full-back by the name of Graham Shaw. Years later, when cleaning the same man's boots, he realised Graham was a cut above.

> . . . he wor' a type different to everyone else: they were lower cut.
> Like carpet slippers. He'd got style and it can rub off on you.

The road to Bramall Lane began on the three pitches belonging to the colliery near where he lived. In an era where the only leisure option for working-class lads was football, a dozen would climb over the fences and play all day. Like today, however, money corrupted the game: 'if you owned a football, you were automatically captain of one of the teams!'

The bad example of their elders was evident, too, particularly after 2 pm on a Sunday lunchtime.

> By the time the clubs had kicked out, there'd be a 20-a-side game
> going . . . half of 'em worst for drink.

Avoiding drunken tackles obviously had its merits, because as a ten-year-old he played at United's Ball Inn training pitch for the school side who made it to the finals of the Wednesday Shield. Selected as a midfielder, he never had any particular coaching and taught himself by watching United and practising in both schoolyard and cobbled street. Mid-teens was an exciting time which saw him recommended for a trial with Sheffield Boys. Not selected for the next trial match, he turned up anyway and, when a full-back failed to appear, he volunteered to stand in. He had a good game and got picked to represent the city. The team did well and lost a semi-final at Bramall Lane to Manchester in front of 15,000. The same year he represented Yorkshire Boys and then England School-boys against West Germany at Maine Road, Manchester. His five Eng-land Boys appearances meant a sacrifice on behalf of his mum. Players had to wear a blazer and had to buy it themselves. The FA were gen-erous enough to supply the badge which they insisted must be sewn on the breast pocket.

He was 14 and could have signed for any number of professional clubs. That he chose United was no mystery.

> It was the only team I ever wanted to play for. Me mum wanted me to sign for them as well.

Having trained with United twice a week, he was signed as one of the 'ground staff' in 1960 on a weekly wage of £6. Mrs Badger insisted that the club teach him something other than football. The outcome was a farce.

> Arnold Newton the club secretary said I could be his student and learn office work . . . it lasted about a week!

Training was not too sophisticated, but it was changing. The early 1960s saw the beginnings of the qualified coach and the desirability of FA coaching badges. Endless lapping of the pitch perimeter was to be replaced by an emphasis on technique. All the same, summertime was not what it is today and Len found himself working as a barrow boy on Parkway market and laying kerbstones for the chairman's building company.

He had no more need to do this, however, when in 1962 he signed full-time professional for a team just promoted to Division One. The wage was now £35 a week, and his seventeenth birthday was spent in Toronto as part of an 18-man United squad on a close season tour of North America. Days later, he was sitting in a Times Square hotel in New York watching a colour TV that had 15 channels. It was a long way from Tinsley. In 1966 Len was part of the United team that played in a tournament in Santiago, Chile. He scored in the 4–0 victory over AC Milan and played in front of 80,000 when the opponents were the national side. He was not even 20 years of age.

His first-team debut came in a League Cup tie at Bury in October 1962; the League debut six months later at home to Orient. Meanwhile, both he and his United team-mate, Bernard Shaw, played for England at Wembley in the Junior European Cup final in front of 45,000. A remarkable team also contained Ron Harris, Tommy Smith, Lew Chatterley, John Salmons and John Sissons, all of whom became First Division players. Having made the United first team, the right-back position was his for the next 13 years and he was to make 457 first-team appearances, scoring seven goals and playing under four United managers.

He was fast, albeit with a sort of hunched-shoulder gallop, accurate in the pass and capable of a terrifically effective slide tackle. He was an attacking player who could also throw a ball a hell of a distance. Between 1964 and 1968 he played for the England Under-23 team 13 times under the managerial eye of Alf Ramsey and later Joe Mercer. Three appearances for the Football League XI came his way in 1967. While never making the full England team, he was part of the squad of 40 selected before the 1966 World Cup, but missed the selection for 1970, as both Keith Newton and Paul Reaney were favoured. Len tells me he was as good as those two and I agree. The former in particular was roasted every match he ever played against United's winger and Len's mate Alan Woodward.

The man who made Len into a fine footballer was United manager John Harris, whom he considers a father figure in a number of ways. Aware of the absence of a male breadwinner at home, Harris gave Mrs Badger a job making tea for the directors in a career that ran parallel to Len's. A club house was made available to Len when he got married and another for his mum; in return, she looked after United apprentices there for 17 years.

The mid-1960s team was remarkable in costing next to nothing and containing nine local players and two others who came from around 40 miles away. The average age of the team was 21 and, at one time, the captain was an 18-year-old Len. When Harris moved upstairs to become general manager, his successor Arthur Rowley was not the man for the job in Len's opinion.

> He was casual and laid back; it probably wasn't the thing a team so young needed.

Relegated to Division Two in 1968, John Harris returned to manage. Three years later, United were back in the top flight following a ten-game unbeaten run to end their Division Two campaign. Then followed a 12-match unbeaten run in Division One—a club record that still stands. Len played in all these matches in a team that attacked mainly down the right-hand side using that astonishing triumvirate of talent: Badger, Currie and Woodward. What memories those names conjure up.

European football so nearly came his way when United finished one point away from a European place under Harris's successor, Ken Furphy. An amazing season gave way to one in which United won only one match in six months and Len found himself on the end of criticism for not getting back quick enough from his overlapping forays. No manager at United ever dropped him, but Len knew his United days were numbered. When Jimmy Sirrel succeeded Furphy, they were over. The newly arrived Scot bought a full-back as his first signing and, in Len's recollection, said the following:

> . . . he said to me, 'You're not big enough to play at the back: be finding yourself another club.' I said, 'I'm 32, and I don't think I'm gonna grow much.'

Another club was not difficult to find. The chap who lived next door was a former team-mate and United's longest-serving player ever, Joe Shaw. He was also manager of Chesterfield. They struck a deal over the garden fence, but United's need to squeeze every last penny caused bad feelings and a bitter departure.

> Joe said 'Come on a free and I'll sort you out.' I thought after 17 years they'd let me go for nowt. Jimmy Sirrel said 'No way! We've a new stand to pay for' and I'd cost £8,000. Even today, I don't know what the deal was, but after all my years of service and what my mum had done for the club . . . well, I said to him, 'Fuck off, I'm off.'

As parting shots go, it was a good one. There were no goodbyes. Collecting his belongings, he left. Days later, it all sank in: '. . . it was like being chopped in half'.

When he next returned to Bramall Lane he cannot remember. The memory of the day remains, however.

> I left in a temper. I had 18 months of my contract left. I would have loved to have stayed, but I wasn't wanted and I used to react like that . . . red mist . . . just temper.

Playing for the first time ever in Division Three with his new club proved a struggle. It was a different world: albeit one that valued a cultured right-back. Then his mate Joe got the sack. His successor, Arthur

Cox, proved good for Len, giving him a renewed appetite for the game and, following a broken leg, got Len fitter than he had ever been in his career and made him captain on his return. A few months later, he broke his leg again. After 46 appearances for the Spireites, he hung up his boots.

> When I was very young at United, I asked a senior pro called Harry Latham: 'How do you know when you want to finish?' He said to me, 'You'll know son, you'll know.'

He knew now. While the football world ended with a broken leg, he was not out on a limb. A business partnership begun years earlier meant he had a paper-producing factory in Derbyshire employing 40 people. Disaster struck when, at the age of 37, he learned what liquidation meant and had to sign on the dole for a while.

Ever resourceful, he was soon working again, this time selling advertising space for *The Star*. An office junior by the name of Steve Thompson shared the same space before becoming a professional footballer and becoming caretaker-manager of United in 1998. Len's attempts at football management went no further than Norton Woodseats in the Yorkshire

The professionals: Len (front),
Ted Hemsley and Bill Dearden

League. He loved the good times and camaraderie the unpaid position provided and still regularly sees his ex-players. But paid work put paid to football when he teamed up with a former schoolteacher and bought a pub and wine bar in the Sheffield suburb of Dronfield in 1982. This venture then saw him move to another pub in north Derbyshire and in 1991 he took over the pub we are sitting in.

Of all the former United players I have ever spoken to, Len is the one who speaks with the greatest affection for his time at the Lane. Some of the jobs he was given, however, made him a liability.

> As a 16-year-old apprentice, they gave me the job of stoking the coal boiler in the dressing room so that they would always have hot water. One day I didn't shut the boiler door properly and hot coals fell out. I burned the dressing room down. When they cleared away the debris, they found underground passages, so, being the smallest, I got in one and followed it until I saw a bit of light. I pushed against the roof of the tunnel and up pops my head into the floor of the boardroom. All the directors were sitting round a table; the chairman looked at me and said, 'What's going on here?'

Young Len was given 50 laps of the pitch as a punishment—not for burning down the dressing room, but for insulting the board!

Whatever the task he was given at Bramall Lane, he was up to it. Given the job of sweeping the terraces, he did it and regarded it as a learning process.

> I knew John Street terraces like the back of me hand. In fact, I knew every inch of Bramall Lane and every smell. I could have walked around it blindfolded.

At one time, in the 1960s, there were five floodlight pylons. Len climbed every one to the top. Why? 'Why? 'Cause it was where I belonged.' The association of emotion and place I always thought was the preserve of fans, but in Len I found the only player who felt the same about the bricks and mortar that represent most evidently what a football club is.

His early career was among a team who enjoyed socialising. The exciting era that was the late 1960s saw Len and others hanging about in the Nether Edge Jazz Club and Sheffield's second nightclub, the Penny Farthing. Saturday nights would find him occasionally in the City Hall and one of my dad's mates remembers Len trying to pull the woman who was with him and who today is his wife of 30 years. The virtue of Sheffield's womanhood was saved somewhat when the 22-year-old Len married. Renting his new home from the club, he experienced for the first time an inside toilet and bath.

By 1970 and on good money, he did what all footballers of that era did and moved to the new housing estates in Dronfield. Only ever on a maximum two-year contract, the renewal in the close season was the green light to try to negotiate a wage deal. The best basic he ever got was £80 per week in the mid-1970s. With a £30 bonus for points earned, he pulled in a career maximum of £8,000 per annum. The biggest cheque that came his way were two five-year loyalty bonuses of £500 and £12,000 from his 1973 testimonial against Wednesday. Investing it for several years meant he had £18,000 to go into business in the late 1970s. Today's wages astound him, but allow him to reflect on what such an income does to football.

> The game never gave you an assurance that you'd be all right. That was what most men had to put up with in their job. Then the gap between those playing and watching wasn't that great. The wages today take you away from your fans; it makes you different.

What also makes Len and his contemporaries different to players today is the longevity of their friendships.

> There was a bond in them days: Trevor Hockey, Geoff Salmons, Tony Currie, Woody, Bill Dearden, me and Ted Hemsley . . . there was a feeling for the club then and even now it remains. We have aged together and meet about three times a year.

They got together in 1986 for Tony Currie's testimonial. In the dressing room beforehand, Len remembers the atmosphere.

> It was like we'd never been apart. When you've shared what we had, you didn't have to say anything.

Talking to this decent chap, whom all the pub regulars and staff like, it's hard to reconcile the happy publican with the hot-tempered younger man he was. The Burnley and Wales left-winger, Leighton James, once went public to the tabloids after Len had got him sent off, accusing him of being a 'talker' and intimidating by constantly winding up the opposition. Was this true?

> Oh, him! He had funny eyes, so I used to talk to him calling him 'Clarence the Cross-Eyed Lion' [from a TV series called 'Daktari']. Usually, we'd face teams playing the 4–3–3 set-up and either me or Ted [Hemsley]

the other full-back would get a winger. If it was me, I'd say to him, 'Fuck off onto the other wing or I'm gonna fuckin' kill yu.' When he did, Ted would tell him exactly what I'd just told him.

Sent off five times—each time for raising his arms to opponents— he dismisses such escapades as 'red mist'. One player he remembers produced mist of another kind. In Liverpool and Bolton's Peter Thompson was an opponent Len dreaded playing against. 'He would destroy me. I couldn't ever get near enough to kick him.'

Another opponent who evaded his attentions in front of a TV audience of millions was a chap called George Best, who you may recall played on the wing for Manchester United. In October 1971 Blades were top of Division One, challenged by Manchester United. A match at Old Trafford saw over 50,000 inside and another 15,000 locked out. With seven minutes to go, it was 0–0; then George decided to take the United defence on and score a goal. On Match of The Day, as the ball enters the net, the figure of Len Badger is seen sliding vainly across the goal. Realising the damage is done, the full-back in the white shirt lies on his back, no doubt devastated. He remembers it well.

It was the most deafening noise I've ever heard in my life when they scored. Blame Ted Hemsley! He got injured and Gil Reece came on as sub. If Ted had been on, he'd have pushed him wide. Gil hadn't a clue what to do . . . he was a winger not a defender!

A few post-retirement charity matches ended when old injuries started playing up. Arthritis in the ankle produces an occasional limp and provides a constant reminder of his footballing career. Not much else remains. His England caps and various medals he gave to an auction to build a sports pavilion, only for the organiser to run off with all the money! But, ever phlegmatic, he took it in his stride, as he does my question on whether he has regrets.

I should've made more of my career, played more times for England. We [United] should have won the cup in the early 1970s.

Attending Bramall Lane as a fan is something he has done since he left. But attending has its difficulties.

United are me passion. Then sometimes I don't go for months. I'm not sure why . . . Maybe I'm selfish: I want it to be like it was and it never can be.

Many fans understand that emotion, and it's good to hear a former player express it. It's somehow encouraging to find that some players share the passion and memories that fans carry with them. Few things in life can equal the euphoria of the great moments provided by a football team for a passionate supporter. That a player can appreciate the same things and still seek that feeling from others when his playing days are over makes me feel happy. Like all of us who reflect, contemporary times never seem as good as the mythical golden age of some distant past, but what Len ends with I think many readers will understand.

> I've mellowed . . . but there'll never by the high in my life that I got as a player under floodlights in front of 40,000. You can't replace that, and that's the problem many have after finishing with football.

A Stable Lad...
Carl Bradshaw

To achieve international football status, play in England's top division for Sheffield's two professional clubs, be handed a six-week custodial sentence and own a converted farmhouse in an area where horses abound, with a charming wife and two kids by the age of 30 is no mean feat for a man whose life began in 1968 on Sheffield's Manor council estate. This district of repute achieved national notoriety when its major hostelry, The Manor Hotel, won the accolade of *The Sun* newspaper's 'Roughest Boozer in Britain Award' in 1989. It is and always has been a tough place to grow up.

For street cred, however, it is a good place to come from, and it makes one appreciate the good things in life. So, aged 13, when Mum and

Dad, wishing to try their hand at being publicans, moved the family of three brothers to a spacious pub home in a better district a few miles away, a new life began in the company of hundreds on a daily basis, none of whom took too many liberties.

A United fan by virtue of being taken to Bramall Lane by an uncle, Carl later attended with mates from the locality, but then stopped attending due to playing every Saturday—for Sheffield Wednesday. A lot of water has passed under the bridge since the 17-year-old made his debut for Wednesday, only to find himself years later at Bramall Lane much vilified by his former fans. In a busy life which has seen many a fracas and much action before thought, Carl can now reflect on football loyalties in a city that does not easily forgive on this issue.

Footballing ability ran in the family. Dad was a good player who had represented the city as a boy, and two of the three sons made it as professionals. Spotted at junior school, Carl was to represent the city from the ages 11 to 15 and play on Sundays for Woodhouse Angel in his elder brother's team, which meant he was two years younger than everyone else on the pitch. Playing as a right-winger, he was small but fast, and both he and his elder brother caught the eye of scouts. The latter was signed by Wednesday on schoolboy forms. Later, aged 14, Carl was offered a trial at United, but watchers were not impressed. Eddie Gray at Leeds was, and tried to sign him. Told by Dad to wait a few months, Wednesday then offered terms and Carl accepted—a decision made in preference to Leeds on the criterion that training with him would be big brother Darren. Under the eye of Wednesday's youth team coach, Albert Phelan, Carl found himself at centre-forward and, once again, the youngest player on the pitch in the Wednesday Northern Intermediate side.

A trial for England Schoolboys meant that, almost inevitably, at the age of 16 he was offered and signed apprentice professional terms with Wednesday. Paid £28 a week, his parents received a weekly stipend of £10 to feed him well. On such miserly money, he then had a trial for the England youth team. This was a success, and between the ages of 18 and 19 under Colin Murphy he played five times for his country in places as diverse as France and China, in a team that contained Vinnie Samways, David Holdsworth, Matt LeTissier and David Hirst—who competed with Carl for the centre-forward position. Signing professional aged 18 under Wednesday boss Howard Wilkinson, his income rose to £250 a week plus bonuses and incentives with a signing-on fee of £9,000 spread over three years. His full League debut, however, came in a Barnsley shirt, where he was loaned for experience. Scoring on his debut, he made six appearances before returning to Hillsborough.

The Barnsley manager, Alan Clarke, wanted to sign him, but Wilkinson soon had him in the first team. Scoring a hat-trick against Sheffield United in the Northern Intermediate League one Saturday, he scored another against Aston Villa in a midweek reserve game. Selected for the first team, he scored on his debut days later at Queens Park Rangers. The 1986–87 season saw nine full-team outings and two goals. The following season he again scored two in 20 appearances. Next season, however, he played only three games and then left Hillsborough. The departure of Wilkinson to Leeds meant the man who signed him was gone. Not seeing eye to eye with his successor, Peter Eustace, meant his days were numbered, and in September 1988 he was transferred to Manchester City.

Moving from one big club to an even bigger, albeit a Second Division, club was a surprise to say the least.

> I knew nothing about it. I hadn't asked to leave and if I knew that Eustace would be manager only three months I wouldn't have gone.

Signed by Mel Machin, Carl managed only five first-team games in his time at Maine Road and for four of them he was substitute. The transfer was rushed, but he could repent at leisure. Three weeks later and not in the first team, he questioned the manager as to how a First Division regular cannot get a game in Division Two. He was told that he was a replacement for Imre Varadi, who was not an automatic choice, and who had gone the opposite way as part of the transfer deal. He was not placated. He continued to live in Sheffield but got tired with the travelling and his weight ballooned.

Into this misery came happiness in the shape of Harry Bassett who took him on loan to Bramall Lane in September 1989 and signed him permanently a month later for £50,000 plus £50,000 more after so many games. He became a regular first-teamer, playing as a right-sided wingback and occasionally as a defender. On signing Carl, Harry, with typical imagery and diplomacy, told the local press that he considered him a 'headbanger with potential'. Obviously, Harry knew a bit about Carl, but Carl had never before come across him and had only once played against Wimbledon when at Sheffield Wednesday.

The money United offered was lower then he was getting at Manchester City, but there was a three-year deal on the table and, as Carl sees it in retrospect:

> Harry did me a favour from the hell-hole that was City. He was in a
> class of his own. Some didn't like him—usually them who were not in
> his side.

Leaving Manchester City weighing 13 stone, Harry put him through
the mill to shift some weight. Long runs and abdominal exercises got
him into shape under a regime he had almost forgotten because the training at Maine Road had been pretty easy—hence the weight gain. It
was Harry who tried him at right-back and it's a position he occupies
today. Made captain of United when the normal incumbent (Brian Gayle)
was injured made Carl 'over the moon' (yes, he actually said it!) and
his time at Bramall Lane was the happiest of his career.

> It was about pride. Captain of the team you always wanted to play
> for . . . great feeling.

What I find intriguing is how such a Blade felt when offered terms
by city rivals Wednesday, which then turns into a situation where he
has to pull on a blue and white shirt and make himself popular with
their followers.

> I was only 14 when I signed, and then it was a lot to do with me
> brother . . . but Wednesday did me a big favour. At 17 I was playing
> in the top league, and as a player it doesn't matter what shirt you wear.

While at Hillsborough, he always looked for the Barnsley result due to
the happy times he had there, and then looked for what the then Third
Division Sheffield United had done.

> You didn't mention United out loud. To be honest, as a pro either you
> just wanted your money—after all it's a short career—or you wanted
> to fulfil some ambition.

He got plenty of stick at the time from United mates but, as many of
these were family, he didn't lose friends by initially signing for the wrong
club.

Admitting to once being 'arrogant and cocky', such characteristics
got him into trouble. We'll look at such incidents later, but I was curious about how, in the 1989 BBC documentary about United, the only
player to give the manager, Harry Bassett, any lip was the young Carl.
Privileged to be allowed to ride the team bus when Harry was in charge,
I noticed again that it was Carl who would say to him things that his
team-mates were merely thinking. The latter always took it well and

maybe, Carl reasons, there was a recognition from Harry that Carl had something of the younger Bassett in him. While probing where such confidence came from, his wife Joanna enters the kitchen and interjects that he was like it at school and in his neighbourhood. Confident and able to speak to people, she adds he was also a tough guy at the school where they met; he could put the fear of death into her. Living in a pub, he agrees, makes for many a precocious child and, belonging to extended family networks, which on his mum's side consisted of three families of ten kids, meant back-up in times of trouble was always available. He never had to be shy or retiring.

Naturally, then, when in a United shirt, he caused a bit of bother here and there. He had annual on-the-pitch run-ins with Kevin Gallacher of Blackburn and, when United played against Nottingham Forest, his name was written in first and the other ten followed. The Forest and England full-back, Stuart Pearce, always got a hard time with Carl, who tackled as hard as he did and could not be intimidated. Then there was Vinnie Jones who, having been a team-mate for years, left for Chelsea in 1990. When the sides met in an FA Cup tie, Carl decided to ridicule his old mate.

> He'd taken to wearing a headband . . . so I ran out with one on like his, then in the warm-up threw it on the floor and jumped on it.

The 7,000 travelling Blades appreciated the joke; the Chelsea fans for some reason did not. Neither did Vinnie who, 30 seconds into the game, got booked for a bad tackle on Dane Whitehouse. The matter was not over yet.

> We got a corner and he's holding the ball and pushes Dane when he tries to get it. I went up to him and he jabbed me in the eye so I head-butted him and punched him. Neither of us got booked, 'cause the referee realised he'd have to send him off for a second offence.

What the ref could not or did not want to see was caught on camera and Sky TV's Andy Gray went through it in slow motion. Next thing, Carl was up before the FA and received a three-match ban. Vinnie got away scot-free.

Various off-the-field activity had also gained him notoriety. In his teens, he had a 'Fighting Irish' motif tattooed on his shoulder blade— and then pulled on an England shirt! When at Bramall Lane, he had the Sheffield United club badge tattooed on his right calf muscle, which probably did not impress his later employers at Norwich and Wigan.

Hold me back: 'Bradders' in a disagreement with Wednesday's Carlton Palmer and Nigel Worthington. Jamie Hoyland attempts to calm him down.

Problems in Sheffield arose when he signed for United and was quoted in the local press stating how United were his team and he always wanted to play for them.

When United and Wednesday met in a Premiership derby in 1992 in the first League fixture between the two for 14 years, feelings were running high. The United victory saw Carl play a big part in winding up Wednesday players both in the players' tunnel beforehand and throughout the match and annoy taunting Owls by kissing his United shirt. A complaint from a female Wednesday fan saw Carl and the United goalie facing a disciplinary panel at the FA, the former accused of making a two-finger sign at the Owls, the latter of running around arms aloft 'like an aeroplane and making a pig noise'. Both were fined £500 for their conduct.

In a Sheffield city-centre pub after the 2–0 victory, a group of Owls starting abusing Carl. Standing for so much, he told his accuser to step outside, but the latter refused, seeing that Carl had an entourage bigger than his. Days later, the Owl, armed with a baseball bat, toured pubs in his district looking for him. He never found him. He, however, was found, days later, by Carl.

> I went to his house with a few others . . . which I shouldn't have done.
> I just got an apology.

Good family connections have always served him well. Later, however, he sought a more tranquil route out of public encounters when he took a course offered by the US personality guru Dale Carnegie. The course followed by the man who wrote the classic *How to Win Friends and Influence People* was meant to build confidence and encourage articulation. In so doing, Carl felt he was addressing a contradiction in his character in that here was a man who could, in a pair of shorts, perform with glee in front of 40,000 yet in a smaller crowd in a pub was 'stand-offish' and insecure with strangers. Whether the course worked, he can't really tell me, but he did claim now to be able to start a conversation, which is a relief because he certainly knew how to end them.

The 3–1 United victory at Hillsborough, months after the 2–0 result, had the Wednesdayites booing his every move. Chants of 'Reject' he could handle, but the one that went 'He only hits fuckin' women' was cruel and therein lay a story that made Carl notorious. An incident in a Sheffield nightclub years earlier is explained to me.

> This lass wanted to go to the women's toilets. She didn't know who I
> was so it was nothing to do with football. Anyway, she just pushes
> past and then pours a drink over me head. I told her to fuck off and
> she points this empty glass at my face so I slapped her.

Arrested next day when other revellers told police who had done it, he was later fined in a magistrate's court on a charge of assault.

Certain Sheffield police officers were also taking an interest in him around the same time because of who he hung about with. When not playing, he would watch the match with Blades his own age. Nothing wrong with that, but some of his peers were on police records as 'hooligans' and, through the eyes of the police camera lens, this made Carl a bad lad by association. A few mates received complimentary match tickets, so police blamed him for facilitating the entry of hooligans into the ground. One told the club chairman, Reg Brealey, that he was playing with naughty boys, so Reg told him to drop the complimentaries. He didn't: he simply left them in the name of a team-mate so that the police who would stand watching at the players' entrance before games never saw him handing them out.

Another drama involved the boyfriend of a former girlfriend who had a child by Carl. Threats and weapons were produced and retributions promised and executed. It was all getting a bit hot.

With the heat on, Carl decided a break from Sheffield wouldn't be a bad idea. Norwich City had 'tapped him up' to see whether he was interested. As it was, he left in June 1994 for £500,000 and a deal whereby United would get £75,000 after 25 games and some other convoluted payment. They never saw such money because a ruptured Achilles, torn thigh and damaged knee ligaments combined with different managers to limit his first-team appearances. Bought by John Deehan, he played under his successors Gary Megson, Martin O'Neill and Mike Walker. It was Walker who sold him in 1997 to Wigan, but only a year earlier United's manager Howard Kendall had tried to bring him back to the Lane.

Leaving United was not easy. Relegated a month previously from the Premier, he was told by Harry that he was prepared to let him go and Norwich, being a Premiership club, was too good an opportunity for a footballer to miss. But loyalty to United made for a difficult decision.

> I didn't want to leave a sinking ship. I wanted to help get promotion, but when Deano was sold I knew things weren't happy at the club.

Have being offered his best-ever payday in football, he and his family moved to a new home in rural Norfolk and a new and more tranquil life seemed about to begin. He took up fishing on the advice of John Deehan.

> I think 'cause of the trouble I'd had at United, he got a bloke to take me fishing as a way of keeping me out of trouble!

Rarely out with the lads, he became domesticated and a very competent cook. On the board at Norwich was TV chef and million-selling author, Delia Smith, and, believe it or not, the pair would swap recipes. Before you start groaning, the Brads everyone knew was lurking amid the bouillabaisse—and it was back with a vengeance in February 1997.

A Sunday match at Bramall Lane saw Norwich defeat United 3–2 and Carl come on as sub. The celebrations began on the coach and Carl and team-mate Andy Johnson decided to continue festivities in Norwich. Around midnight, the two of them took a cab to the training ground where their cars were parked with a view to getting their house keys from the vehicles and continuing their taxi journey home. The remote location and the ignorance of the cab driver produced an argument en route. Arriving at their destination, the driver exchanged words with his occupants. This resulted in a scuffle by the perimeter fence, which culminated in the 17-stone driver sitting on top of Carl. Unable to get him off, Carl bit the driver's finger, which did the trick, so the driver phoned for the police as Carl phoned for Joanna to come and pick him up.

The police arrived first and surrounded the training ground. While three of them hid in the hedgerow watching the two footballers sitting in their car, others further down the road spread out the 'stinger' device intended to puncture the car tyres of miscreants' vehicles. Finding the car park locked, the police called the groundsman who arrived to open it, whereupon ten officers stormed the stationary car and arrested the pair. Unfortunately, when cuffed and thrown into the van, the pair got the giggles, but were not laughing next morning when faced with charges of criminal damage and assault.

The cab driver made four statements, all of which differed. The same man had once faced charges of kidnapping a female passenger, but in court the stipendiary magistrate favoured the prosecution and sentenced Carl to six weeks' imprisonment. He was to serve three of the six weeks, and, when he entered a prison for the first time, he found it 'frightening and atrocious', made all the worse by Joanna having just given birth to their second child. It was exercise time and he entered the prison yard to a chorus of catcalls of 'Hello footballer!', 'Ipswich', and 'Where's your girlie shorts?' An armed robber who knew people who knew Carl in Sheffield looked after him, as did a black lad who had apparently once crossed the Krays in another prison. Kindly prison officers allowed him extra gym time to stay in shape.

Offered the chance to play football, he first went in the net to suss out the level of ferocity and then had a few games in midfield, riding the tackles of the temporarily ensconced pub players. His cell-mate was an old man who was harmless and, in the absence of currency, a prison officer got him a phone card. The hardest part of being inside proved to be the weekly visits from Joanna. Aware that the court process and sentence destroyed her, he then realised what Norwich City had to offer: nothing—the club were to disown him and then get rid of him. Fined two weeks' wages, they let him go shortly after his release on a free transfer.

Relations with both managers and fellow-professionals at Norwich had not been good for a while, though. Too many players had too high an opinion of themselves.

> You'd got to have a flash car. They all wore Armani or Calvin Klein under-pants; me being from Sheffield, I had M&S, so they gave me stick. It just seems to me it was a latest-label-big-time club.

Refusing the offer of a new contract under Mike Walker brought ostracism at the club's barbecue in a situation neither Carl nor Joanna will ever forget. Then came the prison sentence and he found himself transferred two days after his release. He left without saying goodbye to anyone and took up a job offer at Wigan from his old manager, John Deehan. Another offer came from Crystal Palace, but he wanted to return north, and in Deehan he at least knew what he was walking into. The seven months at Wigan have so far been enjoyable.

Sitting in the kitchen of his farmhouse on the edge of Sheffield, a stranger sees only a calm young man in a dream home. He hasn't graced a Sheffield nightclub for nine years and he admits he's changed a lot: not on the pitch—he still gives everything—but off the pitch he will never be drawn into the 'big time' he flirted with at Norwich. As we speak, the issue that preoccupies him is the proposed building of stables on the land he owns in front of the home. With sensible investments and pensions, he has many years before he has to worry about what to do after football. He's happy now; only a return to his one footballing love—Sheffield United—could make him happier.

Heroes

But the idol is an idol for only a moment, a human eternity, all of nothing; and when the time comes for the golden foot to become a lame duck, the star will have completed his journey from sparkle to blackout. His body has more pictures than a clown's suit, and by now the acrobat is a cripple, the artist a beast of burden.

(Eduardo Galeano, *Football in Sun and Shadow*: 5)

The King of the Land...
Tony Currie

I impressed a couple of teachers with my choice. It was quick and unequivocal and, they presumed, obviously well researched. Yes, at the age of 11, my chosen name for the Catholic sacrament of Confirmation would be Anthony. Fortunately, no one asked me why or raised the possibly embarrassing facts that, of the two Saint Anthonys in the calendar, one was the patron saint of hopeless causes and the other renowned for sexual denial. Truth is, it was not a saint but an idol from which I took my name. This was a certain Tony Currie. The day before the ceremony, United beat Watford 3–0 and were back in Division One. The man known to all as T.C. played his part and, until he left United in 1976, held my attention to the point of adoration.

Personally, I believe football support is a form of worship. It allows fans, the true believers, various emotions and it says and does something. Having said that, the true meaning of what it is to be a Blade is not known or agreed upon. What constitutes a true supporter? Does it require years of learning? Regular attendance? Can you be self-taught? Do you need preaching to? Regardless, because we have watched for years and played a bit, we allow ourselves to be simultaneously indignant, intolerant and pious. We reaffirm our devotion weekly and recycle hymns with slightly changed words at the match. Occasionally we curse Fate or Fortune. Each season and before every game we dream a little, and every day and each game die a little. We believe a better life lies ahead and, as devotees, take our support to the grave. An occasional lapse in faith is permitted, but guilt compels re-attendance; football support is therefore similar to Catholicism.

When it comes to players of maestro or genius status, fans are generally agreed as to who they are. But Blades fans have a problem. First, they appear but once a lifetime. Secondly, because of United's status, anyone of such ability will leave for glory elsewhere. Tony Currie, a man forever associated with Sheffield United, was a football genius, but Tony Currie left. The prodigal son has since returned, but in a new life. Herein lies a long story which began 48 years ago in Cricklewood, north-west London.

The formative men in his life were a younger brother and three uncles. Aged four, his father walked out and his mum took the two lads to live in an amazing extended family household of 12. An uncle took him to watch nearby non-League Hendon. Two of three such bachelors who dote on their nephews, Bert and Jim were to watch every game of his career. In the garden, they taught skills and watched the boys whenever they turned out for the school. The kid brother (by two years) helped as well: the pair shared a passion for bouncing a tennis ball off the roof slates to learn anticipation and control.

Talent spotters from Queens Park Rangers signed T.C. on schoolboy forms, but let him go at 15. Days later, he began work with a small building firm; he made tea, painted, did anything he was asked—and loved it! Then the youth team coach at Watford offered a six-week contract extended to six months and he signed pro. One year later, United snap this 18-year-old up for the strange price of £26,500. While he went on to play for England, the other brother, despite a trial at Bramall Lane, never made the grade, but played non-League until aged 40.

Arriving in Sheffield at night and in the rain, his digs provided some welcome in the character of Paddy Buckley, another player in similar circumstances. They looked forward to Friday nights—greyhound racing then ten-pin bowling. Not exactly Stringfellow's, but this young Londoner was easy to please: nightclubs and football babes were never to be his scene. On the pitch, he had a dream debut: he scored and showed maturity beyond his years—something that was to become a feature.

> I was never scared before a match. I never suffered nerves. I was always supremely confident in my ability.

Why should he show false modesty? He could do things most players only dream of. To assist this precocious talent, manager John Harris bought a midfield terrier called Trevor Hockey who had simple instructions: win the ball and give it to T.C.— who then delivers 60-yard passes and scores 40-yard goals. While all this was happening, there were power cuts and a three-day week, sheepskins and silk scarves battling it out on the Shoreham End and a DJ who welcomed everyone to 'beautiful downtown Bramall Lane'. You got your money's-worth in those days.

If that wasn't entertainment enough, he would produce his very own movement: the 'Currie Shuffle'. Somehow, he would flick his right foot and feint to the right, then move the ball past the bewildered defender with the other foot. Had this been a Brazilian, we would hear romantic myths about oranges and the Copacabana Beach. The truth is that T.C. learned it in 1961 from Hendon's Jewish left-winger, Miles Spector (it was a cup match against Kingstonians). Now you know! After a shuffle, T.C. would sometimes wave to the crowd, or blow kisses after beating players. Once, he took the ball into attack only to stop, put his foot on it and gesture in bewilderment for supporting colleagues.

But his most renowned act occurred in 1975. A certain Alan Ball (known to all Blades by his full name, Alan Balls-Zabastad), then of Arsenal, had made disparaging comments about United, days before a match, in 1972. He endured mass Blade chants questioning his parentage and, with Arsenal 5–0 up, the carrot-topped git sat on the ball in contempt. In the same fixture over two years later, United were 4–0 up in 17 minutes and, prompted by goalkeeper John Hope, T.C. made amends for 27,000 Blades—he sat on the ball and invited you-know-who to come towards him. Touché.

For all this, my lasting memory was the time he allowed a long ball to bounce over his head and, raising his right heel put it over his and a defender's head to a United player. Once-in-a-lifetime stuff.

He was among a select few who changed the nature of players' relationships with fans. Like a few others at that time—Stan Bowles, Rodney Marsh, Frank Worthington—he was flamboyant, good-looking, rakish and precocious. There he was: tall, muscular, long blonde hair, shirt outside his shorts and making it all look so easy. He received adulation unknown for footballers in Sheffield. Fans wanted locks of hair; he was the mystery star in 'A Question of Sport'; all sorts of posters at the Lane shop were available as souvenirs. Fans sang that he walked on water and that his eyes shined like diamonds and he was the king of the land. These were blatantly false claims, but he did make United famous. For this reason, many Wednesdayites hated him.

One day, in 1975, he kissed a rival player, Alan Birchenall, as they recovered in a heap from a goalmouth scramble. The moment was captured for the Sunday tabloids' front pages. It wasn't a tonguey, and it was all good fun but, at school, the Wednesdayites had their opinions confirmed: he was a 'reyt puff'. We knew he wasn't; blood was spilt in playgrounds over that incident.

Remember the first time we kissed? Alan Birchenall and Tony Currie relive an infamous moment for the benefit of the photographers.

We knew him as the Messiah, but many knew him as 'Beefy'. A few myths grew up around this title, and now's the time to put people straight. The name had nothing to do with physique or suggestions that he was overweight; it was a word used by team-mates, Mick Heaton and Len Badger, whose idea of a joke was 'Beef Currie' (geddit?).

While we're at it, there's another story he wants to sort out and one that his one-time manager Ken Furphy criticised him for publicly: namely, that he did not train hard and lacked motivation. On the contrary, he loved training, never missed it and gave everything. Those who said he was disinterested on the pitch, listen to the man:

> I wanted to be the best every day and every match. What people don't realise is that the other team want to stop that. At times, there were two men marking me and kicking me, and sometimes that tactic worked. If I did not perform, it wasn't a question of not wanting to know. People don't realise how bloody difficult it was sometimes.

Interviewed in 1993, he declared that never in his career did he ever start a match in 100% condition.

> It was part of the game. It was bloody special to play and, if I played when not fully fit, it was usually my own fault.

Just to add to this statement, let me tell you what T.C. told me. In 1972, while boiling an egg, he tipped the pan of scalding water over his right foot. It ballooned and blistered and he limped to the phone box (he didn't have one at home) to tell John Harris. Less than 24 hours later, and with four pain-killing injections in the foot, he's hammering balls around in United's 2–0 defeat of Arsenal. Remember that when the issue of his motivation next arises.

He played some great games for United, but for T.C. there is not one that stands out. As for his best goal? Easy: the 1972 40-yarder against Liverpool. Of all those who were given the job of marking him, the most difficult was Arsenal's Peter Storey: 'an effective stopper . . . who also scratched and gouged'. He won his first of 17 England caps in 1977 and captained the Under-23 side. It followed he should captain United, and Ken Furphy gave him the armband in 1974—and periodically in 1975–76 when Keith Eddy wasn't playing.

An extrovert on the pitch, the living-god was tongue-tied and ill-at-ease off it. He opened Aston Comprehensive Summer Fête in 1973, with me and 20 others like a pack of small dogs walking behind him

Magic moments at the Lane: that memorable 40-yarder
by T.C. against Liverpool in 1972.

and a teacher for an hour. I realised then that he hated such scenarios:
he didn't really know what to do or say. Not that I cared. In fact, in
contradiction to nineteenth-century French novelist Flaubert, who
advised against touching idols lest their gilt comes off in our hands, I
touched T.C.'s brown sports jacket. My opinion of him subsequently
rocketed. So shove that in your pipe, Monsieur.

I never saw T.C. in real life again; he kept a low public profile. His
social life was his team-mates—John Hope, Ted Hemsley, Len Badger
and Billy Dearden. He also had a lot on his plate, about which we didn't
really know. Sure, we heard the rumour that his wife wanted to go back
to London and, the truth is, between 1974 and 1979 his partner had
severe depressions. It must have taken its toll on him.

I wasn't depressed so much as stunned when he left United. At the
time, I thought only of what we would do without him. And now,
over 20 years on, I can ask, 'Why did you leave?' The answer, quite
simply, is that United got relegated in 1976.

Two years previously, he had signed a six-year contract which would
have kept him at Bramall Lane until he was 30. A year later, he turned
down a move to Manchester United mainly because the chairman, Dick
Wragg, promised him that he wanted to build the team around him.

He did say, though, that, if they ever got relegated, they would let him go. Well, United got relegated and, to rub it in, they sold his good mate, Geoff Salmons. This was not the move an ambitious club would have made. Although disillusioned, the truth was:

> I loved the crowd here and we had a great bunch of players. The contracts I signed were always the ones offered. I never knew you could hold out for more or extras or clauses. For me, a contract was offered and you signed them. I didn't want to leave United; they sold me.

On a team holiday in Gibraltar, manager Jimmy Sirrel told him to report to general manager John Harris upon returning next day. The latter put T.C. in the car and drove up the M1. One hour later, on the outskirts of Leeds, he told him of his fate! The fee was a pathetic £265,000: 'something to do with getting ten times what I cost United'. After 313 appearances and 60 goals, our god had risen, 35 miles north and to a higher division. Within a week, t-shirts were sold among Blades: below his head and shoulders were the words 'Gone, but not forgotten'.

This situation provoked indignation and philosophy in the young me. Watching your idol play in another team must be like watching an ex-girlfriend out with another geezer. Besides, that white or yellow 'Admiral' Leeds kit never suited him: he was always meant to wear stripes. But what really annoyed me was that they loved him at Leeds; they even had badges made—'Hot-Stuff Currie' and 'Currie bends more balls than Uri Geller'. Pathetic.

Next time we saw him was two years later when he was wearing a Leeds shirt. The visitors beat United 4–1 (he scored one). It got a bit silly. When he took to the pitch, Blades cheered him and chanted his name. Then, when 2–0 up, chants of 'Currie is a fat twat' were heard. Approaching the Shoreham End, he lifted his shirt to display a physique that was the lightest of his playing career. He indicated his disgust but was bewildered. 'They'd loved me for eight and a half years and I loved them. It hurt.' He was only half-fit that night; he hadn't played for a month, but lied about his injury just to turn out at Bramall Lane. Forgive us, T.C., we know what not we do.

The Leeds manager, Jimmy Armfield, bought him to replace Johnny Giles and build a new team around him. He became captain, played 11 of his 17 England games while at Leeds and was in a team full of internationals. But, with Leeds finishing only sixth, Armfield was sacked. Our favourite former footballer was to leave as well. After 124 games in three years, he asked for a transfer. He did not want to go—leaving

Gone but not forgotten: the Currie Shuffle
in action against Everton in 1971.

Leeds was, in fact, 'the biggest wrench of my career'—but Mrs Currie had to return south. He cost Tommy Docherty at Queens Park Rangers £400,000 and Jimmy Adamson, Armfield's successor, admitted to T.C. that the deal would get him a lynching, but settled for a sacking soon after.

At QPR he wore the number 10 shirt as previously worn by Marsh and Bowles. In this difficult inheritance, he excelled and popularity came followed.

> Wherever I went, they loved me on the terraces and I was popular in the dressing room.

He captained the team at Wembley in the FA Cup final and, in his four years there, was honoured to be coached by Terry Venables: without doubt, he tells me, the best coach he ever played under. But, after 80 games, it was time to move on. This time the impetus was his left knee, a recurring problem that restricted his appearances—and the Loftus Road

'Astroturf' experiment didn't help. Months after promising him a contract, El Tel sold him for £40,000 to Toronto Nationals. However, the local-born Toronto manager didn't know an offside from his backside, and the five-month contract promising £11,000 collapsed with the club after eight weeks. Tony limped home with just two weeks' pay.

It's a long way from Toronto to Tring in more ways than one. But, aged 33, he made his debut in the Vauxhall-Opel League in an away game for a small Buckinghamshire outfit his brother captained, Chesham United. His appearance helped the Tring coffers—he doubled the gate. Soon after, he was back at Bramall Lane when chairman Reg Brealey had a chat and proposed a three-month contract. However, manager Ian Porterfield was not keen (T.C. was probably too young, considering the ages of the other players he signed). Porterfield never got back in touch, even though, that Saturday, the fans sang Currie's name in anticipation.

Meanwhile, Southend signed him on a three-month trial. But, get this, on his debut, running out of the tunnel and stepping over the touchline, he got injured! He limped back to the dressing room and broke the news to the manager, Peter Morris, who went mad: 'he was chuckin' things about and swearing!' Sidelined for six weeks, he managed two reserve games before Morris told him he wasn't wanted. The spirit was willing but the flesh was weak.

Next stop was Torquay, near the bottom of Division Four. His old QPR mate David Webb was manager, and gave him the following job description: 'Come down Friday night, play Saturday and do your bit on the pitch.' While a cut above anyone else, a lack of pace meant flying tackles sometimes connected. After 15 games, his knee was playing up again and he returned to London to deal with two types of pain: the physical one of throbbing ligaments and the mental one of divorce.

Unable to play for a year, he had plenty of time to reflect, but the future was not looking good. What does a man do when the tools of his trade cannot provide for him any longer? From whom does he seek solace? Wiped out financially following the divorce, he returned to live with his mum. A job in a video shop didn't last and his attempts at cab-driving ended when the car blew up! He admits that he began drinking too much and, out of work and broke, he bought a one-day bus pass and trotted off around London taking photos of historic sights. In 1984 he returned to where it all started in a sense—Hendon. He played five games, but the knee didn't hold out.

Two things were to drag him out of this slippery slope: two knee operations and two testimonial matches. Let's start with the scalpels.

The origin of the injury, believe it or not, probably lies with a former United player. In an early 1980s pre-season friendly, QPR played a bunch of upstarts called Wimbledon. Well, Currie shuffled, but a tackle, followed by an awkward fall, snapped a ligament. It was only in 1992 that the culprit—who was now playing for United—held up his hand. Step forward, Glynn Hodges! But, to put the record straight, T.C. bears no animosity, did not regard the challenge as sinister and, in fact, laughs about the situation. Years after this incident, in 1986, T.C. had an operation, ostensibly to clear up the knee. A week later, he couldn't walk and poison had to be drained from it a month later. A year later, another operation involved a series of holes being drilled into the area. Fluid no longer collects. Then what?

> Well, like a pillock, I thought I could play again. Worst thing I could do.
> But no one said don't do it!

Late 1987, out he trots for Goole Town, managed by ex-mucker Paddy Buckley. After 15 games, the knee went. Today, a round of golf means three days of agony. All this as a result of entertaining you and me.

As for the testimonials: one was Tony Kenworthy's, the other was his own. After the former, he met and married a local lass. More important, though, was that many a Blade realised their old hero could do with a hand. A testimonial was organised and, one Sunday in 1986, 20,000 people turned out for him at Bramall Lane. 'It was the most moving day of my life. They'd all turned up for me.' Some great players gave their time that day—Hurst, Hudson, Bremner, Best, Woodward, Worthington.

A year later, when the Football in the Community scheme was begun, a high-profile name was, ideally, needed. He's had the job for over ten years and loves it, and, at the time of our chat in 1994, was off the booze and in the Sheffield footballer's version of heaven—a detached bungalow in Dronfield with a former fashion model.

We love football for various reasons. It is romantic, nostalgic, allows us self-delusion, a chance to celebrate our city (and, implicitly, our self-identity) and, via that lot over in Sheffield 6, our parochial chauvinism. Part of the love is the pure theatre and pantomime that is the Match made all the better by players who play their roles wonderfully. Those of you under 30 might not understand what I'm trying to convey. Try this. Combine a Gazza without tears and belches with a Hoddle with charisma and you've got T.C. The nearest comparison with a recent player is Ruud Gullit. Wherever he played, he increased the gate. How many players can do that? Today, he watches and wishes he was still part of it all.

> Football's no different today: those with class will always find time and stand out.

If he had a ten-year ambition, it would be to be in football management somewhere, and be happy, with a few bob behind him. He applied unsuccessfully for the vacant job at Sheffield United in the late 1980s.

★   ★   ★

Perhaps, though, it was for the best. A few years after we spoke, his circumstances had changed. No longer married, he was living with someone else and had moved house and was not easily contactable. One senses that matters will never be straightforward with T.C. Genius does come with a price.

Sacks of Goals...
Keith Edwards

Exchanging punches in the early hours of Sunday morning on the drunk-ard buses out of the city centre in the early 1980s was a leisure-time hazard for many a Blade in their late teens and early twenties. But pro-claiming by chant the name of Keith Edwards and ending it with 'Goal Machine' was a good way of annoying Owls that lived along the route who would occasionally by way of reply choose action over words.

The balmy days of the early 1980s, when neither set of supporters had, in reality, little to shout about but did so with a passion when the worse for drink was the era that provokes the memories of United's greatest-ever goalscorer. With boyish looks and a manner that never seemed perturbed by anything, he was, while on the pitch, both brilliant and arrogant. Though many clubs bought him and many good managers tried to do things with him, he never quite made it to his fullest potential. He could have played at a higher level and should have; that he did not probably evinces a character that was not easily understood and did not suffer those he considered fools gladly.

He was born the youngest of four boys in Middlesbrough in 1957 to London-born parents evacuated to the north-east in their early teens to avoid the blitz. Keith's dad, though a good player, did not make the grade but found contentment working as a clerk in a chemical factory. Mrs Edwards was a cook. All four boys excelled in sport at school and Dad took them to their sports venues every weekend. As Keith remembers:

> . . . it was a lovely childhood. As a father of four meself, I realise he was an exceptional father.

One brother played a few games for Coventry and then slipped into non-League status, while Keith made a name for himself at schoolboy level playing for Stockton Boys and Durham County as a centre-forward or in midfield. After scoring twice at an under-15 game at Ayresome Park, then the home of Middlesbrough FC, he was invited to train with the club. He tried it, but didn't like it and left. He had no affinity to his home town club, preferring to play on a Saturday rather than spectate. If he supported anyone, it was Liverpool via Match of the Day highlights.

What Middlesbrough did not pursue, others did. He accepted an invitation to a three-day trial at Wolves, and then had a trial at Leeds. Watching him score that day were Jack Charlton and Billy Bremner, but Leeds didn't want him. With a certain smugness, Keith now recalls that his first League goal was against Wolves and, in 1986, Leeds under Billy Bremner signed him for £125,000. Meanwhile, his school attendance was excellent, primarily because he could play football there, but mainly because, had he not turned up, his mum would have noticed—she was the school cook.

Leaving school at 15, he took a job as a trainee salesman at a dairy. He loved it! The dairy manager was the best man at his wedding years later. With money in his pocket and a company car at 17, Saturdays would find him playing for a youth club team. Then Ken Furphy, the manager of Sheffield United, noticed something in a trial. Furphy recalls that the scout who spotted Keith warned him that this youngster might do nothing for most of the match, but he would usually get a couple of goals. True to prediction, Keith did nothing and then, as Furphy's patience was wearing thin, scored twice. United signed him in August 1975 and he began his professional football life in the reserves under the eye of coach Alan Hodgkinson.

Impressive at this level and scoring goals, he was soon promoted. Five months later came a first-team debut away at Leicester in an FA Cup tie, and a 3–0 defeat to a team that contained many a good player.

> I walked in the players' entrance and the first person I saw was Frank Worthington. I thought, 'do I really have to play against him?' Then I ran out on the pitch and Larry Lloyd was centre-half and I was frightened to death.

The debut boy had an effort cleared off the line and was substituted in the second half. A month later, he made his League debut at home to Queens Park Rangers and, over the next 30 months, made 64 first-team appearances, scored 29 goals and became a crowd favourite. Out of the blue he was then sold down a division by the then-manager Harry Haslam, to Hull City for £50,000, where he bagged 57 goals in 130 appearances. Three years after leaving Bramall Lane, a new United manager in charge of a club now in Division Four paid double what the club sold him for to bring him back for the 1981–82 season. How did all this come about?

It started with Ken Furphy, who seemed to have fallen between stools. His excellent team that finished sixth in Division One in 1975 was built around a core all aged over 30. Knowing their days were numbered, Furphy introduced a lot of promising youngsters—Hampson, Stainrod, Kenworthy, McGready and Edwards—but could not halt the decline and, when firmly rooted at the foot of the table, he was sacked. In recounting this, Keith gets introspective.

> Whenever I signed for anybody, the manager always got the sack. There's never really a happy ending.

There wasn't a particularly happy beginning with the stand-in manager, Cecil Coldwell:

> . . . he tried to kick me up the arse as I was running round the pitch in training. Why? I dunno . . . must have been something I said.

More likely it was something he refused to do. When a permanent replacement was found in the shape of Jimmy Sirrel, first-team appearances became more regular—not that Keith tried too hard in training to impress.

> We'd play matches every day. I got sent off by him in one and all because I wouldn't close the full-back down.

As Keith saw it, his job was to score goals or make them; others had tasks to do which he could not: 'I tried tackling people and it fuckin' hurt . . . so I didn't try it again.'

It would seem that Keith preoccupied Jimmy Sirrel, the dour and strange-looking Glaswegian, in a way detrimental to his health and pocket. Keith, imitating the manager, recounts the story behind the damaged car in which the manager arrived at training one morning in the following way:

> . . . I go through a red light. And why . . . ? Because I was thinking about that boy Edwards.

Explaining to me that Sirrel was the world's worst driver, he acknowledges his good qualities: namely, defending his young forward when he missed open goals. He'd say to those moaning: 'At least he was at the end of the movement.'

Movement was forced on Sirrel in September 1977 when he was sacked and eventually replaced by Harry Haslam in January 1978. In his short spell under Haslam's eye, Keith only remembers confusion.

> He tells me I'm the next Malcolm MacDonald and goes on about 'I always like an ace card up my sleeve.' That was no good to me sat on the fuckin' bench trying to get a game.

Ten months after arriving, Haslam sold him and replaced him with Steve Finnieston from Chelsea. Costing £100,000, he played 23 games, scoring five goals and retired from the game with injuries.

The start of the 1979–80 season found Keith at Hull City's Boothferry Park, a place where he had scored his first away goal two seasons earlier. The man who signed him, Ken Houghton, was sacked a month later! In the three years he remained at Hull, Keith played under Mike Smith, and did very well, motivated by both anger and arrogance.

> I was disgusted with United for selling me. I looked at the ground and the players at Hull and would think 'I'll tear this place apart and leave

for something better.' I did as well: I was far too good a player for that standard.

Some of the most spectacular goals of his career were witnessed at Hull.

> It was total arrogance, but I had self-belief. At kick-off, I'd get the ball and try to dribble through the opponents' half all on me own. It came off a couple of times. What you've got to remember was I was in a team that lost a lot and yet I scored goals, which isn't easy.

Once, having scored a goal, he was substituted. Disgusted, he took off his team shirt and threw it at the manager. Spontaneous chants of 'Smith out; Edwards in' began. Soon after, Hull signed a big lad from non-League football by the name of Billy Whitehurst and Keith was back at Bramall Lane.

Despite liking the club and fans, he always seemed to score against United when at Hull. In a Division Three fixture in 1979, he scored twice in Hull's 3–1 victory and caused a spot of bother.

> I never liked scoring against United, honestly. Also, Tony Kenworthy had the job of marking me and I'd been in digs with him and he was a mate.

The 5,000 following from Sheffield were not aware of this, and directed insulting songs at him. When his second went in, he came over and replied with a few choice words and gestures of his own. For the next 20 minutes, police were pulling Blades out of terracing and it was all a bit messy. Everybody blamed Keith.

> The police wrote to me saying my behaviour had produced a distur-bance and many arrests. United fans wrote me letters saying it was all my fault. I'd been given a load of stick so I gave it back!

His last goal for Hull was against United in 1981 and, days later, he became the most expensive signing in the Fourth Division as he joined Ian Porterfield's new set-up at the Lane. Scoring 42 goals in his first season, he won the Adidas Golden Boot for being the Football League's highest goalscorer. The ceremony was at the London Hilton and at his table were sitting Kevin Keegan, Elton John, and . . . wait for it . . . Freddie Starr, and . . . (drum roll) . . . Lennie Bennett. The top scorer loved it: from a Middlesbrough council house to all this—who'd have thought

In search of a happy ending: Keith in action against Walsall in 1984.

it, eh? The £10,000 award that accompanied the trophy he split amongst his team-mates in a magnanimous gesture.

Strangely enough, he won another Golden Boot in the 1983–84 season and, for some reason—he never found out why—was presented with the trophy by a bloke in the car park at Bramall Lane. There wasn't even a photographer there. Then, four years later, when at Hull, he got another similar trophy. Then aged 31, he had scored 29 goals in one season.

Initially partnered by Colin Morris, Keith seemed to score at will and United walked the Fourth Division. Having gained promotion again two years later, the manager was dismissed when the club were seventh in Division Two. One of the reasons he got the push was the United crowd chanting for Edwards while he was on the subs' bench and the team were losing 5-2. But it started off so well, if not a little confusing.

> It was all daft talk about 'horses for courses'. I didn't need all that crap. You end up seeking an explanation for what he was explaining. Then he starts putting me on the bench for the first 14 games of one season

> when I could guarantee him 20–25 goals a season. It was always impor-
> tant for me to show others where the problem lay.

Who knows where the problem lay? Wherever Keith played, he had rows, invariably with the managers. Most of the 15 managers he played under got the sack while he remained. He assures me that not once did he have any bearing on the dismissal. Every club he played for fined him for something; the maximum he got under Porterfield was two weeks' wages.

He was soon on his way out of Sheffield United when a new young manager wanting to be regarded as a 'disciplinarian' took over. It wasn't long before he fell out with Billy McEwan.

> I won't suffer fools. At the time, all the senior pros had a meeting and
> McEwan said to us, 'We're the best team in this division.' I said, 'That's
> bollocks; we finished seventh: the best finish top.' Then I walked out.

Not the best way to impress a new manager?

> No, but I always spoke me mind and I'd get frustrated. When it wasn't
> going too well, others players never got dropped: it was always me
> that got bombed out. When dropped, I wanted to know why. I was for-
> ever in Porterfield's office arguing with him.

In 1985 he found himself on the subs' bench and was left out of a pre-season tour of the USA. United let his contract run out and he had talks with Willie Maddren at Middlesbrough, but returned to ask United for a one-year extension.

> It's all I ever wanted anywhere I played. I knew that, by the end of the
> season, I would have scored goals and could ask for better terms. I
> did this all my career.

Maybe there is something about centre-forwards. By virtue of the role they play, they need to be self-centred and opinionated. They seek glory; their names are sung more than their team-mates; their mistakes are remembered more than anyone else's bar the goalie. It helps their task to display something their team-mates might not possess.

Having mentioned in our conversation the word 'arrogant' six times already, I decide to pull him up. Having repeatedly used it to describe his character as a footballer, I ask Why? and How? The reply combines ideas of stature and the intimidation offered by many central defenders.

> ... being a short-arse [he's 5' 8½"], when up against some six-foot-three monster, you can't exactly be weak. They might be big and hard, but they were also big and slow. It was easy for me to run away from them. I'd tell 'em how crap they were ... and nobody could hurt me. I never rolled about in agony and was rarely on the treatment table.

He was the fastest player at Bramall Lane and very resilient to injuries. Able to find space, he could play with both feet and had a wonderful ability to shoot on the turn. He could treat the less gifted with contempt; he once dummied a through-ball, fooling both his marker and the goalkeeper whom he ran round to stroke the ball into the net, but only after he had smiled at his admirers on the Kop. His repertoire expanded when allowed to take set-pieces; he was deadly with free-kicks close to the box and could whip over a good corner.

When he did leave United in August 1986, transfer rumours had been around for a while. An admirer was Jack Charlton who tried to buy him when he was at Hull and, when managing Wednesday, was believed to have made inquiries. Then he nearly went to Seville in Spain when a friendly match played over there saw him and Colin Morris run them ragged. United accepted the offer for the pair and the two players and their wives met to consider the logistics of living there, when—you've guessed it—the Seville manager was dismissed and the deal was off. So his last game in a United shirt was in Spain and, after eight and a half years in total, he left with the statistics of 261 League and Cup appearances and 143 goals. Billy McEwan, who fell out with Keith in his first week as manager, finally got rid of him. In August 1986, he sold him to Leeds for £125,000.

His new boss at Elland Road was Billy Bremner: not a man it was wise to fall out with, surely?

> He was brilliant ... my main man. Wherever I went, I would negotiate for weeks money-wise and I could get it 'cause I scored goals. What the hell does a full-back go in the room with? 'I tackled so-and-so, give me a rise'? Anyway, what I ask for Bremner gives me and we have a cup of tea. He'd make you want to run through a brick wall for him.

He may have loved the man, but the tactics he chose did not suit Keith. Too much midfield play meant his style was cramped as he was partnered up-front by the big figure of Ian Baird. Losing in the FA Cup semi-final and promotion play-offs rounded off a season of 28 appearances and 10 goals. A year after joining Leeds, he joined his old boss

Ian Porterfield, now in charge at Aberdeen. The £60,000 fee produced six games and two goals in six months, memorable mainly for his only long-term injury. Hull City then appeared again and give Aberdeen what they paid for him. The manager who brought him back to Hull, Brian Horton, was sacked soon after! His successor, Eddie Gray, and Keith got on really well, but inevitably he, too, was sacked! Yet in 55 appearances he bagged 29 goals: a brilliant achievement considering the club finished the season at the bottom of the Second Division. Significantly, he scored more goals that season than the England internationals, Kerry Dixon and Ian Wright, who played in the same League for successful clubs.

Then his journeys become shorter but more frequent. In September 1989, the former United coach, Danny Bergara, paid a club record fee of £50,000 to take him to Stockport County. He returned the investment with ten goals in 27 League games, but left six months later for Huddersfield on loan who later, with Eoin Hand in charge, buy him. A hip injury, however, started playing up—a year after retiring from the game he was forced to have a hip replacement. The niggling injury made the manager think Keith wasn't interested and, to make matters worse, he was regularly late for training because of delays on British Rail because he was now banned from driving after attempting to do so when slightly over the limit. Released on a free in September 1991, after 305 goals his Football League days were over—and so was his marriage.

Teams still wanted him. A few months at non-League Stafford Rangers was followed by a stretch at lower-division Alfreton Town, a signing made in unusual circumstances:

> I was playing golf every day. The manager was a roofer doing some work on the clubhouse and asked me if I wanted a game. So I signed for them.

It didn't last long. And his attempts at roofing with the manager lasted three days. Out of work, out of luck and out of love, Keith had to reappraise his life and sought a new career. An ex-Blade team-mate tried to help out.

> I hadn't planned too much. I'd made a few quid, sure, and I'd got a big house. I met up with Joe Bolton and took a Class 1 driving course and he got me a job as a tanker driver. I enjoyed it for two years. Meanwhile, I'm getting divorced.

The big house was soon to go and then the kids. The loneliness of driving resulted in a decision he has not yet reversed.

> I was sometimes 14 hours a day in a lorry and I wasn't seeing me kids, so I thought, fuck that. I packed it in and it's fantastic now when I see the kids.

In truth, he hasn't quite found a role to replace football. Many Blades, both at the time he played and years later, thought him a lazy player and too self-centred an individual to be concerned about team-mates. This is a bit unfair in Keith's opinion, because, when at United, he was dedicated to the club and the game.

> I'd never liked running like a silly bastard around Graves Park, but I'd stay back for hours for shooting practice. I never had a day off in my time at United. I loved training, especially when it was fun, but I couldn't see how eight-mile runs could make you a better player.

As for accusations that he was not bothered about what the club did, he sees this more a fault of integrity than nonchalance.

> I suppose my fault would be to appear unaffected by the results. But I did my sulking at home . . . ask my ex-wife. I once played for United reserves at Everton and we lost 7–2. It was no shame to get beat— they had half their championship-winning side playing. It wasn't a disgrace . . . we'd tried but lost to good players, and afterwards in the dressing room I said so. The coach, Jim Dixon, turns to me and says, 'Your attitude stinks.' I told him that we'd learned something and you should respect Everton. Next thing we're brawling . . . me bollock-naked.

He also brawled with a United team-mate on a pre-season tour of Jersey. A drunken card-school led first to an argument, which in turn led to a stool over the head. The reminiscence of this incident produced the contemplative 'I always attracted the idiots.'

Today, with too much time on his hands, he has the luxury of reflection on days past.

> I loved me football, but looking back there's too many gaps. I should have played more games and got more goals. I would loved to have coached. I even wrote to United recently asking if I could help coaching. I said, pay me a pittance and I'll still do it. I didn't get a reply.

He was intending to coach at Hull under Eddie Gray, but you know the ending . . . Eddie got the sack.

Not all players can easily adjust to life after football. Keith has found it difficult partly because he didn't consider football as work, more as a few hours of fun each day with a celebratory drink after a good performance. But, when football ceased to need him, a few things occurred that he had not expected. On a physical level, his health let him down—as we talk, he suffers permanent discomfort and awaits an operation on his hip. He hasn't worked full-time for over four years and, though his task of match-summariser on BBC Radio Sheffield since 1996 has won him many admirers, that only occupies a few hours a week. The visit of his four children is the highlight of his week. Though he lives in one of the best suburbs of the city, his abode is a modest one-bedroom flat with precious few reminders of a footballing career: just the award-winning golden football boots on display next to statues of greyhounds. He hasn't gone to the dogs, but he went to the dogs too often and therein lies much of his current predicament.

Now off the tracks and off the booze, he's pulled himself out of a post-football tail-spin. When I ask him if he's happy, he replies after a long pause by stating how glad he is to be asked that question but how he can't really answer it fully. You see, in many respects he is, but he needs more to occupy his time and so the interview is turned: what do I think he should do? Put on the spot, I suggest he expand his broadcasting abilities and get his own radio talk-show and maybe start a college course and get his CV together . . . and . . . Well, there's always public relations: he speaks very well, is confident in manner and . . . I don't know, to be honest. I hate being interviewed!

He gives me a lift back into the town centre and tells me to call on him anytime. I will; he's good company: a natural raconteur and funny with it. There must be many jobs he can do. He never fulfilled the enormous potential he had in football. All who delighted in his footballing abilities will hope that he can find something as rewarding at this time in his life as playing football was to him at an earlier age.

★ ★ ★

Six months after we first spoke, Keith is working as a fundraiser for Imperial Cancer Research. Hopefully, just this time, there is a happy ending.

Bob Who...?
Bob Booker

About once a decade a player becomes the darling of the Sheffield United fans and is remembered for another ten years with awe and a smile. Usually such players have remarkable footballing ability and usually little is known about them when off the pitch.

An exception to this is Bob Booker, whose four years (1988–91) with United saw him arrive in relative silence, but leave in what was the most unusual departure a United player has ever suffered when 25,000 Blades cheered his free transfer to a Second Division side as he stood in the middle of the pitch. This Watford-born battler had modest skills and ambitions, but had something most players will never have: an appetite for the game, combined with a love of the club and its fans and an enthusiasm based on the wonderment of being allowed to play football and get paid for it. Now youth team coach at Brentford, he was and remains an adopted son of one half of the city of Sheffield and his home is a shrine to his days at Bramall Lane.

By his own admission, Bob had an affiliation with the north of England from childhood. When taken to watch nearby Watford by his dad as a boy, he was fascinated by the Leeds team of Don Revie, and his ever-obliging dad would occasionally drive to Elland Road. Excelling only in running and football at school, he left at 16 to begin a four-year apprenticeship in an upholstery warehouse while playing for a local Saturday team called Bedmond, forming a strike force with Derek French (the United physio between 1988 and 1996).

Attracting Watford's interest, Bob attended a couple of training sessions until a director of Brentford, who was a mate of Bedmond's ex-manager, asked him to attend Griffin Park for a trial. Playing centre-forward, he scored two and was picked for the next few weeks. The manager, Bill Dodgin, then offered a financial package which was not much better than that he got from piecework in upholstery, but he took it. Signed on Thursday in a deal that saw Bedmond receive a set of tracksuits, he made his first-team debut in Division Three two days later away to his home-town team—Watford. He was kicked all over by a centre-back called Ian Bolton who was in later years to become his brother-in-law.

Selected for the next three games, he didn't score and struggled. Loaned to Barry Fry at Barnet, then in the Conference League, he scored a few and, first game back for Brentford, scored a hat-trick. There was no looking back, and for the next ten seasons he was an ever-present, playing over 280 league games and scoring 42 goals. Famed for his versatility, he alternated between centre-forward, centre-half and right-back. Receiving the supporter's Player of the Year in 1982, he had played in every position bar goalkeeper, and that season scored for Brentford in front of the Shoreham End in the visitors' 2–1 victory. A few clubs came sniffing; Portsmouth made a bid. Alan Clarke at Scunthorpe made inquiries, as did a certain Harry Bassett, then manager of Wimbledon. Having taken over the helm at Bramall Lane in 1988, Harry remembered Bob and got him on a free transfer, but we'll get to that story in a minute.

The first season at Brentford wasn't easy; two years later, they loved him. Sound familiar? Anyway, as Bob explains it:

> I was inexperienced; it was hard, but I weren't gonna give in. I knew I could make it in time. I believed in my own ability.

Having won the fans over, his career was modest but doing very nicely until a cruciate ligament injury in 1986. Out of the game for 18 months and with a warning from the surgeon that he might not play again, Bob's head dropped. Was he close to giving up football?

> Never. There's a big part to injuries which is in the mind. If you're not strong-minded, you won't play again. I was, and I knew I'd be back. I can see it in my players today; I know who can come back from injury and who can't.

In his years at Brentford, a few managers came and went. Fred Callaghan succeeded Dodgin; then came the joint administration of Frank McLintock and John Docherty. While Bob was recovering from the injury, Steve Perryman took over and, though he gave him a one-year contract with the intention that Bob got fit by the end of it, also informed him he was not part of his long-term plans.

Aged 30, hobbling in his testimonial year and having been informed that he was surplus to requirements, Bob had some decisions to make. One possibility was to make a wedge from a benefit game and sink it into a window-cleaning business with a mate. Unable to decide on that matter, he got over the injury and Perryman selected him for a game against United in October 1988. A 4–1 Blades victory impressed Bob, and he was touched when wandering around the United dressing room after the game to see that Harry Bassett's flipchart tactics identified him as the danger man. Flattered and jealous, he spoke to his old mate, then United's physio, Derek French, in the bar.

> I thought, what a team! So strong and everywhere. I told Frenchie I was pissed off 'cause I'd got substituted and had no future.

Meanwhile, Blades' midfielder Simon Webster broke his leg. One Sunday afternoon, Bob's phone rang: its Frenchie asking if he fancied a permanent move to United.

> Harry and Steve Perryman had spoken and Harry told me to come up for a chat. I'd never had a move in me life. What do I do? Well, I took me dad with me! We had quarter of an hour with Harry and I'd got a signing-on fee and an 18-month contract and basically more money then I'd ever had. I started training next day, then went out with Frenchie to celebrate.

After only 24 hours in the city, he realised the nature of the support. His tracksuit in the pub gave his identity away and brought him the attention of inquisitive Blades who wanted to know more about him and fill his glass as a welcome. This was new. Recognition in streets and pubs, however, was something he was going to have to get used to.

Life on the pitch was to prove no bed of roses. The inevitable question upon arrival of 'Bob who?' soon became 'boo'. His early games did not show what he was capable of. There were two reasons: he was still not fully fit after 18 months out of the game; and Bassett's style of play took some getting used to. Played as an attacking midfielder, his main job was to stop the ball when it came from the opposition's goalies and defenders and knock it forward when it came from United's rearguard. Meanwhile, his other task was to win the ball in midfield and give it to smaller cleverer colleagues such as Mark Todd and John Gannon.

It all turned out lovely in the end, but the first few months were distressing. His confidante at the time (and still a big buddy) was Mick Rooker in the commercial department. This Sheffield-born Blade of the same age as Bob knew the fans well and, when Bob came to him on a downer after a bad verballing from the boss, Rooker gave him the following advice: 'Give 100%. Don't hide, because Blades will suss you. Acknowledge them at the end of the match to tell 'em you're here and you're not scared of being seen.' He did as he was told and the fans grew to love him.

One match is remembered by fans and players alike as the turning point. A foul night at Mansfield saw United 1–0 down when Bob won a penalty which got the equaliser. Then, everything seemed to go right.

> I was doing something right for a change! It's hard to explain, but in 45 minutes I'd turned that corner.

Other memorable matches followed. An FA Cup tie victory at Barnsley saw Bob taking the applause and shaking hands with fans ten minutes after the final whistle. Another Cup win at Watford saw him on a one-man lap of honour for both Blades and his family and mates at the other end. Very soon there were two chants in honour of the man, the first sung by the chaps went:

> We've got Bobby Booker: he's a dirty fucker
> He's six foot tall
> He cost fuck all

Of wider appeal was the rather daft but infectious

Oo-ah, Bob Bu-Kah
I said oo-ah Bob Bu-Kah

which graced nearly every game he played as well as bars and neigh-
bourhoods patronised by beer-soaked Blades. There was a Bob Booker
t-shirt and a life-size cardboard cut-out which travelled to away games
and met its demise in May 1990.

> After we'd got promoted at Leicester, one of the team got hold of it
> and carried it round when they went on the piss back in Sheffield. In
> Josephine's Billy Whitehurst kicked it to pieces for a laugh.

Without a doubt, Bob was a rarity in football. At a loose end after
training and with his fiancée still living in Watford, Bob would take his
beloved Rottweiler for walks in the park or seek out company in the
Lane. In a sense, Rooker and Booker were meant for each other. The
former needed players to visit fans as part of promoting the club and in
the latter he had a player for whom talking to fans was the most natural thing to do. You name it, he'd appear at or open it. One summer

fête appearance produced a ten-year-old requesting Bob come to the house Monday evening for his tea. To the family's amazement, Bob and Mick turned up, munched meat and potato pie, and stayed for two hours. Within a week, 50 invites arrived at the Lane requesting Bob's presence at various dinner tables. A personalised letter and signed photo appeased the diners somewhat.

There was never a shortage of adult company partaking of other forms of refreshment. He loved drinking in the Blade strongholds on London Road and found it hard to buy himself a pint, such was the generosity of fans. Mind you, some United fans once drank his house dry after he had left the club. After being relegated at Chelsea in May 1993, Mr and Mrs Booker were having a dinner party for four guests when two Watford Blades, the worse for drink, appeared in the driveway at midnight singing the 'Bu-Kah' song and giving it the 'we are not worthy' position. Invited in by Bob, they proceeded to phone for other local Blades. The six of them stayed until 3 am talking football and drank every beer in the house. Bob loved it.

If that's hard to imagine, so is a Premiership player who drove a D-reg Sierra estate and who, upon making his Premiership debut against Liverpool at the Lane, asked the photographers to take a picture of him in front of the Kop for posterity. Modest by nature and modest in what he owns today, he appreciates what he earned from the game and it meant a lot to him to be appreciated. He never had an agent, nor did he earn a four-figure weekly rate; in fact, he never got over the fact that he could be paid for doing what he loved.

One story Bob did not tell me is worthy of recounting. Players' contracts were decided by Dave Bassett, but the nitty-gritty was left to the managing director, Derek Dooley. He and Bob sat and sorted it out and shook on it. Dooley's years as a manager and a director had resigned him to the knock on the door half an hour after a deal had been agreed, usually disputing clause six and the win bonus or such like. Duly, Bob knocked later in the day, but did not dispute a thing—he called to thank Derek for the extension and the rate and, pledging his devotion to the club, promised to do his best. Never having seen such magnanimity, Derek admitted it brought a tear to his eye.

Talking of tears, Bob shed a few in his time with United. Maybe you remember the winning goal he scored at QPR in 1991. A 5,000 Blade following went barmy as he acclaimed the goal that ensured United's status in the Premiership. A picture of that moment adorns his hallway and his memories.

> I watch the video of that game and still well up thinking about it. It's
> fierce, it's fierce . . . I looked up and you could feel the buzz for me.

I look up from writing this quote and poor Bob's eyes have watered.
Then its memory lane time: Leicester away, destroying the home team
and ensuring promotion—and Bob was captain that day and kicked a
rival player who was to go on to greater things.

> I tackled Gary McAllister, gave him a kick and all the Blades nearby
> started givin' it the 'oo-ah'. He turns to me and says, 'What the fuck
> they singin' your name for?'

A few weeks earlier, dozens had sung his name and that of his dog
down the phone at 2 am. The day before Mother's Day, trusted Blades
who had been given the task of driving Bob's car to an away game so
he could drive home to his fiancée in Watford straight after discovered
a couple of cards for his loved one. As good mates, they ripped them
open to find out how embarrassingly soppy he could be. One of the
cards to Christine was ostensibly from the Rottweiler, Bruno, stating
the usual daft stuff: 'To Mummy . . . naughty boy'—get the picture?
Anyway, the match saw Bob get slaughtered to the chant of 'Bruno'
by one section of the Blade following and then receive a drunken middle-
of-the-night rendition of 'How much is that doggie in the window?'
by a room-full enjoying a lock-in back in a Sheffield pub.

His life at Bramall Lane ended in late 1991 after 109 League games
and 13 goals. While Harry offered a one-year renewal, Brentford offered
three years. Not wanting to leave, but at 32 years of age wanting security, he made the hardest decision of his life and left, but in unusual circumstances. Shortly before a United–Wednesday derby and a full house,
he said his goodbyes.

> I told Harry I was off. He thanked me and we had a cuddle then told
> me to get out on the pitch. Dave Kilner [the match DJ] announced it
> and led me out. I saw the John Street boys go into one, but not many
> saw me bawling my eyes out. I didn't wanna come off.

He watched the match, drank too much in the sponsor's bar after and
joined Brentford next day.

The first season back saw him suffer his first-ever relegation. The following season saw promotion, but a renewal of the knee trouble. Told
by the surgeon to pack in, he cashed in his remaining 18 months of
contract and then had a long time to consider his future. Aimless, dif-

ficult and depressed he went off the game and was hell to live with. He turned up at United games and sat with the fans with a team shirt on cheering the team. Occasionally, he was part of the match commentary team for BBC Radio Sheffield. A testimonial against United produced a welcome payday and saw 200 Blades travel to out-shout the 4,000 home fans in his praise. He put packs of beer on their coaches by way of thanks. His first venture back into the game came with a Sunday pub team; then London non-League side Harrow Borough offered terms of £200 a week. Others came sniffing, but he fancied them.

> What swayed it probably was that they played in red and white stripes! I told their manager that, if I turned up Saturday and there was a short-sleeved number 4 shirt and a pair of brand-new size 10 Puma Kings, it was a deal.

His demands were met and he played for a year until the knee played up. The intended window cleaning business never came off. Out of boredom, he helped his mate do some office-cleaning, but Mrs Booker urged him to wait and see what football had to offer. Sure enough, in 1994 a call came from a director of Brentford offering him the job of youth team coach. In his fourth season now, he's won a few trophies and has two of his protégés in the first team. Now aged 40, he harbours managerial ambitions or, failing that, a chance to return to live and work in Sheffield.

The 1988–92 seasons were wonderful years for United fans. The commitment of the players was probably unprecedented in the club's history. Known to his team-mates as 'son of', because Bassett excused him from Sunday training sessions to allow him to see his fiancée, he reflects on the unique spirit that pervaded the club in those years.

> We were a bunch of thugs really, but we worked hard for each other and Harry and never let ourselves down. Sheffield people can't be fooled: they want a team of eight triers who will give it everything and leave it to three flair players to do the rest. That's what we were.

I think he's right about what fans want. Blades are fair fans who can spot a waster when they see one and, by the same token, a trier who gives everything. Bob gave everything and he wasn't a bad player: he was a strong lad who, though limited in skill, was useful at set-pieces and could stop players who were more skilled than him. He was unusual in this day and age in that he played with a smile on his face; he enjoyed

his job and the chance he had been given so late in life to mix with the stars of the game—and his enthusiasm was contagious. What the game gave him he tried to give back by being available to fans off the pitch and making them happy with his efforts on it. Too many players today take but do not give anything in return; overpaid and cocooned from the life of the fans, they care little for the club they are paid by. Players like Bob Booker are becoming an endangered species and that is football's loss.

A Blessed Talent...
Brian Deane

I speak about five words of Portuguese. Unfortunately, none translate to 'What time is it, pal?' Earlier this year, while standing in the spring sunshine outside the huge Stadium of Light, home of Benfica, Lisbon, I spotted a middle-aged chubby chap with the unremarkable features of light black skin and greying hair. Catching his attention and tapping my left wrist with my right hand, my victim shows me his watch. The former Blade I am seeking has still not shown, so I take a seat near the bronze statue in the centre of the roundabout outside the stadium entrance. Dedicated to Michel Eusebio, Benfica's famous Mozambique-born centre-forward in the 1960s and '70s, it is a fitting tribute to one of the world's greatest players. A minute later, I realise that the statue commemorates the bloke I just asked the time off. Christ Almighty! I've travelled 1,500 miles and missed the chance of pressing the flesh with a footballing legend.

My consolation, however, was meeting his successor of 30 years later, also a centre-forward and also black. Inside the bowels of this stadium, built by a military dictator in 1954, I shake hands with the man known to all Blades as 'Deano', forever in the history books as the man who scored the first-ever Premier League goal in August 1992.

As I sit with Brian, the Benfica–Sheffield United link has never been stronger in a strange way. He's gone from one to the other, and, a month later, a former Benfica player scored the winning goal for United, which came days after the burial in Sheffield of the famous United star of 1938–58, Jimmy Hagan. The latter enjoyed great success after United as Benfica's manager between 1970 and 1973 when he coached them to three successive championships. I point this out, and ask Brian if his present club was represented at the funeral. He can't answer this, but you'd have hoped so, wouldn't you, after what he achieved for them? But then again, this is football, and it's a strange world. Outside the stadium, the name 'Hagan' provokes many nods of recognition.

The football club that is Benfica and its environs is a social life for hundreds daily. A Saturday-afternoon junior team game I watched on one of the two pitches adjacent to the stadium pulled an audience of 500. My two further visits saw hundreds of middle-aged and old men sitting for hours in the three Benfica-owned café-bars to talk football in between solving the world's problems. One gets the impression that fans think they own the club and believe they matter. The ground is public property, in the sense that anyone can watch training and, if you sat outside the ground all day, no one would think you a nuisance. Joining such a fanatical football culture means that, when you are the club's centre-forward, a lot of people want a piece of you. Brian is aware of this, having changed the number of his mobile phone days before when a journalist somehow managed to get through. Consequently, he's got to be prepared for slumps in form and possibly a bad press.

> Fortunately my Portuguese isn't very good, so I don't have to say too much and I can't understand what they write about me anyway!

In my experience, players always look bigger on the pitch compared to when you meet them in 'real life'. Face to face with Deano was the first occasion I recall when a player seemed bigger to me off the pitch.

At 6' 3" and 14 stone, this guy is huge with an enormous pair of feet. A Leeds accent and a seeming reluctance to smile makes for a somewhat brooding and hounded presence, which is a bit misleading because the man turns out to be one of the most courteous and polite blokes you could wish to meet. Honest, if not a little guarded, in his replies, one gets the impression of a man in control, with an unshakeable faith in himself and not prone to hysterics. In the footballing world he inhabits, increasingly dominated by hyperbole and arseholes, Deano retains an admirable modesty. This has much to do with his upbringing.

A product of migrants from the Caribbean island of Nevis who moved to the poor district of Chapeltown in Leeds, Brian was the youngest of six children. Hard-working parents provided for a family that stayed together and prayed together—daily, in fact, sustained by an Anglican faith that remains with Brian to this day. Sporting inspiration in the child Brian is provided by an elder brother who represented the Royal Navy at football before becoming a kick-boxing champion. This secure home produced a diligent schoolboy who became a talented footballer, chosen to represent his home city between the ages of 12 and 16. Professional clubs noticed him: Bradford, Barnsley, Notts County and Leeds offered trials, but none offered a contract. In return, he failed to see the attraction of his home-town club when his first (and only) visit as a young spectator provoked racist abuse towards him. If he supported any club, it was Arsenal, mainly through their FA Cup exploits on TV.

Leaving school wanting to be a footballer, Brian meanwhile sought work in advertising, mainly because he enjoyed school classes in economics and commerce. Armed with four 'O'-levels, he applied for a job and, clothed in a suit, entered the interview room.

> It was a rude awakening. This guy looked up and realised I was black. There were no black faces in that firm.

Weeks later, his income was derived from collecting glasses in a Leeds nightclub, a job that obviously affected him.

> It hardened me. I knew what I wanted to do and meanwhile I had a job in a place where all these blokes were trying to impress women. You're a glass collector, a piece of shit to them. You realise what people are thinking and it made me determined to succeed at something.

Today, Brian could probably afford to buy that nightclub and take his pick from dozens of female admirers. But vindictiveness isn't part of his nature. Empathy is, though.

> I've gone from that to being a well-known bloke, but I'll relate to that bloke doing that job. I'll respect someone who respects me.

The humbleness of Chapeltown contrasts vividly with his existence today. As a star player in one of the world's best-known clubs, who play before crowds of 75,000 and who have made eight appearances in European Cup finals, he has, by anyone's standards, made it big. An apartment with a private pool in the chic Lisbon suburb of Cascais with a panoramic view of the Atlantic and good weather all year round is a long way from what he knew in his Leeds childhood. But this is a man who has never, before moving here two months ago, lived more than 30 miles from home, and who shared a house with his brother and even stayed at his mum's twice a week when playing in the Premier League. Of course he misses them: I should not even have asked. The blunt approach continues: now aged 30, has he a seven-figure bank account? The reply is a smile and an oblique reference to business interests out-side football: namely, property-owning and rental, which is accompanied by a philosophy.

> When I finish playing, I want to do exactly what I want to do. It should also give me pleasure to help my parents and brothers.

Sitting in this stadium with a 2½-year contract and a five-figure weekly wage, the life of Brian looks good. A niggling foot injury discomforts, but does not hinder reflection on the nature of his profession.

> I've had an injury-free career and I give 100% a game because, if you don't, you're not going to be a better player. I see a lot in football I don't like; you see the cynical way players are treated: nobody gives a damn in this game.

Renowned for being a model professional in attitude to training and off-the-pitch moderation, this survival instinct that has taught and brought him so much in life is tinged with a degree of bitterness. Some of this was a product of his time at Sheffield United and came from both those that employed him and those that at one time adored him. Before we address this episode, how he came to get here is worth detailing.

Playing for non-League Yorkshire Amateurs in 1985, Brian wrote to the then Division Four club Doncaster Rovers for a trial. The chief scout there was from Leeds and remembered the big man from school-boy days. He recommended him to the manager—Billy Bremner—who signed him on a part-time basis while Brian studied physical education at Doncaster College. Succeeding Bremner in 1987 was the former Sheffield Wednesday player Dave Cusack, who made Brian a full-time professional for the reward of £60 per week! Doing quite well at Donny, scoring 12 goals in 66 games, he asked Cusack to put a word in with any big clubs after a centre-forward. Though the manager was a big influence on Brian's career, he initially thought him 'too soft' to be a professional target man. Furthermore, he wasn't impressed with his heading ability and once described him as 'like Bambi on ice'. The United manager Harry Bassett saw something he liked, however, and, in July 1988, paid £30,000 with a further £10,000 promised should Brian ever make 30 first-team appearances. The rest is history: Brian stayed five years, made over 200 first-team appearances and left the club for nearly 30 times what he was bought for.

As all Blades can testify, Brian had remarkable ball control for a big man and tremendous heading ability. The softness accusation was nonsense, and Harry publicly stated in his early days that Brian would improve when he ceased apologising to rival players after he had flattened them. A pre-season friendly at Skegness saw him for the first time in a United shirt, then a League debut at Reading saw his first full appearance. He scored in both games, the crowd took to him immediately and the chant of 'Deano' was heard at almost every game for the next five years.

He could score from almost anywhere: flick on headers from both low crosses and high crosses, lift it over the goalie from six yards, 20-yard strikes. A partnership with Tony Agana produced three hat-tricks for Brian and 60 goals between them in one season. Fast, strong and level-headed, he was willing to listen to advice. For this he thanks Harry, whom he credits for allowing him to 'extend' himself. International recognition came in 1991 when chosen to play for the England Under-21 team, which saw 200 Blades travel to the game at Walsall to chant his name (and boo the Wednesday player also in the team!). Later in 1991 and 1993 came full international honours. A total of three caps made him the only post-war centre-forward from United to play for England (the other two, George Headley and Arthur Brown, played at the turn of the century). Now aged 30, future international appearances are unlikely.

> I think I should have had more! Moving to Leeds was perhaps a bad move. When I left United, I was in the England squad. What I'd done at United didn't happen at Leeds.

One thing that did not happen anymore was getting overdrawn at the bank. When at Doncaster, he was permanently in this state; then his wages improved over time, but this is where some annoyance creeps in. His first season at United saw him take home £250 a week. When in the full England team, he was on £700 at Bramall Lane and he was learning some football truths.

> I'd sit in the dressing room with the rest of the squad telling me what they were on at other clubs and I realised something was not right!

This caused a rift at the time with the manager which still resonates.

> He used to find it within himself to hammer me in the papers saying that when his players were away they were always talking about cars and money . . . yet there was only me in the international squad. I think he thought I'd been tapped up when on England duty. But no one was trying to sign me. It hurt me.

A few things bug him about his times at Bramall Lane. Perhaps we should put the historical record straight and then explore Brian's version of events.

The final game of the 1992–93 season saw his last goal for United before departing two months later to Leeds for a fee of £2.7 million. In 221 team appearances he had scored 106 goals. In four of his five seasons he was almost an ever-present and he was sent off only once. When he was sold, the club was in boardroom turmoil. Amid the various sagas, the chairman was technically Reg Brealey, who had resumed control in the absence of Paul Woolhouse who had fled to avoid the police, who wanted to question him about various 'lost' sums of money. In 1992, Brian had signed a two-year contract with a gentlemen's agreement that he could leave after a year. He had ended the season as the club's top scorer with 20 goals but, with a year remaining of the contract, was prepared to move on, and submitted a written transfer request. Two clubs wanted him: Leeds offered £2.7 million then Wednesday offered £3.2 million. Instructed by Harry to talk to Wednesday's manager, Trevor Francis, Brian had to decide where it was to be. As he saw it, he had a 'no-win' situation. He chose to join the former Owls boss Howard Wilkinson and so, having signed a four-year contract, returned home to Leeds:

> It would have been easy to go to Wednesday, but Blades would have hated me . . . but if I'd stayed they'd hate me for asking for a transfer.

The transfer turned into a media circus, and Brian became the pawn in a power struggle between chairman and manager. The manager presented the situation as one of selling his best player while he was on holiday: on his return, Bassett found only £1 million available to replace his top goalscorer. The chairman said there was no choice given the financial status of the club, but all fans asked was: 'Who got the club into such a state?'

The following season, United were relegated. Brian, when facing his previous club, was booed throughout by sections of the Blades following and received chants of 'Judas!' and 'one greedy bastard', based on their belief that the only reason he left United was for more money. This was a bad time for him: things were not going too well at the new club and at his old club his name was mud. What did he do?

> There were so many clichés written about me . . . so I shaved my head and thought fuck them all. It would have been easy to wilt away and go to seed, but I had too much about myself to let that happen.

As for his previously adoring audience turning on him?

> I don't hold any grudges. I got a lot of bad publicity in the tabloids and certain people were believing it all. The fans slaughtered me when they came to Leeds and probably blamed me for the relegation. But I'd got over 100 goals in five years. They should have been happy; I'd worked hard for them.

The fans at his new club were happy. Popular with them, he was not, however, totally popular among his fellow-players, and the move was proving a nightmare.

> They played with four midfielders; they'd all pass it around, so the ball doesn't come to me quickly enough. I didn't know how to handle it. I'd scored goals for five years and now what am I supposed to do? To be honest, my career stood still at Leeds. The manager didn't know what he wanted. I was played out wide for six months out of the 2½ years I was there. I just gave 100% and got on well with the fans.

Pity about his team-mates, however.

> There was a clique—a couple of players: one in particular was unhappy at me earning more than he did. In fact, there was a lot going on I wasn't happy with. I don't understand it; I was never jealous about other people's money.

Though not given to envy, we might examine the other six deadly sins in the light of his religious convictions. Well, he's not avaricious: the car in which he drives me to the railway station is unremarkable and he was a man who once played for a £60 wage at Donny. He is not subsumed in wrath, preferring to play the game than make a name brawling. Sloth is not a word that describes a hard-working player who trains very hard; neither is gluttony for a man whose idea of a late night is 10 pm and who would take wine only with his Italian meal. That leaves vanity and lust. The former is just not Deano, and the latter, while having made space for it by still being a bachelor, has probably produced the realisation—to paraphrase a well-known biblical quote—that singleness is next to godliness. Before a rich professional footballer there is no shortage of temptation and I'm told that someone special from England flies out to Lisbon to see him.

Guided by a personality that seems to lack envy, his time at Leeds wore him down and, after 110 games, he decided not to sign a new contract and sought pastures new. That was the idea, anyway. A few clubs made offers, including Feyenoord and Strasbourg, but he ended up back at Bramall Lane in July 1997, convinced by the new chairman and his right-hand man, Charles Green, that things were all sorted out and the club had ambition. The transfer fee was reported in the local paper to be over £1 million. Brian doesn't know how much—does anyone? Will fans ever find out? Anyway, according to Brian, the deal offered to him personally was 'half-decent' and back he came, with an assurance he would be played as a central striker and some trepidation.

> I was scared. I thought maybe things had changed, but I loved it. I've always found it easy to relate to the people at Sheffield . . . easier than people from Leeds and I'm from there.

The fans welcomed him with open arms and he did his bit. In 28 first-team games he scored 13 goals and his trademark goal acclamation of arms aloft with index fingers pointing down was a welcome sight to success-starved supporters. Then he left, this time without drama or protests. The status of the club that wanted him silenced any criticism, because all fans knew that, offered a chance to play for Benfica, who was going to choose to remain in the First Division? Also, fans were by now so resigned to the club selling players to the detriment of playing success that they realised protest was pretty useless. So, how did it all happen?

> . . . very quickly. The chairman and Charles Green told me they'd had
> a good offer and I had to say yes or no. What do you do when a club
> like Benfica come in for you?

You sign for them, Brian. So he joined Graeme Souness in the Portuguese sunshine and, as I speak to him after just six games, has scored
two goals and is well liked by the crowd. But at least United got good
money for him, do I hear you say? Can anyone tell me how much the
fee was and when it was paid into the club's account? Can anyone tell
me why a club on the verge of promotion sells its two leading goalscorers in the same week?

Having left one boardroom struggling with financial problems, he
joined a carbon copy, albeit one with a much grander scale of publicity.
Unpaid transfer fees have brought Benfica an admonition from FIFA.
The new chairman—*elected* in 1997 by a narrow majority from the 20,000
voters—was rewarded with the problems of sorting out massive debts
and refuting allegations that organised crime controlled the game in Portugal and that the club profited from prearranged victories courtesy of
bribed referees and match-fixing. A year previously, one referee was
jailed for 15 months for accepting such payments and in this milieu 40
well-known academics, trade unionists and politicians declared their future
support for FC Barcelona of Spain as a form of protest against what was
occurring in Portuguese football. It makes the shenanigans of United's
various chairmen pale into insignificance.

One distinction Brian holds is being the most popular black player
in the history of Sheffield United. When I asked him who his mates in
the game are, two things stand out: first, they are all players who promised
so much but never quite made the big time—Rod Wallace, Chris Fair-
clough, Franz Carr, Ade Littlejohn and Tony Agana; secondly, as you've
probably noticed, they are all black. Should I read anything into this?

> Not really. When you're black, you have to be a better player; you have
> to do things a bit better than a white player: the moment you can't,
> they'll start with the 'I knew he'd let me down' stuff.

Whatever Brian has been put through by dint of his colour, his is not
the kind of personality given to bitterness or grudges: just, it would seem,
a quiet sense of solidarity with fellow black footballers. These days, he
certainly has nothing to prove and his goalscoring record will not be
challenged for many a year (if ever again) at Bramall Lane.

Shortly after his second departure from Bramall Lane, the United manager Nigel Spackman spoke out in disgust at the sale of his leading goalscorer and then walked out. The chairman then called the manager names in public—only to resign himself when he gets called names by fans. And so it goes on, and who really cares? The answer, strangely enough, is Brian. He rang mates in Sheffield that same week to find out what was happening at his old club. Now he asks me what Blades fans think of him, and I find it touching that he occasionally refers to 'us' when talking about United. When Blades next see him on TV as he scores in the Champions League—or, who knows, in the Premier League?—with his trademark acclamation of a goal, think what might have been had those in power at Bramall Lane over the past decade been able to get their acts together. He was a modest lad who loved his time at Bramall Lane; he never let anyone down at Sheffield United and he was not a Judas. Other people, in selling him, sold the fans out—twice in fact. Sadly, those same fans never got to see the benefits of the 30 pieces of silver.

Injury Time

Businessmen buy him sell him, lend him: and he lets it all happen in return for the promise of more fame and more money. The more successful he is and the more money he makes, the more of a prisoner he becomes. Forced to live by military discipline, he suffers the punishing daily round of training and the bombardments of pain-killers and cortisone to forget his aches and fool his body. And on the eve of big games, they lock him up in a concentration camp where he does forced labour, eats tasteless food, gets drunk on water and sleeps alone.93

Bouncing Back...
Dougie Hodgson

Working as a bouncer in high-decibel discos and pubs for five years teaches such an employee to lip-read to a degree. This can have unexpected consequences. Years later, two young ladies in a car pass the team coach and the ex-bouncer is in it returning from a professional football reserve game. He mouthed a request to one of them while indicating his mobile phone; a number was mouthed in return from the car. A phone call and 40-mile journey later, boy and girl meet in Sheffield and Bob's your uncle.

As I face Doug in his garden in the sun, the car-driving vision appears wearing sunshades, micro-skirt and high heels. She smiles and sits with us. Noticing my distraction, Doug smirks. The shady lady merely shows leg and attitude. As a cleaner gives the house a once-over while two mates recently arrived from Oz suck on tubes of beer in the kitchen and messages from females work the ansaphone, I am reminded of why I still want to be a footballer.

Millions of men would love to be professional athletes; many women love male sports stars; and, in Doug's home-country of Australia, men and women love their sport. The country has one of the world's highest percentages of participation in sport. Inevitably, academics have attempted to explain why, but the most plausible explanation I reckon was offered by that distinguished Antipodean philosopher by the name of Dame Edna Everage. For her, all this exercise and activity was down to three factors: one was the moderate climate which permitted all-year-round pursuits; second was the plentiful diet of meat and fruit which sustained the sporting body. However it was the third reason that she felt was most important: namely, the total absence of any intellectual distractions. Maybe the Aussies are a nation of 'doers' rather than scholars; certainly, Doug left school as soon as possible. Working from the age of 15, he was soon a big strong lad who burned the candle at both ends. For millions of Australians, it's a good life: much of it lived outdoors and celebrated in particular with team sports and communal drinking. This was not always the case.

In a country founded on transported convicts and their conquering of warrior natives, Australia produced a frontier mentality. For 50 years from the late eighteenth century, Britain shipped its loaf-stealers and sheep-rustlers to this penal colony—140,000 arrived this way. From 1830, people arrived by choice: Dougie's folks were among those who paid their boat fare and arrived in Melbourne from Sunderland 30 years ago. A few years later, Doug was born. The old man (a cricketer with Durham County and an amateur footballer) progressed from construction work to owning a poultry farm, while running a football club in his spare time.

Until the past 30 years, life out there was tough and, for many, it was a hard and violent existence. With the conqueror mentality no longer the accepted norm, sport has provided a semi-legitimate avenue for many to intimidate and throw punches—a fact that does not seem to perturb the authorities over there. In fact, TV stations sometimes show footage of on-field scraps in various sports as a way boosting the game's popularity. No one turns the TV off for fear of watching a fight.

Possibly because of its relative tranquillity, football is third in terms of male sporting participation behind rugby and Aussie rules. Crowds at football matches are modest by British standards, with only Sydney Olympic capable of averaging 5,000. Millions, though, watch English

and Italian games on TV and, occasionally, the game gets a higher profile, such as when the national side qualifies for the World Cup, as they
did in 1974 (and narrowly missed out in 1986, and 1998 with El Tel).
A national football league was formed in Australia only as recently as
1961. Consisting of teams from the big cities—in particular Sydney and
Melbourne—the football clubs are usually products of immigrant Italian,
Greek and Yugoslav communities with club names that represent their
origins. For some reason, no clubs represent English, Scottish or Irish
émigrés. Explaining why is difficult. Some obviously wished to sustain
ethnic identity and did so via football; others no doubt migrated to forget what they had previously known. In Doug's case, there is no great
attachment to another land or nation: despite holding a British pass-
port, Doug is an Aussie, and proud of it.

The young Doug played the game from the age of four and, by his
mid-teens, had represented the south Australian state of Victoria, but
was also representing them at cricket and was a local tennis champ. The
longer-established national sport of rugby league never appealed, and
Aussie rules was just a brief flirtation.

> It's really just an excuse for a scrap. They all get white line fever. Soon
> as they cross over one, they go fuckin' crazy!

Recent years have shown that football down under is in a healthy
state. In the 1991 Youth World Cup, the Australian team came fourth
and achieved a similar position in the 1992 Barcelona Olympics. Some
excellent Australian-born players have lately made a living in English
football—Craig Johnstone, Tony Dorigo and Mark Bosnich are the big
names; dozens of others have gone to teams in Greece and Yugoslavia.
For all this talent, the basic problem is that the game over there suffers
the stigma of being seen as the pastime of recent migrants. Because many
of these have tanned complexions and speak a different first language,
using typical white-settler sensibilities, millions of native non-participants
dismiss the game as 'wogball'.

Back in the 1970s, the Irish comedian Dave Allen described Australians
as the most balanced people on earth, an attribute caused by his belief
that they had a chip on each shoulder. Dismissive of the newly arrived,
many are equally dismissive of their former rulers, i.e. the Brits, better
known as 'the poms', and enjoy nothing more than beating them on
the sporting field. Though they can seemingly do this at will in cricket
and rugby, football is still a game they haven't quite got the hang of.

Every so often, the English FA sends a team out there to put them in their place and remind them how far they have got to go. For 70 years now, the Old Country has sent its representatives to fly the flag and, in a sense, patronise (and beat) the colonists. So far, an England side has never lost. Funnily enough, it was around 70 years ago that United last had an Australian on the books. This was in 1922 when Bob Muse joined from Durham City; he lasted a season, but never made the first team. So Dougie flies the flag for his nation: he is both the Australian cultural attaché and diplomat for Sheffield. He performs the task very well.

Subtlety and discretion, however, are not always his strong points. Most United fans got to know of him via his mouth. Newly arrived and injured, he was asked to commentate on United matches for Radio Sheffield. He proved a natural narrator with memorable one-liners. Shortly after coming out of hospital where he had enjoyed cocaine for pain-killing purposes, he was asked on air to comment on the then-recent Paul Merson drug-taking affair.

> I just said, he's a loser: he paid for the stuff I got it for free. I thought it was funny, but the boss heard it and told me it might be true, but you can't go round saying that.

He has a natural exuberance, not intimidated by British broadcasting standards. When players started fighting on the pitch at a match against Sunderland, Doug's radio shouts of 'They're into it!' and his later opinion that the fights were the best part of the game, though true, was not what the football authorities and radio officials wanted to hear. One game saw him leave the microphone when fans sitting nearby started giving him some lip. Doug went on the Aboriginal masculine rite of passage known as 'walkabout' and, once among them, suggested they quieten down! His professional co-commentator meanwhile gibbered away, frightened Doug would chin a few or get chinned himself or ask him for back-up.

Before anyone gets indignant about such a scenario, it might be useful to know that fans brawl at matches in Australia. One famous kick-off took place a couple of years ago between Preston Macedonia and Heidelberg Alexander. Dougie played for Alex that day and remembers it well.

> Christ, it went mad. I kept bootin' the ball into the crowd so I could watch the fights in the grandstands. Everybody was brawling, police were everywhere and we had to be smuggled out of the ground in a police van.

And all because of events 10,000 miles away. The home team consisted of Macedonian migrants; Heidelberg was a Greek team and their fans Greek migrants. The former did not take too kindly to Greek military manoeuvres on their homeland and took it out on their Greek neighbours. The police had to get the helicopter in to control the fracas! Soon after, the Australian FA, in the interests of promoting both peace in sport and ethnic integration, ordered all teams to drop names that indicated ethnicity, but failed to realise the reason such clubs existed was the belief at one time that the sports ruling body would not pick ethnic players for Australian representative teams. Although our man has an ambition to represent the national side, he, like many colleagues, only ever wanted to play for a British club.

Aside from his family, the biggest influence on his desire to become a footballer came from satellite TV, via which Doug supported Liverpool, his hero being Kenny Dalglish. His first attempt at the big time was when he came to England, aged 13, on a family holiday and had trials with Sunderland and Watford. The latter had a manager called Graham Taylor who told him to come back when he was 16. He would have, except that fate in the shape of a drink-driver intervened.

Aged 15, Doug was one of seven car passenger victims of a driver who was so pissed he didn't see a 'Stop' sign. Compared to some of the others, Doug got off lightly with broken ribs, jaw, neck and head injuries, or so it seemed initially. Later it was found that whiplash and concussion had caused serious injuries which were to plague him for the next five years. Wearing a neck brace for three years and in and out of hospital, this prodigious teenage athlete had his life curtailed.

> There's a file as thick as my arm on me in Melbourne hospitals. My nerve-endings caused me spasms; I could collapse without warning, and when this happened I'd be rushed to hospital and pumped with all sorts of drugs. Then they'd let me go after being delirious for days. Then it would happen again. Eventually they had me in for a lumber puncture and took fluid off my brain.

This situation almost destroyed him. The best years of many people's lives were for him years of severe pain, sedative drugs and occasional despair. He admits to mood-swings and serious depression, which required him to visit the head doctor: 'They tried to get me doing hypnotherapy . . . all I got was cold sweats!' A variety of psychiatrists came and went because Doug became a late-teenage handful.

> I became a violent man. At 17, I was going out on the piss too much. My mum and dad were coppin' it off me and one night I had a rush of blood with some bloke in a bar and mates had to pull me off him. I know now I could've killed him. It was all down to frustration at my situation; the way I was going, I was going to end in prison.

Although unable to articulate how he did what he did, the end product is that, five years later, this physical wreck was a professional footballer at Bramall Lane. The best explanation he can offer is the following.

> I taught myself to relax. The mind is amazing and we know little about it. A sports doctor taught me how to put myself out of it, sort of switch off from some experiences. Now I can do it anytime I want.

He still had downers, though. Winning substantial compensation in court from the drink–driver cheered him up, but even that could not stop the black moments.

> I'll admit it to you: I was suicidal to the point of thinking of the best way to do it. For me it was gonna' be a shotgun in the gob and we had guns on the farm . . . but I knew deep down that wasn't the answer.

Realising he had to do something, he combined physical exertion with self-analysis. The former technique saw him buy a punchbag and speedball and take up kick-boxing and martial arts. His efforts here produced a disciplined mind and body, but one that still suffered dreadful pain and exhaustion—after some sessions, he could not walk. To avoid depression, he somehow convinced himself things could get better.

> At 16, the doctors told me it's all over with the football: forget it. Three years later, I'm still being fed all sorts of shit drugs and I'm basically a guinea pig for the medics and none of it's working. One day, I threw them all away; I said to myself: it's time to get on with life and put mind over matter. I put my anger into the punchbag and onto the football field: this gave me the will to live day to day.

This helped him to contain the pain he was suffering and to manage his anger—which was good news for the merry revellers of Melbourne. I say this because, between the ages of 19 and 23, Doug was a licensed bouncer. In fact, he worked 15 hours a day at times. A one-time landscape gardening job then became steel-fixing; oil rig work was then followed by painting and decorating. Bouncing four nights a week meant the other two nights were reserved for football training. Through his fitness regime, his strenuous daytime jobs and night-time interventions, he discovered both physical and mental courage and also realised he was capable of becoming fitter than he ever thought possible.

> I've been toughened in various ways and, I'll say it myself, I am hard. I've no fear on a football field. Maybe it's anger, maybe stupidity, but I'll stick me head in anywhere. Also, I'm a late developer. I'm nearly 27 but, remember, I lost years of my life. These guys training every-day since they were 16: look at them . . . look at how little hair a lot of them have. They've got old bodies!

With such a life story, it was inevitable that he came to the attention of Sheffield United in dubious circumstances. All the same, another English club could have bought him two years earlier and far more cheaply. He impressed the ex-Hull City star Ken Wagstaff who was coaching out there in 1992 and who recommended him to his old club. A couple of games in Hull reserves impressed the manager Terry Dolan, but they could not afford the £20,000 fee Heidelberg demanded and so he had to return.

> I was out of my rut and wanted to be a pro footballer in England. They wouldn't let me go. I was fuming, kicked in the teeth. I dropped the bottom lip for a few weeks, then got on with it and hoped another chance would come.

Off the pitch, however, activities with the bouncing fraternity had brought him to the attention of the Australian legal system and its uniformed representative. Let's just say that, because of a couple of incidents, he had to get out of town for a while and reckoned another club a few thousand miles away might be just the ticket. The fortunate team was Dinalya Serbia (not being national league level, they still retained an ethnic name) and the city was Perth, Western Australia. His demands were modest.

> I said, I want a job, a house, a car, good money and a game. I got it all. It was like goin' from the English Premier to Division Two, so I could easily handle the standard. I got a job painting and decorating and, by midday, would be on the beach with beer. Meanwhile, I'm winning the radio phone-in player of the week.

Then United turned up to play a Western Australia Select side. Though not a Western Australia player, he somehow got himself picked and he was out to impress.

> I went on a week's fruit diet, and I was not gonna' give anything away.
> I had a good one, even though we lost.

It was a game a few United players remember. One told me that his memory of Dougie was of 'a big daft bugger who wanted to fight everybody'. After a few clatterings, the United centre-forward Nathan Blake tried to explain to this big centre-half that it was only a friendly; and the gasping Glynn Hodges, while bent over, had Doug's thumb enter his backside cleavage. Apparently, as Doug remembers it, Hodges laughed, which is not a bad reaction when the perpetrator is 6' 3" with a strange stare and crooked smile.

United's manager at the time, Harry Bassett, saw something he liked in big Doug and took him on the rest of the tour, then bought him for £70,000. Landing in Sheffield, his first task was to get as fit as the pros. He did well and got a first-team run-out in an autumn Anglo-Italian Cup fixture. Then the script gets confusing.

> The boss says I've got 'til Christmas to settle. Then he goes and gets
> a centre-half on loan for three months; he's already got five on the
> books.

When he made his first-team debut, it was coming on as sub and playing centre-forward (a position he played for five years in Melbourne). After a series of injuries and an inability to make the first team regularly, Harry tried to unload him. First stop was Plymouth, who were prepared to pay £100,000 and better the wages United offered. Then, out of the blue, Bassett called him back for the first team. Then it got more confusing.

> I'd just played two great games and we'd got the first clean sheet of the
> season and Man of the Match and Harry says to me, 'You're just not doin'
> it', and says I'm going to Lincoln for £60,000. I refused to go, and said,
> 'Put me on the list and get me a decent club.' They were bottom of
> Division Three and I rang their manager and, when I asked him how
> long he was gonna' be there, he didn't know! He was out weeks later!

A possible move to Mansfield fell through; then Bassett left and Howard Kendall took over and something about Doug obviously impressed the new man.

> I got an 18-month contract. That said, he told me I'm not an automatic
> in his first XI. I've got to prove I can be.

He played five games in a row in a defence that conceded only one goal. Though forever grateful to Harry for discovering him, the constant ball-work in training which the new manager emphasised suited Doug down to the ground.

A year earlier, however, pain and misery returned to haunt him as he lay for a total of 32 days in a hospital bed. A clash of heads in training, ironically with a colleague with whom he shared a house, left him with a double fracture of the nose. Headaches and breathing difficulties followed. Three operations were needed to realign the nose, and problems occurred. Basically, he kept losing prodigious amounts of blood before medics realised he was allergic to the drugs they were pumping into him.

> There was one time I lost two pints of blood. Fuck, it hurt! At one point, they stuck a foot of cotton wool up each nostril then had scissors in there to pull it out. Mind you, some of the bed baths were lovely . . .

A couple of incidents with nursing staff are recounted at this point which are possibly libellous and without proof so I won't repeat them. What is an undisputed fact, however, is that, around this time, there occurred a Dougie drama on an aeroplane returning from Cyprus. Basically, the altitude caused his nose to sort of explode. He lost pints of blood again and caused a right commotion! The nose is fine right now, and so is Doug, but back in hospital how did he feel?

> You lay there thinking, why me again? After all I'd been through, I didn't need it. Then I got philosophical; I thought of all the bad things I've done in me time and realised maybe they've come back to me . . . y'know, what goes round comes round.

The man's a Methodist and he doesn't know it! But it's not a morbid moment. With a grin, he explains his everyday philosophy learned from a grandmother: 'It's nice to be nice to people.'

Regardless of what some rival players might think, Doug is a genuinely nice fellow; he loved Sheffield and had many people (mainly United-ites) who wanted to look after him and who regularly called to his house for a drink and a laugh. Some visited him daily in hospital, which was appreciated from a man 12,000 miles from home who got so homesick shortly after arriving that Harry let him go home for two weeks when injured to cheer him up and who, on receiving a card from Mum and Dad on his first Christmas here, sobbed at the kitchen table.

Wherever Doug played he was a crowd-pleaser, but some form of controversy was never far away. His debut at Heidelberg was eventful.

> I broke a rival player's jaw. It wasn't really intentional. Afterwards, a bunch of their fans were waiting for me. Luckily, I had the nun-chucks in the back of the car . . .

Eh? Imagine a British footballer facing such wrath, and responding to it, and in such a matter-of-fact manner explaining that a martial arts weapon just happened to be to hand. There was no hysterical tabloid headlines, no FA inquiry—nothing. Violence around sport in Australia is not viewed in such a hysterical way as it is here. To date, the only time he made the English national papers was recently when a Millwall centre-forward called him an 'arsehole' via *The Sun* after an on-the-field run-in. Blades at the match may have noted Doug's refusal to shake

the hand of Uwe Fuchs, but none heard Doug's offer as to where and how the pair could settle their ding-dong—which the German wisely refused.

Apart from the said gentlemen, nothing and nobody much winds him up. This caricature of the Australian icon Tom Ocker retains a good humour, wit and a willingness to try anything and is relaxed with people, regardless of their social standing. When not on the team, he would sit with the fans chatting away and, when his first team appearances increased, he received a lot of invitations to appear, present and open things in the city.

When we met in 1996, he had not scored for United, but he almost got one on his debut.

> They'd have had to send me off if it had gone in—I'd have been havin' a wank in the middle of the field!

As long as team-mates don't feel the need to emulate, I suppose it beats pretending to sing into the corner flag or pulling your shirt over your head. But I felt Doug had to learn that what might be appropriate for Australia could, in England, both set a bad example to the lower orders and frighten the horses.

He was awfully keen to succeed. On the pitch, he would talk to himself, punch the palm of his hand when he knew his efforts were close and, at Arsenal once, though he played for only a couple of minutes, he acknowledged the thousands of Unitedites at the end by kissing the club badge on his shirt. Fans got the impression he liked what he was doing.

> I'm happy as a pig in shit. Since the age of 15, I was gettin' up at six o' clock to go to work. Now I get up at half-nine and run around for a couple of hours and get big money for it. All I ever wanted to be was a footballer in Britain.

I phoned him in February 1997 with a view to blagging a couple of free tickets for the next United match. Having played 13 straight first-team games he had, it seemed, finally made the breakthrough. The distraught replies to my call told me he was leaving, sold to Oldham hours earlier that day for a deal which, whatever it was quoted in public, was not what actually exchanged hands. In return, plus a cash differential, United got Nicky Henry, who played a few games and hasn't played for over a year now.

Never wanting to leave, he realised he had to in order to play regular first-team football. Oldham offered a wage packet superior to that at Bramall Lane and a package that included relocation fees and two flights to Australia. They could not, however, offer a better standard of football. Relegated a few months after he signed, Doug has since played in Division Two both at centre-half and centre-forward. Inevitably, a few months after signing, he broke his nose badly and needed an operation on it and, inevitably, a week later in training he broke it again and needed another op and a month to recuperate.

He phones his old mates in Sheffield every week and misses Bramall Lane and the fans.

> I've such fond memories. United will always be my club: after three and a half years there, it's my second home . . . the fans are fantastic.

He speaks highly of his two managers at the Lane, Harry Bassett and Howard Kendall. When I ask why Kendall sold him, he seems stumped: '. . . I dunno . . . I never did ask the bastard.' One question he did ask was on Valentine's Day in 1998. Standing in the Eiffel Tower, he asked a woman he had met in Sheffield to marry him. The good news? She accepted. The bad news? She's a Wednesdayite. Perhaps it was a good thing she was not present when Doug scored his first League goal for United on Boxing Day at Bradford.

French Dressing...
Derek French

Imagine Norman Wisdom running for a bus wearing a fluorescent pink cap. Got it? Right, now imagine a bloke who invades the pitch, alone, every match, without getting nicked or looking too daft. Combine these scenarios and you've got Derek French, United's physiotherapist between 1988 and 1996, the man with the bag, who, we believe, has a magic sponge which allows our favourites to continue the good fight.

A simple job brief—'to treat and rehabilitate injured players'—is, in practice, one hell of a task. With 40 professionals and 30 youngsters on the books in his era, there was plenty to do. But, as anyone at the club at the time would tell you, he was always more than his job description. In this closed fraternity, he was Father Confessor to many—the level of management that spends, at times, hours alone with players. Many players considered him a bit special, and even those not under treatment saw him as something of a cult figure. He was, after all, the only physio in United's history who received a chant requesting a wave when he entered the field of play.

No player goes through a career without picking up injuries. Most, thankfully, are trivial. Some are so serious they end a career; the physio deals with both kinds. The day we met in 1995, the club had two men with the title of physio: one only recently appointed full-time. Although they shared the same title, Frenchie was *primus inter pares* and the man for all first-team games.

Now, before we go any further, a few people asked me to ask him the following: What's the story behind the pink cap? and, What's in his magic bag? Well, the cap advertises a golfing equipment company and he wears it for two reasons. First, it protects a balding head from the cold and, secondly, by wearing it, he gets a set of golf clubs for product endorsement. It originated years ago with a good mate of his, a Mr Vincent Jones, who got him a similar cap as a joke. This footballing colossus owed Frenchie a favour after he recommended him while playing for Bedmond (the village in Hertfordshire in which Frenchie grew up) to the manager of Wimbledon, a Mr Dave 'Harry' Bassett. As the man himself explains, 'It's the only bit of scouting I've ever done. I don't think I'll bother with any more after him.' Just the one find, but what a diamond. As for the bag, well, it's a bit of an anti-climax: a couple of squeezy 'Lucozade' bottles full of water, a towel, Vaseline, splints and adrenaline solution to stem bleeding. There is no sponge.

There were days when bag-men really did have sponges. Traditionally, such men were called 'trainers', later dignified to 'trainer-coach'. They supervised training and fitness programmes and entered the pitch to attend the injured. United's most famous and probably the world's longest-serving was George Waller (1894–1930). Much respected, his benefit match in 1923 against Wednesday drew a staggering crowd of 25,000. Such a job got a bit technical in the 1920s: trainers became partly skilled masseurs and got a basic knowledge of physiology. The successor to Waller reflected this. Tom Radcliffe was masseur to the England cricket team in 1930 and his successor, Dougie Livingstone, had proper physiotherapy qualifications.

By the 1950s, United used two of their ex-players as trainer-coaches assisted by a part-time, fully qualified physio. On top of them, for serious problems, was the club doctor—United have had one since 1920. In fact, one of the first-ever directors of United was a medic. By the 1960s, the job of trainer was totally different to that of physio. A match programme (October 1967) pictured the physio at work—fans knew instantly what he was: he looked serious and wore glasses and a white coat over a shirt and tie. Beside him was an embarrassed-looking Len Badger, de-bagged on the 'massage plinth' attached to an 'Impulsathon'. Furthermore, readers were told this gizmo was German. The club had also bought a 'short-wave dithering unit' (no, not one of the late 1960s defenders) and club joiner, Norman, had banged together a pulley system for weight-training. Who needs *Vorsprung durch Technik* when there's British technical wizards like Norm around?

Anyway, enough: let's find Frenchie. Unfortunately, he tells me, they all do find him: he can't hide anywhere at Bramall Lane and it's a non-stop, nine-to-five job. Then there's Saturdays and alternate Sundays, and it doesn't end in the summer. His little empire is two rooms of equipment and a corridor with various contraptions in it, but his door is only there to be opened and there is a continuous flow of wounded.

The match is the minor part of his job. The main part is facing up to longer-term injury, which means he sees players in various states of mind. It's an emotional job and tears are spilled when injuries get players down. He remembers well the courage of some he has treated: Simon Webster had the worst leg-break he's ever seen. The bravest player he has ever dealt with, though, was Mel Rees:[7] 'Nothing could compare to that man's bravery.' Frenchie was one of the first to know of the man's life-shortening condition. He also mentions the club coach, Wally Downes, who came through a lot of pain to continue playing.

As a physio, his word is gospel with regard to what players should not do. Trouble is, he can get it wrong and those whom he praises can then dump on him. Thus, when Frenchie was out of earshot, Wally Downes offered his version of events.

> He's such a good physio he failed to notice three out of my four broken ankles. Three times he ran on and said there's nothing wrong, definitely. I couldn't fuckin' walk. He got it right the fourth time, but I made him a fuckin' expert in broken ankles . . . at my expense.

The pair at one time shared a house and are very good mates, apparently.

Among the playing staff, Frenchie was famous for two things: his one-liners, usually abusive and personal (and very funny), and his penchant for working to music. The music box pumped out jazz, acid, rave and

---

7. Mel Rees was a goalkeeper who played eight first-team games for United in 1992. Diagnosed as having cancer of the bowel, he died a year later at the age of 26.

jungle (yes, jungle) and the 47-year-old would get on down as the players limbered up.

In hindsight, warned of his one-liners, I asked for it. Do you get attached to players you see daily for months on end? The answer, straight-faced: 'Not half as much as I'd like to get attached to some of their wives.' Prompted, Wally Downes throws in his one-line philosophy on relationships and the wired-up and massaged defender has a giggling fit. Normality resumed, the correct answer was 'Very much so, but that's football.' It works both ways. Former Lane favourites phone him regularly or drop in for a chat. Furthermore, one ex-United player with a long-term injury at his new club was recently unable to come through a practice match. The manager went mad, telling him not to come back until fit. Hearing this, Frenchie sent word for the player to call and see him.

The job, as he sees it, is all about body and soul. Though legs are still the most injury-hit parts of the body in recent years, the club emphasised upper-body physique for 'springing and shielding'. Muscle power and strength here are also useful in a fight, but Frenchie didn't mention that. As we all know, footballers play with their heads in more ways than one. At one time, thanks to Harry, United got seriously involved with some headcases. So, into the dressing room all the way from the USA arrived disciples of Dale Carnegie and Tim Robbins. They preached personal growth and, well, I'm not sure what else. Their legacy was various bits of psychobabble on Frenchie's walls. Alongside the poems 'If' and 'Go Placidly' and a not-too-flattering reference to Australia were various slogans to muse over while under treatment: 'He who angers you conquers you', 'Healing is a matter of time, but is sometimes a matter of opportunity' and 'No matter what you do physically or mentally your own determination produces the outcome'. It's all way above my head, but some of the players enjoyed the sessions these various gurus gave, so that can't be a bad thing.

Other forms of alternative medicine were made available under Frenchie: shiatsu, acupuncture and aromatherapy. 'They're all adjuncts to normal procedures and they work for some players. We do anything for a change; we need to stimulate the brain.' The players have had aerobic instruction and used the speed-burst-recovery training method from Scandinavia known as the *Fartlek*. Training at one time ended with drinks of mineral water and vitamin supplements and three times a week a fitness and diet consultant arrived to give advice. The emphasis was on pasta and not getting plastered.

Once a year, the squad went away into a sort of retreat. These preseason trips to army camps, while hard physical work, were also considered good for morale; and that, in football, is always half the battle. The idea is that a happy squad reflects its camaraderie on the pitch. Such excursions provide for good times. The downside is the occasional nightmare scenario when an injury ends a career. How do you approach that one?

> Fortunately, it's not really down to me. The orthopaedic surgeon would be the one to break it. But, being honest, the player would know if his progress was not right.

In a sense, the physio selects the team. Only he ever has the authority to tell the boss if a player could play or not. If he considered an injury on the pitch worrying, what then? 'I think I could insist a player be brought off.' What about when his precious bodies are battering themselves in the line of duty?

> I tend not to get involved. If I was particularly incensed, I might have a row with a player, might tell him his recklessness might get himself injured.

Not all injuries occur on the pitch. Some circumstances fans learn about through gossip. Do such situations present a problem?

> If a player has picked up an injury outside of football, I'd get to know the circumstances eventually. There could be some feud in the club which I'd get to know about. A player might be unhappy about a million things. His attitude could affect his recovery.

So, what do you do?

> Sometimes the boss don't need to know everything. He can get too involved with his players. I won't always tell him every circumstance.

Some players might use injuries as a form of protest. A disgruntled player could spin an injury out: then what?

> If I thought he was, I'd have words with the manager—tell him he's not putting the work in then he gets him in and sorts it out.

The physio is powerful. He must also be trusted. Though his face suggests much of the time that he's holding a smile back, at your expense,

or that one wrong word might produce a punch, it's a face you can talk to. Furthermore, he's tremendously open and honest himself. If ever you get the chance, ask him about the time the squad were in a hotel in Sweden when a wedding party held a reception. It's unbelievable, but true. I can say no more.

His work has extended beyond Bramall Lane. An interest in ortho-paedic medicine has seen him attend operations on the players. If a player has an illness or injury, the club doctor diagnosed and Frenchie super-vised treatment. He would then chat with the club surgeon and the club doctor who visited three times a week. In the case of a pitch emergency, a procedure was enacted: two hands in the air would see the Doc run on and the ambulance crew get the stretcher out. The wounded would be taken from pitch to ambulance to hospital accompanied by the Doc and painkillers. In 1994, the club hired a radiologist for all home games. With his scanning machine, results could be produced in ten minutes, permitting the player to know the extent of his injury and the boss to know who was available or not for the next match.

Rather like cars, footballers are traded, and buyers look for a good motor, decent bodywork and not too much mileage. But, when money rules the game, those selling might not wish to highlight deficiencies. Ideally, players come with a medical history—their equivalent of a log-book—but this cannot always be relied upon. So how do you know you're not buying a ringer? This is a job for the Doc and Frenchie. Under Frenchie's eye, players undergo tests for strength, endurance and flexibility. The Doc looks for abnormalities and anything dodgy will result in a Magnetic Resource Imaging scan, an all-body, non-intrusive X-ray that doesn't miss much. On top of this, Frenchie rings his counterparts elsewhere and has a word. In days of old, a semi-fit player might have received a few needles to sort him out. Not anymore—or at least not at Bramall Lane under Frenchie. Now there are strict guidelines from the FA: all injections have to be notified to them in writing. Though cortisone is still used, its purpose has changed:

> You'd never give it to a player to play. Normally, it's four weeks after such injections before they can play.

Today, such players might receive electric currents to improve blood flow, or H-wave pulses, or be attached to anything that beeps and whirrs. Players under such control who got too lippy risked an increase in voltage. How flippant he could be about an injury depends on his evaluation of the player.

> You can laugh about the situation with some. Others you can't. It's all about man-management. We tell them and tell the boss what we expect of them.

This is true. When in his company, the boss and the coaches all asked Derek about respective players; he could answer immediately about their progress, and charts and dates against the names of those under treatment were there for the record.

When the team was chosen and the day of the match arrived, Frenchie's day was a long one. For the midweek home match against Burnley, he was in before 9 am treating the long-term injured. By midday, he'd seen six of them. The afternoon saw a continual flow, both established and potentials, who needed help. By 6.30, various players selected to play need attention with their own personal strappings. Others out injured wanted more treatment before watching the match. Meanwhile, in the dressing room, players would push, stretch and bend assisted by various coaching staff. After the pre-match on-pitch warm-up, the mood got serious; the volume of the music box was lowered as the boss gave commands. Wally shouted his wisdom and captain Paul Beesley snorted Vicks-Sinex—and probably helium, judging by the pitch of his voice and subsequent ranting. In all this, Frenchie took a back seat. He watched quietly; he was available, but not needed. Soon the show would be all his.

The 90 minutes saw him in action just three times. Following a fifth-minute diving header, Blakey stayed down. His sore neck was relieved by cold water and sympathy. Then, after 35 minutes, a set-piece (always a danger sign to a physio) resulted in a defender staying down: Scotty got a punch to the face, but cold water revived him. The final call to action is in the seventieth minute, when Gannon held his rib following a challenge. A 20-second consultancy suggested insignificance, but two minutes later he walked off to be substituted, unable to breathe properly. After the match, the same man received a painkiller from the Doc and an X-ray. Within ten minutes, everyone knew it was not a fractured rib; the Doc prescribed anti-inflammatory tablets, the taking of which would be supervised by Frenchie. With Gagey's knee cleaned and dressed by the other physio, the players could now go to their other practice ground—the players' bar. After a 13-hour day, Frenchie downed a few with Wally as the one-liners continued. This time, the match officials enjoyed the jokes.

Talking of refs, here's an interesting story. When at Wimbledon, Frenchie probably saved a referee's life. At half-time, he started hyperventilating in a state of pre-heart attack. Putting him in the coma position, Frenchie looked after him until the ambulance came. A year later, the same ref, at a match at Tottenham, sent him off the touchline for swearing at the linesman. There's gratitude for you.

He never made the grade as a player: a trial at Watford didn't produce a contract, so he played a bit of non-League football, but the highest he got was at non-League level with Barnet reserves. Meanwhile, working in the Kodak factory, he saved up and bought a cab. He entered a career in football via another door: a mate was reserve team coach at Barnet and, after playing a couple of games, Frenchie became physio/

trainer. Reaching 30, he decided to take the FA physio's course. Thus followed three years of study: a combination of distance-learning and residentials at Lilleshall. He studied strains and sprains between stretches behind the wheel; cabbing paid the fees. To do this needed dedication: of the 40 who began, only six finished (four are currently with professional clubs).

Soon after, he became Barnet's physio and, alongside manager Barry Fry, was there three nights a week, rolling the pitch and painting the gates. Fortunately, glamour club Wimbledon stepped in. Their assistant manager knew Frenchie and knew that Harry wanted a new physio; he put a word in while Frenchie put in a low wages bill. 'It was ridiculously low money. I was the cheapest of the four applicants.' No doubt the boss loved him for that. But he obviously impressed, because eight years later he followed him to Watford before landing in Sheffield.

In Frenchie, United had one of the best physios in the business. But he was also chosen by the boss for another quality—he made people laugh. 'The boss liked an atmosphere. He liked to see the squad laughing. I'd play a part in that.' He is genuinely funny: players enter his room at their peril. At one stage, the boss and Wally were in with him when one injured first-teamer was receiving the round robin of being slaughtered for his accent, hairstyle and clothing. He could only sit there and take it.

Maybe it's all good practice for when they step out in front of the fans. Being a footballer is arduous and often a painful line of work. Should they avoid a challenge, fans give them a piece of their mind. Under Harry Bassett's reign at United, no player shrank from challenges; that they could also trot out regularly was thanks to the dedicated man fans could see every Saturday but who, along with those in a similar role, never received the acclaim they deserved. Many a career relied on his patience, care, encouragement and counselling. In more ways than one, Frenchie was the headcase at the club.

When Harry left United in 1998, Derek remained for a few months, then also departed. Having developed a client-base, he fancied his chances at running a private clinic. Furthermore, the club made it known that they were not willing to pay for two full-time physios. Feeling that he had run his course, he left without malice, but found the private clinic tough going financially, and he missed the day-to-day crack that so many years in football had brought. His former manager came looking for him in the autumn of 1997 shortly after taking over at Nottingham Forest. The part-time position became full-time in April 1998.

About to marry and with a second child on the way, Derek has decided to put roots down in Sheffield and keeps a few private patients because as he has learned so well that 'In football you never know what's around the corner.' In view of his longevity in his profession and his reputation as one of the best in the business, I ask my final question, which was whether international-level recognition had ever been offered (i.e. had the England set-up ever asked for his services?). He knew what I meant, but it wouldn't be Frenchie if he gave a straight answer. What I got in reply was: 'I once shagged a bird in Finland.' I feel better already.

The Real Mesters...
Dane Whitehouse

The bloke who inflicted the injury was the subject of a £1.5 million bid by a Premier League team on the same day that I met his victim. The latter had not played a game for nine months and it would be another six before he could start full training. Even now, there remains the slight possibility that even time cannot fully heal the damage done. The 1998–99 season begins in three weeks for his former team-mates. He, meanwhile, watches the juniors put through their paces while we sit in the dugout at Bramall Lane, sheltering from the sun.

This popular local lad has enjoyed a decade of footballing fame and a latest-model flat-top BMW declares 'made it' in the local culture. But the football cliché that you're only as good as your last game is painfully evident to this man who had it all and who had it temporarily taken away by a dreadful challenge from a player who could not find it in him to offer his apologies, but who earlier this year nearly paid dearly for his forgetfulness when faced with the father of the man he maimed.

Like all readers, I have no problem understanding the concepts of jogging, stepping and weight-training but, when Dane tells me about pro-pro reception and neuro-muscular facilitation, I'm lost. Apparently, the latter technique is commonly used for victims of a stroke to encourage their minds to engage with the part of their body that is paralysed or unreceptive. The idea is that the brain can be trained to stimulate feeling and this is what Dane is attempting in an effort to get feeling other than the sensation of pins and needles into the lower right leg. Combined with one-legged squats and balancing exercises, this process is akin to learning to walk again. What I learned from others was that, post-operation, he was woken from anaesthetic and asked specifically to move his toes. That he could meant the leg was not dead of all nerve stimulation. Failure to wiggle the toes could have meant amputation of the leg. The injury was that bad.

No one from any walk of life should have to suffer such a calamity. That it happened to a chap in his tenth year as a professional footballer is neither here nor there. That it happened to a chap who has bounced back from two previous serious injuries only serves to show what a fighter he is. That it should happen to a Sheffield-born lad who comes from a humble background and remains close to childhood mates is a blow to the very essence of the game, in my opinion.

This local-boy-made-good has never courted controversy, never been flash and is obsessive about keeping in touch with his peers from the large council estate of Woodthorpe. Known to all as 'Sid' after his locally well-known old man, the junior version grew up with brothers and sisters both biological and step from a second marriage. Both parents were United fans, but Sid Senior did not take the young lad to many games because of other commitments. As Dane puts it: 'He was locked up much of the time.' A builder and nightclub bouncer, big Sid was, in Sheffield parlance, a 'big hitter' and one of the 'real mesters'. He was also fiercely protective of his kids, even when they were 28 years of age.

It sounds a bit strange, I know, but the demands for academic achievement issued by the head teacher of Woodthorpe Primary School meant that the school could not have a football team. A teacher had spotted his talent in schoolyard kick-abouts, however, and got him a trial with the under-11 city schoolboy side. He impressed and was selected and remained in the team for the next four years. At big school, Dane was suspended a couple of times for fighting and, like many of his era, did not have the incentive of participation in organised sport to give him an interest in school generally. An extended strike by teachers in the

1980s involved a boycotting of extracurricular activities, which included Saturday teams. So, for the last three years of secondary school, there was no school team. In earlier years, a Sunday team run by a mate's uncle kept him busy—and kept rival managers interested so much that, at the tender age of 11, he was poached to join a more prestigious Sunday team called Sheffield Rangers. With them, he won the league and cup for two consecutive years. Eventually, the crack Sunday outfit known as Junior Blades ask him to go with them. Now aged 14, and on associate schoolboy forms with United, Rangers were good enough to wish him well and encouraged him to play for a side that is, in effect, United's nursery team. Scoring up to 30 goals a season while playing as a winger made him a valuable commodity. The involvement with United changed his outlook.

> . . . it was a different style of training. You'd do things like stretch off before the match. It was team effort, not a case of just turning up and every man for himself. The emphasis on passing and control, espe-

> cially at the School of Excellence, stayed with you and you put it into
> your game come Sunday.

Training twice a week and every school holiday, he learned the ropes from the three 'Macs': Ray McHale, John McSeveney and, later, Billy McEwan.

Associated schoolboy was not much of a deal. Financially, he got nothing; in return, the club got first refusal on him until he was 16. Liking what they saw, United retained him under the Youth Training Scheme (YTS) for the princely sum of £27.50 plus travelling expenses. Of this, £10 went weekly to his mum and £20 monthly went towards a bus pass. Lunch was crisp sandwiches from 'Bri and Irene's' corner shop adjacent to Bramall Lane.

Things improved a little when Harry Bassett took over as manager in 1989: the Club fed the youngsters in the Social Club after training. In his first year on the YTS, Dane was part of a junior team that came second in the Northern Intermediate League and, at 17, played three reserve games under coach Danny Bergara. The dismissal of Billy McEwan as manager could have been a major blow because he had managed and nurtured Dane from the age of 15, but Harry saw something he liked, and his youth team coach, Keith Mincher, made Dane team captain and gave him another year's contract as an apprentice professional. Continuing to learn and impress, he was promoted to the reserves in 1988 and, after only six outings, made it to the first team at a Division Three away fixture at Blackpool.

All Sheffielders love a day at Blackpool, Dane was no exception. Believing he was going along for the ride to experience what top-class football was all about, Harry ruined things 90 minutes before the kick-off by telling him he was playing. How does the 18-year-old handle this?

> He said, 'Go out and enjoy yourself.' It was red hot; we were top of
> the League, so there's a lot of pressure not to make a mistake. I was
> up against fully grown men. I didn't play badly.

Then, of course, he had to face 5,000 travelling Sheffielders.

> Warming up was incredible; over the Tannoy I heard them reading out
> the team and, when he said 'Whitehouse', I could hear a lot of people
> saying 'Who?' At the end, I went over and clapped them; for years it
> was me on the terraces clapping players.

It was a mutual admiration. Dane was soon to become and remain a favourite with Blades of all ages. Honest, hard-working, tough-tackling and always liable to score goals, for a decade now he has been the fans' favourite local lad. Initially playing as a winger, Harry told him to 'tuck in' a bit then backtrack to close down opposition full-backs. When times demanded it, he proved adept in midfield and even left-back. When a job needed doing, he did it effectively—and without a tantrum, if not chosen in his favoured attacking role.

Such a 'can-do' attitude impressed the manager. Dane can reflect how the 18-year-old in him learned maturity and responsibility from Harry Bassett without being subject to threats or discipline.

> You could do what you wanted with Bassett: turn up smelling of beer, but as long as you did the business on Saturday he was happy.

A few years ago, a team-mate told me that Dane was Harry's 'blue-eyed boy'. Was this the case?

> . . . [laughing] when you've got players together taking the piss, they've got to have something on each other. In training, a few would say to me, 'He loves you', and say things like, 'Are you sure he's not your dad?' . . . Were it Hodgy and Tracey who said that?

The atmosphere Harry generated has never been re-created at Bramall Lane. A great social life existed in the squad, but maybe times have changed on the pitch which militates against too much of a good time off it.

> The game has changed. You need to be fitter. It's more physical now than ten years ago. You have to watch your food intake and realise what isn't good for you.

The best preparation in the world, however, could not prevent two serious injuries. Torn knee ligaments, the result of a blocked tackle, saw him carried off in an FA Cup quarter-final against Manchester United in 1989. Out for nine months, he put on weight, the result of drinking with mates. It was a struggle to get back into the first team.

> I was on professional terms and on good money. When injured, I was out shagging and potting [drinking pints]; when I tried to make a come-back, I wasn't up to it. Harry tells me that at my age I should be playing more first-team games than I was and he gave me another chance.

He took the chance and, through intensive training and abstinence, became a regular. Then, less than two years later, he broke his right leg following a late challenge by a Bristol City player. At the time, he was being watched by the England Under-21 coach and big clubs were sniffing around. He had to start all over again. The fact that he did, and once again became a first-team choice, speaks volumes of this unassuming man's inner strength. But how does he find the resources to fight career-threatening injuries for a third time in a decade?

In seeking an answer, the starting point is maybe to describe what happened. The venue is an away match at Port Vale; the time is November of 1997. Early in the game, a very high, reckless challenge shatters his knee and all its contents. I ask tentatively if he would talk me through it. He does so without emotion.

> . . . it was in the first five minutes of the game. I'd touched the ball once and the next thing, I'm finished. Did he do me on purpose? I don't know. Early on in a match is when fast challenges are flying in—there's hundreds every match and there's always one bad challenge.

'Bad' is a euphemism for what this player was attempting. The cruciate ligament snapped as did the patella tendon ligaments.

> I knew straight away it'd gone. The knee popped out the other way to me ankle. I was carried off in terrible pain. I was in shock. They packed it with ice and I went home on the team coach.

Next day he awoke in agony. On Monday morning, Sid drove him to the club surgeon who performed a scan and realised just how serious the injury was. A four-hour operation was completed two days later and then began a three-day nightmare.

> It was the worst pain ever . . . excruciating. I lay in hospital in tears. They gave me morphine and put me under. I was high as a kite! I wouldn't wish it on anybody: only relatives could come to see me and over those days I nearly broke down.

The battle of mind over matter had only just begun. He now had to face awkward answers to questions he did not really want asked.

> The surgeon saw the scans and said I needed a total rebuild of the knee. I got a lump in me throat, but it was me dad who was more upset. I said to the surgeon, 'What are me chances? Will I play again?' He said

he'd give it a 70% chance. That's good enough for me: I had summat to aim for.

Meanwhile, he was told he had a year of basic recovery to endure. Following his stay in hospital, he was kitted out with a leg-length brace for ten weeks, which was gradually adjusted to allow varying degrees of knee bend. Unable to bath or shower, he had to stand naked and scrub down with a sponge. Unable to finish reading a newspaper, and unable to live alone, he moved back to live with mum and dad and it became apparent that, in such circumstances, many other people suffer for the injury. Inevitably, close family endured the frustration, then good mates who had called to wish him well.

> They didn't know what to say to me. I'd say to them, 'Say what you want; just don't give me any crap.' It got to me though . . . I'd be arguing with me mother and father; I'd shout for food or the phone and they'd bring it on demand. I got sick of seeing me mates.

Deciding that his psyche needed the discipline of fetching his own food and phone, he moved out to live alone.

> I looked rough, lost a stone in weight. Easiest thing would have been to say 'fuck it' and have some beer, but I was older and I understood meself better. I tried to give meself a chance so I didn't drink for seven months. On New Year's Eve, some mates picked me up and took me to a pub. I had one swig of Budweiser then left it. I told them I wasn't ready for it.

A recent holiday in Tenerife with mates saw him back to old tricks, but his team-mates still cause him pain him without realising.

> I can't watch 'em train. That's when you start thinking, 'What have I done to deserve this?', and I should be in the five-a-side team and taking shots on goal.

In such circumstances, it is not trite to state that recovery is as much a mental process as it is physical. With a year left on a three-year contract and insurance policies that cover loss of career, income is not a problem. But he will not countenance doubt and he will not accept that his injury is career-ending.

> I don't want them to ever say that and I won't ever accept it. I think it would finish me. I wouldn't know what to do. I've no exams; I've nowt

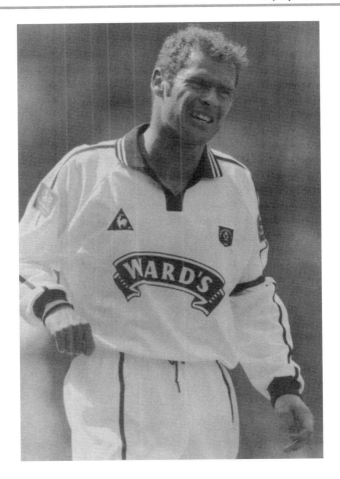

behind me. I'd have money behind me, but I don't want to be cashing that in.

Sid Senior, however, wanted to weigh someone in. When Port Vale visited the Lane five months after the incident, he made his move after the match and got onto the visitors' coach looking for the perpetrator. What would he have done?

Ripped his head off! He took it worse than me. I thought, 'I'm injured, that's it.' But when I didn't get a visit or a letter of apology from him who did it, that got me dad mad. He wanted to confront him and ask him why. Me dad had a couple of beers during the match and tried to find him.

Fortunately for the target, two security guards hired for the day by Port Vale in expectation of trouble stood in his way. A couple of United players came to the scene to help calm it down. Bundled into Dane's car, police followed behind in a vehicle but did not make an arrest.

The following Monday, Dane was surprised to see the old man at Bramall Lane. Regretting his action, he made his apologies for embarrassing his son. The then manager, Steve Thompson, born only a mile from the Whitehouse home, dismissed the apology saying that, as a father, he would have felt the same. A week later, a letter arrived from the perpetrator: it contained an apology, a promise that the tackle was unintentional, and an appeal for empathy, the perpetrator describing how he himself had once sustained a broken cheekbone. It had taken five months and a team-coach drama to force him to put pen to paper.

Now 28, in his testimonial year and currently the club's longest-serving professional, Dane is at a crossroads and only time and fate can move him on. Being one of only two Sheffield-born players in the squad makes him a bit of a throwback to bygone days. Only five years ago, the inseparable triumvirate of local-born Blades—Bradshaw, Ward and Whitehouse—had an on-the-pitch ethos that, if one was kicked, three exerted reprisals. Known to their predominantly southern-born team-mates as the 'Three Sharpshots', in honour of the strange brothers in an ice hockey film starring Paul Newman, today only Dane remains at Bramall Lane. A transfer was rumoured, but only one firm offer ever got back to him. The way it was handled says little for the practices of football management.

> It was last year. I was on holiday in Tenerife and I phoned home and me dad told me I'd signed for Birmingham! When I came home, I went straight to Charles Green's office and said, 'What's happening?' He tells me they've accepted a £1.5 million bid, so I said, 'Fair enough, but I want a word with the manager.' I said to Nigel Spackman, 'Am I in your plans?' He said I was, so I told Green I was going nowhere and what did he think he was doing selling me without asking?

Who cares what answer he received to that? I'm touched that loyalty to a team still counts for some players.

Happy in his heartland, Dane may well be the last-ever local-born player who serves the club from youth scheme to professional. Popular with team-mates, he also has dozens of childhood mates whom he sees socially and whose football loyalties are divided between United and Wednesday. For this reason, trouble does not come his way when out and about in city-centre bars. In his words 'happily single', he has a lot of living yet to do. Let's hope he has another decade in the game. Football grew and was sustained by generations of blokes from places such as Woodthorpe. Their attitudes and ideas don't always fit the market-led middle-class utopia the professional game now pursues, but people such as Sid Senior and Junior will be the lifeblood of the game long after the corporate crowd have moved on to the next passing fashion or profit-making venture. Many feel that football will be better off and in safer hands.

Managers

In the old days there was the trainer and nobody paid him much heed. He died without a word when the game stopped being a game and professional football required a technocracy to keep people in line. The manager was born. His mission: to prevent improvisation, restrict freedom and maximise the productivity of the players, who were now obliged to become disciplined athletes . . . The manager believes football is a science and the field a laboratory, but the genius of Einstein and the subtlety of Freud isn't enough for the owners and the fans. They want a miracle worker like the Virgin of Lourdes with the stamina of Gandhi.

(Eduardo Galeano, *Football in Sun and Shadow*: 10)

Managing Well...
Ken Furphy

The black Mercedes awaits my arrival, then it's away we go to the golf course clubhouse. I have not seen my impeccably dressed driver for 24 years. Now aged 69 but looking a decade younger, he is acknowledged by all on the nineteenth hole. Many want his comments on England's penalty shoot-out defeat at the hands of Argentina last night. But a refusal to mix work with leisure means he deflects the inquiries and settles down in a quiet corner to an orange juice and memories. We part five hours later in another village four miles away, following a tour of Devon coastal retirement villages. In between, the manager of United between 1974 and 1976 tells me why he has never returned to the club that sacked him a few months after he managed a side that finished sixth in Division One, missing a place in Europe by one point. It was all a long time ago and the man tells me he does not hold grudges.

A successful life in football management brought many accolades and a good income, reflected in a retirement lifestyle that many aspire to. Frequent holidays, a good golfing handicap, a bit of a dab hand at crown-green bowling and a football summariser on local BBC Radio makes for a busy life. But then, this man knows no other way. Managing a variety of clubs in England and the USA, he moved home 36 times in 40 years and suffered all the ups and down the game could offer.

Born in 1931 in Stockton-on-Tees to strict Methodist parents, Ken and his brother were taken by their dad to watch the local team: Middlesbrough. A childhood ambition to be a professional footballer was somewhat thwarted when he was accepted into the local grammar school, where only rugby was played. Showing what proved to be characteristic stubbornness and inventiveness, he first of all ran away from the school and then, having been reinstated by his mum, formed an out-of-school-hours boys' team of his own. Refusing to play for the school's rugby select got him banned from all sporting activities. On games' afternoon, while classmates rucked and mauled, he did Latin translation. Living for the weekends, he found a game with an under-15 junior club and turned out whenever they wanted him and played in whatever position had been vacated that week by an absent regular.

Second-hand clothes, a convivial home and football on cobbled streets combined with Latin and art and woodwork classes to make him both a useful footballer and imaginative handyman. An art teacher saw potential and got him to design the label of a sauce bottle for a local firm. The manager was so impressed, he offered Ken a job! But it would cost £10 to buy the 15-year-old out of school and, at the time, Ken's dad couldn't afford it.

Returning home from military service in 1946, Furphy Senior removed his son from school and got him an apprenticeship as an electrical fitter with Pickford's Lifts. Told to file locks endlessly, the tedium got to him and at 16 he walked out. An uncle who ran an auto electrical garage took him on and, while learning about wires, became a regular in the Stockton Boys' team and got a trial at Hull City. Eased out of his position at Stockton by a player known as 'Twinkletoes' Sinclair, Ken moved to Portrock Shamrocks and, playing inside-forward, scored a couple of dozen goals in a championship-winning team. Then a Northern League side called Evenwood Town offered a trial. The expenses claim Ken submitted for nearly five shillings saw him receive an envelop containing £3, at a time when he was earning £1 a week at the garage.

Evenwood proved a good move and seemingly offered a more real-istic future in football, particularly after a trial at Middlesbrough proved fruitless. But an Everton scout liked what he saw, and Ken went to Good-ison Park for a week's trial and was asked to sign on. A wise father refused to let him go full-time, insisting that he sign part-time and that the club also provide a job in the city's Ford factory so as to complete his apprenticeship. While he attained his City and Guilds, his relative isolation from the full-timers saw him play just six reserve-team games. But watching the great Brazil team on TV and studying tactics made him aware that the 'push-and-run' style promoted at Everton was not for him. Having been given a roasting one match for running with the ball, he knew a separation was inevitable. The nearby non-League team Runcorn gave him a one-year contract and £3.50 a week which, on top of the £5 a week he earned from the car industry, meant he had a good income. Married in 1952, his income dropped dramatically when called up for national service, hitherto delayed because of his apprenticeship.

The RAF decided that he could be a physical training instructor. Finding allies in a sergeant and a corporal who took a shine to him, he negotiated time off to play for Runcorn. The RAF bigwigs refused to let him play, but his squaddie income was so meagre that his wife now lived with her mother. While Ken was unable to afford a mug of tea in the NAAFI, the corporal quietly suggested that, each Saturday lunchtime, Ken simply walk out of the unattended officers' gate of the barracks and play anyway. A fan who owned a sweet shop gave him digs in Runcorn every Saturday night, and the money he made was sent to Mrs Furphy. Days before winning the accolade of best all-round recruit at the base and due to pass out as an officer, his moonlighting with Runcorn was discovered. Told by the squadron leader that this was behaviour unbecoming of an aspiring officer, his passing-out was refused and he was sent to Weston-super-Mare barracks to become a mechanic. Everton, meanwhile, retained his registration and refused to let him turn out for nearby Bristol Rovers.

Obstinacy and independent thought saved him from going to the Far East during an emerging crisis. Instructed to take the mobilised squadron to Bristol for their injections against tropical diseases, he found a queue a mile long and four deep with military personnel. Discovering that there was insufficient serum to do everyone that day, he decided to return the men to the barracks. The squadron missed the draft because they were not immunised! A year later, he missed another draft when, upon returning from weekend leave, he found the air base deserted as everybody had been removed to Germany 24 hours earlier. Given the job of cleaning windows while recovering from an Achilles tendon injury, the squadron leader told him to pick a place—anywhere!—and he would send him there. Choosing the nearest air base to Stockton so as to be with his wife, he thus picked up both his marriage and footballing career.

Writing to all north-east clubs, only Darlington bothered to reply. Offered a trial game, he heard nothing. So, after a few weeks, he contacted the chief scout who told him he didn't think he had the stamina the game required. This riled Ken, who was at the time running 11 miles every day from home to barracks to build up the Achilles. Some days, the task was too much so the local bin men parked their wagon same time, same place each morning on the expectation he might need a lift on the final stretch to the barracks!

Invited to have a chat with the Darlington manager, a football career was built by virtue of what the team was short of. Already having good midfielders, they wanted a full-back. Despite never having played in that position, Ken said he was one. Playing 12 reserve team games at full-back, he then made the first team as right-half. He played 380 League and Cup games over the next nine years in what was the Third Division North. Paid £10 a week at his peak and given one-year contracts, he also worked afternoons at his uncle's auto electrics business. Big clubs came looking. Leeds nearly signed him and Chelsea offered £15,000 after a Cup tie which saw him mark their star forward, Jimmy Greaves, out of the game. The day they came to sign him, however, he played a stinker and the deal fell through.

It was at Darlington that his first attempts at coaching began. Asked to teach schoolkids by the player-coach at the time, Ken found he liked it and, judging by the increase in numbers, the kids liked him. In 1958, he attended Lilleshall and gained his full coaching badge under the tutelage of Walter Winterbottom and Stanley Rouse, both of whom thought highly of him. Soon he was coaching the local RAF team, then an Army side and local youth clubs. Then, in 1960, at the request of Stanley Rouse, he went to Nyasaland in South Africa. Accompanied by an interpreter, driver, Land Rover and a hundred footballs, he coached hundreds of kids over hundreds of miles for three months. Unsure of who paid him the £30 a week, he eventually coached the national youth team and was probably the first-ever British professional to coach in Africa in a missionary ideal that Ken explains was 'something to do with the last chance to stop independence'.

Returning from this safari, he was offered the job of player-coach at Darlington. After 45 games in this position, he was told at the age of 32 that he was surplus to requirements. A joint testimonial match brought him the princely sum of £125. 'That was a downer . . . I sent my mother-in-law on holiday to Scarborough with it.' Still living in a council home, he was now out of the game and the auto electrical business was wobbling due to a business partner's drink problem. He made a decision to make a go of it in football and applied for the manager's job at Workington FC, then in Division Four. At the interview, he found a club with only ten professionals, but a 13-strong board of directors. Two of his answers got him the job. One question was: could he play right-back because the club didn't have one; the other was: what would he do if a training session was interrupted by rain? The answer that he would train in the rain resulted in his appointment.

Within two years, crowds were up five-fold, a reserve team and youth team were established and the club was promoted. They were top of Division Three when Ken decided to take stock. Aware that such a sleepy town could be the graveyard of ambition, he applied for the manager's job at Watford.

Leaving the Cumbrian hills was hard, but Watford were ambitious and offered £4,000 a year, a club house and a club car. A 5–1 defeat in his first game convinced Ken that, even at 34, he could do a better job than his two full-backs. He played for the next four years, taking great pride in being, even at 38, the second-fastest player in the squad. Gaining promotion to Division Two and a series of good FA Cup runs brought club and Ken to the attention of the football world. It also brought him into conflict with his chairman in what was to become a familiar theme throughout his managerial life. Much of this at Watford has to do with a certain young player by the name of Tony Currie. Allow me to digress.

A precocious 18-year-old impressed Ken when no one could get the ball off him in a five-a-side trial match in the club car park. He signed him immediately. It was Ken who discovered Tony Currie, and it was Tony who made Ken pack in playing.

> I made him inside-right, moved Terry Garbett to right-half and put Welbourne at right-back. That was me out of the team.

The manager was fascinated by elements of Tony Currie's life.

> He lived with about six uncles. He'd ask me for my suits for them. I used to give them to him as well!

Aware that he had a diamond on his hand, he was troubled by the young prodigy's motivation.

> I never knew what was going on 'upstairs'. One day I got a call from a referee who'd done a reserve game. He told me he'd never heard such language from a young player as he'd heard from Tony Currie. I got Tony in the office and gave him a one-month ban from any Watford team . . . and I gave him cleaning jobs.

Unfortunately, one of the items that needed cleaning was the manager's brand-new Humber Sceptre. Days later, as Ken remembers it, a close-to-tears Tony Currie was brought into the manager's office by his trainer and told to tell the manager what he'd done. The shame-faced Tony explained that, while cleaning the car, he fancied having a go in it, but a misplaced gear manoeuvre had made him reverse it into a telegraph pole. His punishment? 'I told him I wanted two free tickets when he made his debut for England!'

The departure of Tony Currie from Watford to Sheffield United caused arguments between manager and chairman. The latter, having paid £30,000 to have more seating installed at the ground, wanted his money back. The United manager, John Harris, had been watching a match with a view to buying Stewart Scullion but saw Tony Currie and bought him as well—for around £30,000. The angry Ken demanded money to buy three new players or face what he knew would be a certain relegation battle. The chairman refused. By now coaching for the FA in European seminars and on courses at Lilleshall, Ken decided that the inevitability of relegation would reflect badly on his ability and decided to resign. Fortunately, Blackburn Rovers had been trying to approach him for months. They now had their man.

Rovers were then languishing in Division Three and in financial ruin with out-of-condition players, but Ken made nine new signings in two weeks and achieved a 19-game undefeated run. When they were top of the League, John Harris asked him if fancied his job at United, as he was about to take up the post of general manager. Rumours at the time had it United wanted Jack Charlton as manager, but this came to nothing and Ken joined in 1974 on a salary of £10,000. Aware of ground developments, he sought assurance from the board that he was not employed to help fund a grandstand.

> They told me they'd got £250,000 in their account: a £500,000 deal with a supermarket behind one goal and a £250,000 deal with a petrol filling station on one corner . . . the stand would pay for itself.

Six weeks after he joined, the City Council refused planning permission and the development plan was in ruins. On the pitch, Ken saved the club from relegation and the following season the team finished sixth and beat every team above them. It was a monumental achievement, but, in Ken's opinion, not sufficient.

> We should have won the League. We lost it by drawing at Coventry and losing at Arsenal. They were fighting relegation and they were a disgrace. The first thing they did was kick Tony.

Controversy ensued after this match when, at the press conference, Ken spoke obliquely of looking forward to leaving London and returning to the clean air of Yorkshire.

One of his first acts on joining United was to kit the squad out with snazzy new tracksuits. He then briefly made Tony Currie captain. Then, hoping to buy new players, he discovered the true state of the club's finances. The newly built South Stand meant big debts, and he was instructed by the board to search for players aged between 23 and 26 with a resale value. Forced to sell top-class player Geoff Salmons, he brought in a few players from Watford and Blackburn with mixed success. The biggest letdown was the club's then most expensive signing,

Chris Guthrie. Realising he needed a centre-forward to replace the injured Bill Dearden, Ken agreed a deal in the summer of 1975 to buy Manchester City and England forward Francis Lee for £100,000. The board refused the deal, arguing that such money was not available. A few weeks later, a relatively unknown Third Division forward was signed for roughly the same fee. So what happened?

> Guthrie had scored a lot of goals for Southend. He was a tough bugger and a Geordie—I could always handle them. I bid £40,000; they said, forget it. So I did. Then United's chairman, John Hassall, phones me, asking me, did I get permission from the board to approach a player? The Southend chairman had been onto him. He wants to interfere, but I'm having to explain the nature of the game and how you always offer less than you're prepared to pay. He then tells me to come with him to meet the Southend chairman on the motorway. Anyway, in some motel I said £50,000 plus Terry Nicholl. Southend said, 'No way': they wanted £90,000. I said to the chairman, 'Let's go; he's not worth it.' He then says, 'Okay, we'll give you £90,000.' I looked at him and said, 'Are you sure?' He says to me, 'You want him, don't you?' I said, 'I do, but not at that price.' The chairman bought him in effect, not me.

The relationship between chair and manager went downhill as the team hit bottom of the League.

> He'd come in at nine o'clock and ask me what I was doing today. I'd reply, 'Letters and correspondence, then first-team training'—I never missed a training session—'then after a sandwich I'll take the reserves, then I'll be off to Wrexham to look at a player and be home about 2 am, and back at nine in the morning.' He came every week and asked the same questions.

Maybe he was seeking an answer, like the fans were, as to how a team on the verge of qualifying for Europe could be relegation fodder only months later.

> We got off to a bad start and never recovered. It was all down to a pre-season tour of Tunisia. John Hassall was invited to send the team to play a match to open a new stadium. It was worth about £10,000 to the club, but I said, 'No way': we needed a month's training to gradually get harder or we'd be getting injuries. A board meeting decided in his favour and, in Tunisia, three players got injured. In the first few games of the new season we had three reserves in. That was the start of it.

More disputes followed over tactics and signings. One was about Tony Currie, whose habit of sitting down too long after being tackled infuriated Ken. Having done this twice in a match at West Ham, Ken threatened Tony at half-time that he would be substituted if he did it once more.

> . . . Hassall told me not to because it would devalue his transfer price. This was news to me! Anyway, I pulled him off.

The sparring continued when Ken signed Cliff Calvert from York City. Believing he had lesions in the groin, Hassall told Ken not to sign him. Ken in response hired a Harley Street specialist to prove their was no problem and got his own way.

While managing United, Ken was also the England Under-23 team manager and tipped in some circles for the job of future full-team manager. After finishing sixth, United gave him a new two-year contract and a salary of £13,000, making him the highest-paid manager in the country. Then, months later, at a match at Birmingham, photographers gathered around the visitors' dugout and the Sunday tabloids begin to speculate on his successor. Six months after being told he was doing a great job, he was out of a job, but in a dispute.

> I said, 'Pay me up!' Mr Jackson, one of the directors, shook me hand and said it would be settled in a month.

It was not really settled, ever. Eight weeks later, Ken got a call from New York Cosmos offering him a job managing the mightiest team in North America in the initial attempt to sell football to the USA. Considering this, he found he had two options in relation to United: sue them for wrongful dismissal, which he considered he would have won, but at that time a maximum payment of only £5,000 was permitted. The other approach was to take legal advice from Queen's Counsel and fight the club in the courts. But this could have taken years. He knew he would have to take a job, but, when he did so, only the difference in salary (if lower) was what United would pay him by way of compensation. Having accepted the USA job, on the morning of his departure he spoke to Mr Jackson, who passed on the word from his chairman that the club would pay £10,000 on condition he never divulged this fact to anyone. The club then calculated a sum and backdated it, which meant he paid 80% in tax. The cheque he finally received was for £2,400, of which £900 went to pay the fee of the Queen's Counsel.

Soon after his departure, his son was released by United, despite scoring 13 goals in the reserves. Then the supporters' club for young fans that Ken had established—the EDS: 'Educated, Dedicated Supporter'—was disbanded. This innovative scheme to get young fans and their parents involved in the club and to counter the game's hooligan image at the time involved open days and tours of the ground. Thousands went to such occasions and thousands joined the scheme which permitted cheap access to the EDS pen on the Kop and cheap away-match travel supervised by adult volunteers. Its demise was an act of spite to erase any legacy of Ken.

He was an honest man who would do anything to benefit his club. At Watford, he drove a horse and trap in a publicity stunt to raise the club's profile and was the first man in football to introduce American cheerleaders, courtesy of the American College in Watford. 'It only lasted one match. The chairman's wife thought they were unsuitable!'

Commerce and corruption existed in his day. One First Division club he turned down promised £250 a week in cash to pay players off-the-cards bonuses. At United, though, the president, Dick Wragg, was as straight as a die. So was Ken, who, to this day, would not consider feeding a parking meter if it meant breaking regulations. Teetotal all his footballing life and reluctant to swear in front of women, Ken was and remains a man of his time. Always well groomed with a collar and tie, his philosophy would seem to be founded in hard-working and self-help Methodism. A social reformist zeal saw him attempt to introduce closed-circuit TV cameras in the Bramall Lane ground in 1975 both to film the match for training purposes and to film hooligan miscreants for the benefit of police. The board ruled against the idea. It was somewhat inevitable that middle-age would see him active in the local Rotary and golf club of an affluent seaside resort.

His career in football management in England ended when he left Bramall Lane. Offered a deal in New York that doubled his salary at United, he was the ideal man for an innovative scheme. He spent seven years in America managing a side that contained Pelé, then coached for the FA in Bermuda, and managed the US national team in a bicentennial tournament against Italy, Brazil and England. He then managed Detroit Express (later becoming the Washington Express), where he coached a player called Johann Cruyff and put him in his place when he offered an unsolicited opinion!

His last offer of management from England resulted in a betrayal from that arch-betrayer, Robert Maxwell. On the advice of Bobby Robson, the bouncing Czech, then chairman of Oxford United, promised him the job over the phone, only for Ken to learn next day that Jim Smith had taken the position.

He considers himself the most successful player–manager in the English game, if one looks at matches played and not trophies won. In 34 years in football, during 21 of which he was a manager, he was recognised by the best of his peers. Bobby Robson employed him as a scout and Graham Taylor, when England manager, had Ken as a European scout. At one time, his 'soccer camps' in the US catered for 1,000 kids, and he could earn $1,000 for two hours' coaching, transported there and back in a light aircraft. Failing to get the vacant manager's job at Exeter in 1984, he decided to get by with a couple of sports shops in Devon, which provided a decent income but introduced him to ten-hour working days in one place. Selling up, he retired three years ago.

He's seen it all and is in the process of writing a book about his life in football. He has no six-figure bank account, but he has something more precious: a serenity supported by a certainty on many issues. We separate and I thank him, not just for the interview or for the lift, but for the team and times of 1975–76 and the season that no one over the age of 35 will ever forget and which has never since been bettered.

Marching Orders...
Billy McEwan

On the choicest private housing estate in Rotherham, the nearest thing to anarchy and decay is probably an untidy garden. In their expensive but tasteful homes, the good people of this side of town collectively seek a life of privacy. An August Sunday afternoon in blazing heat is, for many citizens, the appropriate time for sloth or excess of some variety. Not, however, the man I've come to see. The football club that employs him had a game on Friday night and two games morning and afternoon on Saturday; he attended all to watch the various selections in their 1998 pre-season friendlies. Sunday afternoon finds him alone, his wife out working but he's still active—mowing the lawn. The well-kept front and back are a credit to his work ethic and a well-deserved orange juice is some reward for the effort. On the patio I sit with the man who was, in the 1980s, the youngest man ever to hold the status of manager at Bramall Lane. The journey to that position was a circuitous route; the departure clean and quick. Few people had ever asked him about his two years at the Lane but he proved willing to reflect on a turbulent time in his footballing life.

Some great managers came from a similar background to this man—the Lanarkshire coalfields produced Bill Shankly and Jock Stein; the mining village of Wishaw produced Billy. His grandad mined coal and his father worked on a machine at the vast Ravenscraig steel plant outside Motherwell. Such places, similar to South Yorkshire, produce footballers, and the game as played there has a passion about it found in few other places. Dad wasn't a player, but watched the game in his role of secretary at the junior league club called Coltness United. This little outfit had produced Tommy Gemmill and Joe Baker in the 1960s. A split loyalty in the young Billy saw him follow the juniors and support the local professional side Motherwell and, because of his Protestant upbringing, Glasgow Rangers.

The McEwan family produced some promising footballers. Billy's older brother Stan went on to captain Blackpool in a nine-year career and later play for Hull and Exeter. But page two of a national tabloid was made by another sibling: namely, Billy's sister, who, as a short-haired underdeveloped 14-year-old had been so outstanding in a girl's game that no one believed she was a girl. Under a photograph was posed the question: 'Is this a boy or a girl?' The question was answered in later years when she was selected to play for Scotland's women's team.

Billy himself made the county squad but not the first XI and, after a trial at Hull City, was told by the assistant manager John McSeveney that, at 5'2", he was too short. Local team Motherwell had him training twice a week and Hibernian, managed by Bob Shankly (Bill's brother), offered him apprentice forms. The old man would not permit him to sign and, instead, Billy started an apprenticeship as a painter and decorator. Nine months of painting skirting boards wore him down and he, in turn, wore down his dad who allowed him to contact Hibs and take up their offer in 1966.

A three-year deal saw the 16-year-old's pay packet rise from £2 and 17 shillings a week for painting to £17 plus board and travel for running around with a precocious bunch of youngsters—Peter Marinello, Colin Stein, Peter Cormack, Alex Cropley and John Brownlie. Turning professional 18 months later, he was soon in the first team and played in Sweden against Malmö in the now-defunct Inter-Cities Fairs Cup. A change of manager did not affect him too much, but Shankly's successor, Dave Ewing, lasted only six months when 'too much running produced a players' revolt' and Willie McFarlane took over in 1970.

Under him, Billy played against Liverpool, marking Emlyn Hughes in another Inter-City tie. Chosen mainly as a full-back, he captained the Under-18 Scotland team and played for the Under-23s managed by Tommy Docherty. A top-level career looked inevitable.

Though a career in football followed for the next 14 years, it was not at the highest level. Things went wrong after a European match in Oporto, Portugal. Drinking infected milk gave Billy a blood infection which left him bedridden for three months. Resuming training, he realised he had lost a lot of speed and, months after trying to re-establish himself, the Hibs manager—by now Eddie Turnbull—advised him in 1973 to go elsewhere. On that same day, he learned his wife was expecting their first child. Blackpool FC, then in Division Two, came to the rescue. Manager Harry Potts offered him a trial in the reserves and then signed him. Pulling a hamstring limited his first-team appearances to only four when, six months later, he was signed by Brighton under the managership of Brian Clough and Peter Taylor.

The wily Clough saw something he liked and, for £30,000, got Billy shortly after his side had been slaughtered at home in an FA Cup tie by the non-League outfit Walton and Hersham. He signed 16 new players in two weeks only to leave six months later! His partner Peter Taylor took over, but the arrangement didn't work out and, two months after Clough's departure, Billy signed for Chesterfield in a swap deal which pleased the manager who was also the longest-serving Blade ever: Joe Shaw. He, in turn, was sacked in 1976. Billy then took instructions from Arthur Cox, but there seemed little to wait around for and, when offers came from Blackburn and Mansfield for the now midfield player, Billy moved to the latter in January of 1977.

Winning the Third Division Championship brought the club to the attention of other teams. One man who noticed Billy was a former United player now managing Peterborough by the name of John Barnwell. Paying £35,000 for Billy in late 1977, Peterborough missed promotion on goal difference. Less than a year after signing for the Posh, Billy found himself at Millmoor, Rotherham, as their record signing at £35,000. He remained there for the next seven years before going to Sheffield United.

Rotherham proved a good move initially; then Billy twice broke bones in his back which effectively ended his playing days. The first time was the result of heading a ball in training: he played on, as the injury was not diagnosed for a while! When it was, he was out of the game for 16 months. Aged 29 and rehabilitating, he was found tasks by the new

Rotherham manager, Ian Porterfield, who sent him scouting and doing match reports on opposition teams. Making it back into the first team, he suffered a similar injury when he collided with a goalkeeper. He never played again. A surgeon in London bolted his spine together and a lengthy rehabilitation began. At this time, he had two kids and little future. The fact that he also broke a leg while at Rotherham seems almost incidental.

With Porterfield tempted away to manage at Bramall Lane in 1981, Emlyn Hughes succeeded him and got Billy to look after the reserve team. When not at the ground, Billy studied sports medicine at Lilleshall and at home. Then, in the middle of this three-year part-time course, he moved onto an FA coaching course and was appointed youth and reserve team manager.

At one time, Rotherham were storming the Second Division with eight straight wins which saw them just miss a promotion. The following season, however, the same spirit was no longer there and, with no money to buy players, Emlyn left. George Kerr took over as manager with Billy as his assistant, but Billy had other plans and was asked by Ian Porterfield to join him at United as youth team coach in 1984. He proved an instant success.

Initially, however, there was some ambiguity about what it was he was going to do. Appointed in the vague capacity of physio-coach—even though he was not fully qualified as a physio—Porterfield told him to take the School of Excellence coaching badge. This meant he would coach both the juniors and the reserves. As a coach, he was paid less than half of what he had been on as a player at Rotherham. It was long hours for not much pay.

> It was a living . . . but football had only got me money through signing-on fees.

His reward of sorts was watching his juniors win the Northern Intermediate League for the first time in 23 years. Ably assisted by two former local schoolteachers, John Stubbs and Jeff Lees, the team contained many a promising player and indeed many made the grade in professional football, though not necessarily at United.

A year previously, Billy had passed his full coaching badge at Lilleshall with flying colours. Under the course run by Charles Hughes and Colin Murphy, Billy had got the top marks—as chairman of the FA Dick Wragg, who was also United's president, got to know. Realising that Billy could possibly do the job and that his young lads were the future, Billy became first acting manager and then manager in March 1986 when Ian Porter-field left after a series of dismal results. Called to the board meeting days later, Billy was expecting to be informed of his own dismissal when Dick Wragg asked him to be caretaker-manager until the end of the season.

> I didn't want to say no because I thought I might get the sack. It was the same money, I think—that was the last thing on my mind. I needed a job because I had a wife and two kids.

The season's nine remaining games produced three of everything with a team that included players who had won European trophies elsewhere: Peter Withe, Phil Thompson, Dennis Mortimer and Ken McNaught. Some were older than their new manager.

> I wasn't frightened of them or the job. I knew I could make them better. I'd been at Lilleshall with Withe and I believe I had his respect. I cer-tainly had faith in my ability.

The directors were uncertain and the names of managerial candidates Don Howe and Steve Burtenshaw were mentioned in meetings. Then came a dreadful 6–1 defeat at Blackburn and a train of events that Billy believes got him appointed manager on a permanent basis.

> We got hammered . . . it was embarrassing. Mostly from set-pieces and free-kicks. Many players didn't carry out orders or did what they wanted and thought 'Who the fuck's he?' You see, they believed, or some of them did, that having got Porterfield the sack they'd do the same to me. Now Derek Dooley was very good to me: he realised what I'd inherited and, after this match in the dressing room, I said to them, 'Back on the coach when you're ready.' They didn't have a drink and they were back training at ten next morning. This was unheard of. I used the morning to go through every goal and point out who didn't do what they were supposed to.

It did not endear him to the team. My memories of the time came from a couple of players who told me of a dressing-room sweepstake as to who among them would be the first to assault the manager. As far as I know, nobody did hit Billy. Those Upstairs, however, liked what they had seen.

> They'd seen I could handle the 'big hitters' and it got me the job. They'd let themselves and the fans down and tested me. The ones that didn't let me down were the big old guys.

One young player of repute both on and off the pitch once refused to do abdominal exercises. Told in front of all by Billy that, if he did not, he could come back at 2 pm that afternoon and do them alone. He thought about it and decided to do them there and then. According to Billy, years later the same player thanked him for putting him in his place.

One place Billy now entered was the manager's office. Until appointed as full manager in May, he would not enter the room, preferring instead to run the club from the room given him as a coach. One place he could not enter, however, was the transfer market. Learning the club had no money, he was instructed to produce players and was told by Reg Brealey to get rid of the 'Dads' Army' old players who were on good wages. In their place came youngsters who were, in hindsight, not up to the job, but were blooded in desperation. Players offered to Billy included Peter Beagrie, Dean Saunders and Mark Bright—he could have bought all three for under £100,000. In the end, he got Beagrie for £15,000 and Martin Pike for £18,000 and sold the club's highest goalscorer.

> Keith Edwards didn't like me and was causing aggro in the dressing room. There was a lot going on and he wanted a bigger club, so I rang Billy Bremner at Leeds and he took him for £125,000.

That was one problem less but also one less goalscorer. A replacement was found in Richard Cadette, who was at the time the top scorer in England, albeit in the Third Division. Joining United for a fee of £130,000, he never made it at the Lane and a couple of injuries limited his appearances. The beginning of the 'Blades Revival' scheme (see the Andy Daykin section) saw welcome money arrive which went towards the purchase of this player, but he was not able to halt the decline. The club was in a mess: Reg Brealey had decided to cut his losses and sell up, but nobody wanted the sinking ship that was Sheffield United. The inevitable departure of Billy came after a 5–0 home defeat by Oldham which saw fans chanting 'Sack the board' throughout.

> . . . it was soul-destroying. I knew then why managers go grey and have heart attacks. You sit there and you feel for your wife and kids and think, 'What are they going through?'

At half-time during the Oldham game, the board held an emergency meeting. At the end of the game, their decision was broken to him by Reg Brealey.

> He said to me, 'It's not working out; they want you to go. I don't want
> you to go, but I can't back you.' Then he broke down and cried.

Another director by the name of Paul Woolhouse was showing his cards
with a view to becoming chairman and Billy knew of the backroom
politics, but could not go to the media and tell them to tell the fans
how his hands were tied. When told by Reg that he was about to sell
the club, Billy resigned in front of the board.

In hindsight, the deal Billy got was not ideal. For a start, he was lumbered with the man who told him he would never make it—John McSeveney,
who had been Porterfield's assistant—who did not leave for months,
even when the man who employed him had been sacked. Then the
chairman brought in a former United coach in the shape of Danny Bergara
to tend to the youth team. Only Phil Henson was Billy's choice as reserve
team coach. Does he look back with regrets?

> If I'd been able to have the players I wanted, who knows what I might
> have achieved. I don't look back now; all I know is that I was right.

Such certainty is needed in football management and, when calls of sympathy came his way from Wednesday's Howard Wilkinson and Manchester United's Alex Ferguson, Billy never lost faith in what he believed
he could achieve.

With one year of his two-year contract left, the club paid him up in
a deal with which he was content and he left without speaking to his
players or shaking hands with anyone.

> I was gutted—disappointed. I'd done nothing wrong, but I couldn't say
> anything to the press about the state of the club. I'd worked such long
> hours; my missus even brought my dinner to my office because I couldn't
> get home some days. Days later the Sunday papers were queuing up
> to get quotes out of me, but I wouldn't speak.

His first job after Bramall Lane was working as a scout for Alex Ferguson at Manchester United. Within a year, however, he was back in
football management at Rotherham. The chairman, Ken Booth, remembered Billy from his earlier days at Millmoor and gave him the job. Months
later the team, having won promotion, were top of Division Three. But
Billy was refused money to buy a couple of players, which would have
sustained the promotion push, and the team finished eighth.

It was early on in his days as Rotherham manager that he returned
to Bramall Lane in a League Cup fixture and got a 0–0 draw and then

beat United 1–0 at Millmoor. The return wasn't bitter: he had only good words to say about Derek Dooley and George McCabe. Reg Brealey phoned him for advice on players only a few days before I sat with him—ten years after his departure.

Fortunately, Billy always had friends in the game, which is just as well because jobs came and went pretty frequently at one time. While at Rotherham, two Second Division teams sounded him out for their vacant manager's job and, a year later, he wished he'd accepted when Rotherham built one of the finest training grounds in the country but financed it by the sale of three players. At the time, attendances were averaging over 5,000 and even topped 14,000 for a Cup tie against Manchester United. Now the team was bereft of three good players and Billy was rowing with the chairman. Eventually, the chairman barred him from coaching the team and then barred him from the ground itself as Billy sued him for breach of contract.

While that was going on, a former Blade, Ray McHale, then managing Scarborough, offered him a job as coach and the following year Billy was made manager at Fourth Division Darlington on references given to the directors by Alex Ferguson. Things at Darlington were even worse than at Rotherham.

> They were skint . . . not a penny. Free transfers only and no signing-on fees.

Finishing mid-table in his first season, the next season saw the team going nowhere. He hated living in digs and travelling to and fro and decided to leave.

> I told the chairman, 'I'm going.' The players were washing their own kit, and it all got me down. Managing at that level is about survival and, to be straight, I could do a lot better for myself than Darlington. I was wasting my time.

Seeking a coaching job in preference to managing, he found employment a month later at Derby County under Roy McFarland. Made reserve team coach, he also assisted Roy with the first team daily. When Jim Smith took over as the boss, he retained Billy and appointed him manager of the reserves. Nonetheless, he accompanies the boss to all first-team games. With a brand-new stadium, foreign imports and a good Premier League set-up, Billy has not done badly for himself and still gets clubs sniffing around asking if he's interested in managing. Coaching rather than managing is his passion. In Derby, he has a club that can afford to send him abroad to attend coaching seminars by European stars and, now aged 47, still believes that he could manage the right club: 'I'm better prepared now than I ever was.'

This brings me to an issue that interests me in this interview: namely, the need I perceive throughout his life for order and discipline. I ask who he considers his managerial mentors.

> Eddie Turnbull at Hibs, Brian Clough at Brighton . . . and Alex Ferguson. When he joined Manchester United, he asked me to bring Sheffield United over for a friendly because he wanted to try out a new system. As a young manager, I'd always phone him and ask his advice.

All three were very successful and all three were renowned for their strict regime. Is this significant? 'The best managers and coaches have got to have ground rules.'

There were a few rules at Sheffield United imposed by Billy that failed to impress some of the players. Long hair was not permitted; neither were earrings; and one player arriving for an away game in club blazer and slacks but no socks with his designer shoes was told to find a pair or face being dropped! The regimented dress code was not popular with some of the squad, and I wonder whether it was all a bit petty. Being so young, was he trying to be a disciplinarian in order to impose a sense of respect? That is easier, I guess, than winning it.

> This disciplinarian thing has followed me around. I don't know why. We had players at United in my time who thought they were better than they were. I stood up and said, 'That's not right.' Bad timekeeping or not being clean-shaven in any other industry would see you docked money or lose your job. Same if players go out nightclubbing and letting the club down by misbehaving. The image of the club is to be positive and to set standards. You want dedicated professionals, not pissheads.

I know what he means to an extent, but I've never gone for the disciplinarian approach, be it in teaching or parenting. Was there not a role for tea and a cuddle?

> There was loads of that. Most of my work at United and even now is one-to-one and is helpful and encouraging.

Perhaps he should smile a bit more. The dour public persona of Alex Ferguson apparently conceals a wicked sense of humour to those whom he knows well and trusts. Billy reassures me that he smiles all the time;

maybe people just don't see it! So where does he go when not on the training pitch or at football matches? The answer perhaps reveals a lot.

> I don't have time to socialise. I'm too busy working—as daft as that sounds.

Asked about when he last went out socialising, he has to think; and then the company was not exactly local, and he hardly drinks anyway. You do end up wanting to tell the man to relax more and maybe don't take the game so seriously. But he was always like this, and such an attitude of sobriety and discipline is taken by many as synonymous with efficiency and capability.

Strength of character got him the managerial position at Bramall Lane at the tender age of 34. No doubt he was a promising young manager, but I also suspect that, having made a mistake in awarding a ten-year contract to his predecessor, who then treated a lot of people with contempt, the chairman was wary of ever promising a man the same deal again. In Billy, he had an easy and no doubt cheap replacement. It was a gamble, but it did not work. Dressing-room unrest, youngsters not quite ready for the first team and no money for decent players would conspire against anyone, regardless of age and experience.

What could have broken many a man did not seem to worry Billy unduly. Billy is doing just fine and will be in football for another decade at least. Look in this interview for an admission of personal failure; look for self-doubt. You won't find it, but seek in its absence what replaces it: a working-class Protestant ethic not concerned with doubt or self-pity, but one that can sustain in times of crisis. Perhaps the sense of certainty that sustained generations of men of his background is what makes for footballing success.

Banjos and Backsides...
Dave Bassett

The first time I met Harry was in the boardroom of Bramall Lane after a home defeat. Standing alone, looking contemplative and holding a fluted glass that contained pink champagne, he presented a contrast to the man of 20 minutes earlier, who had attempted to assault a rival player who was later to become the most expensive transfer in British football.

Two United players had been sent off and, on the final whistle, near to the players' tunnel, the star forward told Harry what he thought of his team and style of play. The subsequent lunge and grapple saw other players and trainers and even the Bramall Lane community police officers jump in as a heap cascaded down the tunnel and out of sight. Only the lucky few, who inhabited the front middle seats of the John Street Stand, got the full view. The incident never made the news. Now, sipping champagne, the assailant was calm, rational, funny and hospitality itself. I phrased my questions carefully, but didn't have to: the man met me another half-dozen times over the following four years and was always kindness itself. I, like many footballers and all fans of Sheffield United, owe him a lot.

I always find it hard to believe that he is in his early fifties. In fact, for many people, it's hard to believe he's a successful football club manager. In a world of 'disciplinarians', moaners and men who talk through their blazers, up pops Harry Bassett. In another life, he's your favourite uncle: the one who, at family gatherings, is liked by everyone, yet still has time for you, his young nephew. He's your mate in the school team's dad who watches each week, encourages, is a good laugh and wears decent clothes. In reality, he was the United manager for nearly eight years, and it was with United that he provoked much uninformed opinion in the football world. Not that United fans ever worried: his persona kept the club in the media limelight and fans knew that it would take more than 'expert panels' to change or worry him.

The man who was to become famous for his expletives and smile was born in Willesden, north-west London, in 1944, the only child of a bus conductor, called Harry, whose passion was football. Due to him, for some inexplicable reason, Dave was known to all as 'Harry' for the rest of his life. Harry Senior and a grandad took the young Dave to watch Arsenal, QPR, Fulham and Chelsea 'without falling in love with any of them'. If pushed he is (or was) a Chelsea fan. Showing youthful footballing promise, he represented the county and, soon after, Fulham offered an apprenticeship, but he turned it down in favour of a 'ground staff position' (not quite an apprenticeship) at nearby Chelsea. A few youth team games did not produce a contract, so Dave turned his talents to other money-making avenues. Armed with five 'O'-levels and aged 16, Dave began work in an insurance company. Having learned by experience and night school the ins and outs of pensions and investments, he was running his own brokerage in his mid-twenties; he remains a partner in the company even today. Surprised? I was. Appearances can be deceptive.

When not trying to make the big time at Chelsea or on the stock market, the man turned out for Hayes Town in the Isthmian League and, for six months, Wycombe Wanderers. Aged 21, fame came knocking at the door when a scout from Watford offered a trial. He signed on under a man who was later to become United's manager: Ken Furphy. A few reserve games, occasionally alongside a promising youngster called Tony Currie, impressed those watching but, offered pro terms, he turned them down. Why? Because he had now got a company car, favourable mortgage rate and steady job. Combined with what Hayes would pay him on Saturdays, Watford's deal was not comparable. More important, though, was a realisation that, at 21, maybe he was not good enough for the very top of English football, where, he realised, the real money was. Never a starstruck dreamer, Harry saved himself the disappointment of not making it and meanwhile ensured a job for life outside the game should he need it. Shrewd.

Any lingering doubts about his chosen path were soon shattered— literally. Playing with mates in a Sunday morning pub team he broke his leg. Watford lost interest and, 18 months later, recuperated, he was back with Hayes. Here his reputation began. A charitable writer might, in footballese, describe his role as a 'midfield general'. Harry prefers 'kicker'. Furthermore, his physical abilities are complemented with ones that border on psychology—he had 'The Stare'. (We usually see it accompanied with a smile; take that away and pretend he's a foot from your nose. See what I mean?) He also talked to opponents and it was rarely about the state of the pitch. The kicking was either accurate or effective, because very soon he was captain of Walton and Hersham who, in a 1973 FA Cup tie, humiliate Brain Clough's Brighton 4–0. The same year Harry received the FA Trophy in the Amateur Cup final at Wembley, and then was selected to represent England's amateur side. Doing well in football and with his own company, life was good.

The happy days continued. When Alan Batsford, the manager of Walton and Hersham, left for Wimbledon, he took half the team, including Dave. For Batsford, a 20-year downward spiral began; for Bassett, a fairy story began, Harry played against Leeds in two FA Cup ties in 1976 and was a regular in the team that won the Southern League three years in succession. When they were promoted to Division Four in 1977, he played 36 games and was appointed assistant manager. When Batsford's successor, Dario Gradi, left to become manager at Crystal Palace in January 1978, Harry took the hot seat. Departing with Gradi was the Wimbledon chairman, Ron Noades. One of the remaining directors, Sam Hamman, bought Noades's shares and became the new boss.

For the next six years, it was tickety-boo between the two, but then problems arose. The end product was Harry's achieving two distinctions in football he'd rather not have. First, he holds the record for the shortest reign of a Football League manager (three days); secondly, he was the manager of two clubs both of which were relegated in the same season.

Let's start with the first claim to fame. It was now 1987 and Noades, having sacked Alan Mullery, convinced Harry to take the job of Palace manager. He accepted, no doubt peeved that Sam Hamman wouldn't pay him what he asked for after all he'd achieved there. But the Wimbledon team were about to begin their first season in Division Two; he made that team, and deep down he wanted to be with them. Three days later he was back! Shrewd Sam had left the door open: Ron was not too gutted—he and Dave are still mates, which was just as well because, ten years later, Harry took up the job offer! However, things were still not right at Wimbledon and, shortly after, he left to join Watford as manager. Their chairman, Elton John, wanted him because Graham Taylor was going to Villa; Harry took over the next day.

In hindsight, this is where the problems began: there was no time between the departure of the man considered God (or, considering his appearance and that of his supporters, maybe Billy Graham) at Watford and the arrival of his antithesis—flash, brash Harry, who in retrospect reckons the appointment should have been left for a few weeks. Maybe Shakespeare's Hamlet character was a Watford fan. His old man dies and mum marries too quickly—you know: 'the funeral baked meats did coldly furnish forth the wedding table'. Like Hamlet, the Watford fans sulked. The squeaky suburban family club couldn't take to him; he wasn't their type. He was a cockney, of sorts; he swore—damn it, he even enjoyed life. The other directors were peeved because Elton hadn't consulted them and some reptile on the local chip-wrapper dug up stories from 20 years before of a notorious Sunday-morning pub team in a local league. The 21-year-old player-manager was a certain Dave Bassett and the team had, er, 'disciplinary problems'—a few blatant off-the-ball chinnings and off-field lager frenzies. Par for the course in Sheffield, but not Hertfordshire. Watford decided they didn't want a man with such tendencies (the journalist reminded them of his prodigies at Wimbledon: Vinnie, Wisey and Fash), so he left after seven months, 'mutually'. Their loss was Sheffield United's gain.

In late 1988, the United chairman, Reg Brealey, contacted his mate Ron Noades for advice when looking for a new manager. The latter recommended Harry. His impact was immediate. Four months later, United were relegated to Division Three and Watford were relegated as well.

Two years later, United were in Division One after 14 years' absence, and he was the greatest thing since sliced bread in the red half of Sheffield. After so many dreadful performances, attendances falling, the Pigs always on TV and doing very well in the top flight, up pops Harry. He didn't so much arrive at the Lane as breeze in. This word seems to epitomise him: he breezes in and out. However, when the breeze had subsided, he realised he had a difficult brief. With only 15 games to go, the team lost nine and won five, finishing third from the bottom. They then lost the play-off with Bristol City and went down.

But it was not the end of the world. He was media friendly; he laughed; talked to fans; made news headlines while out on the team's piss-ups; he even chose videos along London Road and waved to the lads standing boozing outside various pubs. Meanwhile, United won just about every week for two seasons and the fans made a hero out of one of his signings—a man who couldn't get a game in Brentford's reserves and was about to start a window-cleaning round. Football's fun and didn't the fans love it? So what if the players are escorted by police from various aeroplanes or out of nightclubs (see the sections on Billy Whitehurst and Carl Bradshaw).[8] Did the fans care? Match days were magic and United were back where all fans knew they belonged: Old Trafford, Highbury, Villa Park. What other manager could fail to win for 19 games and never hear a chant calling for his head? He appreciated that. Relations between fans and players had never been so good as under his time: at the five-a-side G–Mex tournament in 1992, he and all the players sat with the United followers. In this era of celebrities and straw dogs, Bassett was authentic, honest, fun and talked sense, and on the pitch United finished for two seasons in creditable mid-table positions in the Premier League.

It all had to end sometime, and it did with the last kick of the match at Stamford Bridge in May 1993. Losing 3–2 was not sufficient to send United down, but all the fellow-strugglers picked up points, some in

---

8. In 1989 the playing squad and management out on the Christmas party made front-page headlines in *The Star* when an off-duty policewoman went public over the players' antics. In reply, Harry caustically opined that he hoped that when on duty she did not have to deal with incidents more boisterous than those in which his players were participating. Two years later, eight players were arrested on board an aeroplane as it prepared for take off for an end-of-season holiday (see the Billy Whitehurst section). Two years later still, six players were thrown out of the hotel in which the squad were staying while on an end-of-season holiday in Tenerife, allegedly for their involvement in horseplay around the hotel pool. Months later, returning from an exhibition game in Brunei, the team were subject to complaints about their behaviour and language from a passenger. Police called by the flight captain awaited their arrival, but no arrests were made.

Harry with his back-up staff of (left to right)
John Dungworth, Geoff Taylor, Derek French and Keith Mincher

dubious circumstances. As far as Blades were concerned, there was never a crueller relegation in the history of British football.

Disappointment is part of a supporter's life, but what role does it play in a manager's? Look at what happened to Harry: he made Wimbledon, turning them from a two-bob non-League outfit into a First Division side, and, a year after he left them, he was at Wembley watching them beat Liverpool in the Cup final. Instead of leading the team out, he was commentating, courtesy of the BBC. He admits that such a passive role was hard: after all, half the team were his signings. But the good moments are legion: the various promotions with Wimbledon; promotions with United at Wolverhampton in 1989, then at Leicester 1990; the 3–2 win over Forest in December 1991 ending 19 games without a win; and the defeat of Newcastle in April 1993 when everyone thought United had thereby avoided relegation. In his eight years as United manager, I personally, as a fan, had more good times and retain more memories than the previous 12 years. But what is it like to lose Premiership status in the final 30 seconds of the season? Harry had a premonition.

I looked up, saw Wisey with it and Hoddle in the area. Now, he's never been in the fuckin' area in his career; seconds later, he's nudged it on and we're down.

The manager ran to the dressing room on the final whistle. Devastated? An understatement: he could hardly talk; he couldn't even cry. He'd arranged to go out for dinner with friends that night, so confident was he of surviving. He kept the appointment, but was hardly a laugh-a-minute. It hurt for months, and the moments of sadness remained for about a year, as he explained to me at the time: 'It's like a cloud: initially it was there all the time now it comes in intervals.' When flying out of Manchester Airport a month later on a pre-season tour, the realisation came that, for the foreseeable future, his teams were no longer going to play in the stadiums of Manchester United and Manchester City, which he could see below. He and the players had their own wake in Australia. Over a beer or 12, they thought they had got it out of their system. I'm not sure they did. The following season the club did nothing and finished mid-table.

Nevertheless, he had a proven record of success which was always done on the cheap: the clubs he managed always had little money to spend. But how did he do it? His answer is that there is no mystery or hidden agenda. Certainly, it's hard to put his management style into a category. Those in the South Stand at Bramall Lane would see his two personae. One sat in the directors' box, serene and interested, but giving nothing away. The other was a jack-in-the-box impression while in the dugout. There was inevitably one somewhere in between, usually 15 minutes into the second half, when he would walk from seats to dugout. This indicated to fans either a substitution or a bollocking, or both. But what went through his mind when watching? His apparent unemotional state was a sign of him analysing events, no doubt seeing things we did not. At other times he admitted to being so bloody nervous he was unable to show emotion! And, for all his shouting, he reckoned 'I'm not as cruel and calculated as I should be.' Sometimes, with ten minutes to go, he knew the team were going to win—which was more than the fans did! At other times, he admitted to 'shitting meself' and being unable to understand the crowd's confidence of victory.

His ability and career as a manager will always be judged on how many games he wins. In his pursuit of success, he was pigeonholed—you've probably heard all the comments: 'Crazy Gang'; 'long-ball game'; 'hod-carrying hooligans'; 'ghettoblasters' . . . But isn't it funny, though, how those early exponents of the long-ball tactic—Graham Taylor, Jack Charlton and Howard Wilkinson—aren't remembered for it a decade later, just Harry. But, hold on a second, what's wrong with the long-ball game? This tactic got Wimbledon from non-League football into sixth place in Division One, and Harry learned his game from Dario Gradi (Alan Batsford's successor at Wimbledon), who produced dozens of top-class players, and from Charles Hughes, the FA's director of coaching.

But mud sticks. When United played Manchester United in the League at Bramall Lane in the early 1990s, they lost 3–0. Drawn against them soon after in the FA Cup Harry put five across midfield and left one man up-front. It nearly worked, but there were criticisms from the TV panel about stifling the game, etc. Months later at Wembley, Big Ron (Atkinson) used exactly the same tactic against Manchester United and won the Littlewoods Cup. The difference is he's considered a tactical genius. Various other teams played this formation against Manchester United throughout the rest of the season. Where did they learn it? My guess was TV coverage of United's Cup match. Was any credit given to Harry Bassett? Dream on.

Or consider this. One Sunday tabloid at the end of the 1992–93 season made United bottom of their value-for-money entertainment table. Others slagged the team all season. Yet, apart from a couple of games, things were not that bad and, as Harry found out, marks that match reporters gave the team performance were changed (reduced) by their editors. It's as if some people always wanted him to fail.

Despite his critics, he's got some good mates in the game—Lenny Lawrence, Sam Ellis, George Graham and Howard Wilkinson, to name a few. Others in the game, who remain nameless, are 'nice as pie to my face but say snide things in other company'. Football is a small world: words travel fast and secrets are shared—Harry knows who you are. He offended football 'purists', but he chose sides and tactics according to the standard of opposition. He had to make do with limited resources and his record of achievement is excellent. This provokes analysis about the philosophy of football support. As a supporter, my only ambition is to see my team win; entertainment I'll accept as a bonus, but I don't have time for honourable defeat.

In pursuit of winning, the club acquired under Harry a poor disciplinary record. Committed they were, but not cynical, and there were few moaners to be found in any Bassett side. But among referees word gets around that it's Bassett's team and, you know, give a dog a bad name. As a player, he was no angel and he encourages a sense of fun in his players. He seeks 'neither robots nor goody two-shoes'.

Like most of his managerial colleagues, he enjoys a post-match moan, but he has also acted and innovated. Instead of just verbally complaining about refs, in 1992 Harry put a video together of what he considered inconsistencies against his team. What a brilliant idea! Whether the FA acted on it is a different matter. Another innovative idea was a strange chap Harry brought in for the day: a 6'7" teeth 'n' tan Californian by the name of Tim Robbins. Preaching a quasi-evangelical ideology called 'constant and never-ending improvement' ('CANI'), this smooth operator would get audiences shouting 'Bangstab' and 'Yowie' in pursuit of something called 'self-actualisation'. Having bought his book and video, followers made him tens of millions of dollars richer. The players liked the session, so it did some of them some good.

So what about the old days? For him, the 'Crazy Gang' at Wimbledon were never as daft as the media made out; they just enjoyed the image. He never tried to re-create it elsewhere as it was a unique bunch of players at one particular time. What did follow him, though, was the pre-match noise generated by the ghettoblasters. That was down to his physio, Derek French. Apparently, while at Wimbledon, the medicine man thought it would help the team to import the Brazilian training-to-music technique. The idea was only to get the players mood up but, as Dave soon found out, 'it also pissed off the opposition' in the adjacent dressing rooms. When managing United, the same ruse was adopted and at Coventry, apparently, the former England captain Terry Butcher went apeshit over it.

Harry can't half talk! But one of the worst aspects of being a footballing public figure is having to bite your lip at times. His outbursts at refs have got him into trouble. On other occasions, he has offended both football and society's politically correct. Always good for a quote, he could be relied on, when ruffled by the game, to say something memorable. Thus the three-sided ground at Bramall Lane between 1992 and 1995 made for a 'poxy atmosphere'; defenders who did not do as they were told were, in his universe, 'fanny-dangling with the ball'; and the reluctance in one season of any referee to award United a penalty saw him suggest that the only way his club would be awarded one was if one of the team 'got gang-banged in the box'. His players were occasionally 'brainless'; he had forwards who 'could not hit a cow's backside with a banjo'; and he never liked his selections rolling about feigning injury like 'poufters'.

Ebullient by nature, well dressed and occasionally very funny, Harry was destined to become a TV panellist, which he did for Sky. Not backwards in self-promotion with favoured sections of the media, he knew when to plant a story and who could be trusted. Nevertheless, he generated trust and wouldn't have his players talking out of turn or giving away dressing-room secrets. He once used the term 'village' to describe the people with whom he could talk about anything in the understanding that it never went further. The early years of phoning up certain reporters to rant at them for what he considered unfair comments on him and his team ended when he mellowed and, in a sense, subverted their copy by getting inside the corridors of power.

His attitude to his players was in marked contrast to most of his contemporaries. In his early days at Wimbledon, food fights on the train home from games and not letting team-mates off at their stops produced many a laugh and many a complaint from other passengers. Never wishing to acquire authority by virtue of aloofness, he would come down hard on those who transgressed the few things that annoyed him—in particular, trust. He would sign players with a history of being troublesome because he believed he had the ability to sort them out. Reputations did not worry him; his memorable phrase on signing Vinnie Jones was:

> When you're building a team, you're looking for good players, not blokes to marry your daughter.

At United, he was forced to continue to rely on his remarkable ability to shop for good players in football's bargain basements. This kind of talent-spotting, he considers, is no act of genius. In his years in amateur league circles, he has acquired many contacts that he knows and trusts. Players are recommended to him. But he's too modest: such good contacts are surely due to his personality, honesty and hard work. Scouting for untapped talent requires hours of driving and watching.

Somehow, you can't imagine him relaxing, but he tries. He'd like to know more about classical music; he reads autobiographies; and, when in London, he goes to the theatre. But he's in demand: he's often on London regional TV or Sky as match summariser for games and he's popular on the after-dinner speech circuit. He actually enjoys driving: it allows him privacy and a chance to think. At other times, he's out with his wife (the daughter of a Watford player) and his two teenage daughters. They're his closest team.

One thing Blades never saw in Bassett's reign was an overpaid prima donna who couldn't give a damn. He was notorious in football for paying low wages and he would not tolerate drama queens. If he has a phi-

losophy, it is in wanting each man to play with pride and respect for both himself and his employers (indirectly, you and me). I'll drink to that. Put another way, he specified that, when looking at a player, he would ask the following. Does he understand the game? Is he athletic? Is he brave? Is his character sound?

In his years at Bramall Lane, dozens of players came and went, some in not totally amicable circumstances. Not every player wants to give their all for the cause: some, as he sees it, pull their feet and heads out of challenges once too often. They are soon away. According to him, players leave for one of the following three reasons: they're not good enough; someone's come through to supersede them; they've not got the 'bottle' required. He is adamant that no one ever left because he didn't like them as a person.

Prone to being stubborn in some things, he also admits his mistakes. In the cruel world that is football, he was, according to the youth team coach at Bramall Lane, Brian Eastick, 'soft' when it came to deciding who among the juniors were to be retained for another year and who had to be 'bombed out'. His informal management style combines respect that must be mutually earned with a desire to have a laugh. There is, in his management style, always time for work and time for play. 'Play' included the occasional piss-up, which Dave was usually in the thick of, but age is beginning to tell: 'As I've got older, the age gap's opened up. I'm not what I was ten years ago!'

But a manager has to deal with another set of men older (supposedly wiser) and more secretive than the players. When the subject of the board of directors arises, Harry is always diplomatic. Various people sat in various chairs in his eight years at Bramall Lane. Surely, this must have had some effect?

> I've got used to them. We disagree, but I don't take it personally. I can't tell them what to do or what not to do. I have to accept it.

Offered a place on the board in 1992 by one chairman, he turned it down because he couldn't see how the two jobs of manager and director were compatible. Nonetheless, as he points out, if he had accepted, he would have had the casting vote over the sale of the United centre-forward, Brian Deane, sold to Leeds in 1993! Think about it: you find a puppy, nurture him to show-winning status then, while you are on holiday, someone sells it and keeps nearly two-thirds of the money! The club were then relegated, having spent most of the season without a goalscorer.

As a popular manager, he found himself drawn into the boardroom dramas that afflicted Bramall Lane for around eight years. The mention of the name Reg Brealey does not evoke fond memories and he admits that his final year as manager was a time of personal struggle between himself and the chairman. When Deane was sold, only half a million of the income was put at his disposal. When he went public, saying the club needed new players, Brealey replied by asking why were the 39 on the club's books insufficient? Then came the fan movement against Brealey, which saw crowds plummet and mass protest action during matches. Amid all this, Harry had to try to keep a team in good spirits and get results. But, as he puts it: 'We were at war and I hated it.'

His version of the sale of Brian Deane is this:

> I never wanted to sell him, but he'd made his mind up he wanted to go. Trevor Francis offered £3.2 million and I thought, at that price we

can let him go. Reg then interferes and he goes to Leeds for £2.7 million. Why did the club take off half a million?

It was December 1995 when he decided to leave Bramall Lane after eight years. Mike McDonald had become the new chairman in September and Harry realised the new man wanted him out. Why? 'I think he thought I was too powerful a figure at the club.' Some of the board wanted him to stay: in particular, Steve Hinchliffe, who talked with him until the early hours.

I told him it'd gone too far. The club had stagnated; we'd lost 2–0 to Huddersfield and I thought it was the right time to call it a day.

Knowing Howard Kendall (who succeeded him as United manager) was in the crowd for a couple of matches before he went did not make

for a reassuring time and, knowing the new chaps in charge did not want him, he was neither pushed nor jumped. He thought he had come to an amicable agreement.

He thought wrong. The new men seem to have had other ideas when it came to honouring contracts. On his final day, he found that the money owed to him was not to be paid in full. He wasn't going to take this lying down, and an argument ensued. When a certain person offered to settle it physically, Harry called his bluff and the offer was promptly withdrawn. Many people know the full story and also know of further attempts that the same individual made at such diplomacy with other people. The final word on this comes from Harry.

> I would have loved to have had the chance to take negotiations further in the car park. He didn't want to.

He could have begun a new managerial job the day after he left, but decided to have a few months off to reflect. Interviewed twice for the Ireland national team manager's job, he was approached by Sheffield Wednesday and finally accepted a job at Manchester City—only to think about it on the way home and turn it down a few hours later! The thought of another interfering chairman was too much to contemplate after what he had been through. One chairman who knew him from their days at Wimbledon was Ron Noades at Crystal Palace, who appointed him manager in March 1996—and this time he lasted longer than three days.

By cruel coincidence, his first match in charge was against United. The visiting Blades gave him a good welcome and the game ended with honours even. Then Palace went on a great run and ended up in the play-off final at Wembley. A last-second goal defeated them in a scenario that Harry had seen before. The next season saw Palace doing okay and in line for the play-offs when, after 13 months, he upped and left for Nottingham Forest who were relegated from the Premiership as Crystal Palace replaced them, beating Sheffield United in the play-off at Wembley.

Realising that Forest had no money, Harry went public with the realisation that, when in trouble, clubs seek him out or, as he put it: 'It's gonna be my epitaph, innit? "Deep in the shit where he started".' The following season Forest went back up as champions and, as we chat, are about to play their first game of the season at Arsenal. The clubs he has managed have never stayed in the same Division too long. The three years he kept United in the Premiership was the longest stretch for a club under his guidance without a change in status. At the time of writing, he has enjoyed seven promotions with three clubs and three relegations also with three clubs.

A month or so ago, a strange thing happened at Forest. A year of boardroom struggle had given birth to a fan movement who were vociferous in their condemnation of the newly arrived, whom they considered were asset-strippers content to sell the best players to line their own pockets. While on holiday, one of his best goalscorers was sold for £3 million without his knowledge. Sound familiar? So, what is Harry's next move?

> Yeah it's déjà vu, innit? Maybe I've mellowed, but I've got to accept it and get on with me job.

Don't be fooled. What he calls 'mellow' is probably a new line in diplomacy and I've a feeling there will be fireworks over the Trent before the season's out.

Bad Lads

Not all players act with their legs alone. Some are masterful actors in the art of tormenting their fellow players.

(Eduardo Galeano, *Football in Sun and Shadow*: 12)

A Celtic Lament...
Jimmy Johnstone

Next time you're in the Mediterranean, sitting in a bar talking football with Demetrius or Manuel, ask them to name the most internationally recognised player Sheffield United has ever had. If you're trying to answer this, I would suggest that you forget the name Tony Currie: the accolade belongs to a chap who only played 1 Cup and 11 League matches during an 18-month stay at Bramall Lane that was largely forgettable, his name subsequently eliciting mainly derisory comments from Blades about drink. But, in and around Glasgow, this man is adored by tens of thousands, despite last playing a game there over 20 years ago.

The man in question signed for United, aged 30, in November 1975 following 14 years with Celtic. He had a good few years left in him, but it didn't work out: the club was in a dreadful mess and his time reflected it. All the same, he regrets his wasted time in Sheffield and, to all Blades' fans, offers his apologies about the affair. Yet, in 1975 it seemed that a brave new world was beginning for the club. What went wrong?

The answer lies in a combination of events connected to over-ambition. The 1974–75 season had seen United in their highest League position for 13 years; finishing sixth in Division One, they missed a place in Europe by one point. The high-profile manager, Ken Furphy, had bought well and put together a very neat side. A few pundits even tipped United as an outside bet for the Championship the following season. Off the pitch, building work had finished on the new stand: the three sides and a cricket pitch were to be merely a memory to an older world. Built on the premise that United would remain in Division One and on crowds averaging 30,000, the club, to convince fans of their ambition, bought a high-scoring, lower-division centre-forward, Chris Guthrie.

The opening day of the 1975–76 season went to script. Guthrie did well, the stand was opened and 31,000 watched a draw with Derby County. Within two months, though, United were bottom; Furphy was looking for a new job having been sacked and Guthrie had proven to be a waste of space.

To get them out of this mess, United turned to the 53-year-old Glaswegian, Jimmy Sirrel. Still a 'tracksuit' manager, he had performed wonders at Notts County taking them from Division Four to the brink of the First. Chosen, probably, because he was cheap, on seeing what talent was available in the squad and learning that little money was available, he offered his resignation within two months. His second signing at no cost was Jimmy Johnstone, who arrived to find a football world unknown to him. Yet this was a man who breathed football and knew all about passionate loyalties in a divided city.

Glasgow doesn't really have footballing neutrals. If not Celtic or Rangers, you're a Partick Thistle fan. Even so, fans of the big two reckon Partick fans are, deep down, either green or blue thistles. They, in turn, like to think they are Glasgow's nice little club, whom no one can be bothered to hate. Maybe—but there's plenty of hatred elsewhere! Everyone should go to at least one Old Firm game to witness the hyperbole and religious overtones; everyone should enter Celtic Park—sorry 'Paradise' (so called because it's adjacent to a graveyard)—chant with the green mass in the 'Jungle' end and learn the words for the ritualised exchanges with the 'auld enemy'. What one side suggests that the other do to the Queen and the UDA, the other replies likewise regarding the Pope and the IRA.

Okay, Sheffield's passionate, but, apart from the mutual term of abuse of 'Pigs', it does not have historical-political memories or pretexts to shout about. The religious thing up there is a world unknown to the mainly atheistic Sheffield population. It's hard to understand but, put simply, the Glasgow teams are meant to reflect the virtues of nationality and theology. It's all a bit dubious, but a lot of them believe in it. Thus, Celtic in their play are skilful, tricky, precocious Irish. In contrast, Rangers are a team of big chaps: unelaborate, uncompromising, chin-up-and-boot-it British. At no time was this polarised relationship expressed more clearly than the years when Jimmy Johnstone faced the big and ugly features of Rangers' John Greig. While Celtic fans chanted 'can you see a handsome Hun? No-oh, no-oh', Jimmy did his bit for stereotypes: small, with an Irish-Catholic background, ginger-haired and a bit of a paddy on him if riled. In such games, 'bastards' abounded: some were prefixed by accusations of being Fenian; others were 'Dobs' (dirty orange ones).

It goes beyond religion. Because they sponsor Rangers, Celtic fans don't buy McEwan's beer or Adidas sports gear or even wear blue clothes. Public spaces have real or imaginary bias: various pubs and council estates ('schemes') have known or suspected football loyalties. I know it's similar in Sheffield, regarding colour prejudices and the Blade belief that Owls are mainly from the big estates in the north of the city, and I know that certain products have football loyalties, but the overtones aren't the same. Nevertheless, there is, arguably, a parallel between United and Celtic in terms of status. Like Rangers, Wednesday is considered the club with links with the political and business powers-that-be in the city and, like Blades, the fans of Celtic live in a state of antagonism towards the local newspaper, believing it biased towards Rangers. It might not be true, but the fact that thousands believe it is more important.

With that to muse over, let's have a look at the man United signed over 20 years ago. Born in 1944, the youngest of five children to an Irish-born miner in the Lanarkshire town of Uddingstone, wee Jimmy was an intense little lad. Conscious of his smallness and stigmatised by a scalp rash, the balaclava he wore to school was removed by a sadistic teacher to the ridicule of the class. Such insecurity seeks outlets: some creative, some self-defeating; Jimmy pursued both. He needed to be good at something and it was in football that he shone.

> A ball was all you wanted for Christmas. I took it to bed with me and it went with me to the shops. Between the age of 12 and 18, I'd play about five hours a day. At home, I'd walk it round rows of milk bottles in the house or I'd play it off gas lamps outside.

Weighing next to nothing and standing at 5' 3", he was a pocket dynamite. Such dedication produced precocious skills, which attracted Manchester United scouts, but it was Celtic who signed him on schoolboy forms; in return, he got to be a ball boy on match day. So, who were his footballing heroes?

> Stanley Matthews. I watched the '53 Cup final and saw what he could do and decided I wanted to be that man.

Hearing that Matthews trained in a pair of leather brogues so as to appear light on match day, Jimmy went one better and borrowed a pair of his dad's pit boots to run in the mud. Discarding them, he would then, in stockinged feet, balance on the tubular fencing of his junior club's ground to learn poise. Such techniques are not taught these days at the FA School of Excellence. Mind you, his diet was not textbook stuff either, but we'll come to that later.

Aged 17, he signed pro forms for Celtic under Jimmy McGrory. Loaned to Scottish junior club Blantyre Celtic to learn his trade against grown men, the Celtic first-team debut came two years later; Celtic lost 6–0 at Kilmarnock. Soon, though, he couldn't do a thing wrong: he was a permanent fixture in the most successful side in the club's history and the most easily remembered Celt of all time. Acclaimed then (and now) as, variously, the 'wee man', the 'flying flea', but, more respectfully, as 'Jinky', he was a spirited player, very courageous and occasionally liable to fly off the handle with rival players and authority figures. You could see his point of view. Kicked in the air several times every Saturday, he still went back for more. At times, his team-mates were instructed to get the ball to him and await the subsequent clattering and booking which meant that a rival would remain on tenterhooks for the remainder of the game. Faced with hammer-throwers, he used his own psychology.

> Over 30 yards I was very fast. If anyone clobbered me, I used to think, 'I've got a dancer here. I've got him.'

Contemporaries speak about him as a man who could not be intimidated and one who, if rivals got rough with him, simply taunted them by getting the ball more. One game in 1974 against Atletico Madrid in a European Cup semi-final saw a vicious campaign to stop him. The end result was three Spaniards dismissed. When the refs didn't protect him, he was capable of doing it himself. He was sent off seven times at

Celtic and he could do his own jockeying (anyone who's ever been chased by a Jack Russell would understand) and he had (and still has) a stare and red face as good as anything offered at midnight Saturday in a Govan bar. You mixed it at your peril with this fellah.

Look at this for a record: 23 Scotland caps; League Championship medals annually between 1966 and 1974; four Scottish Cup winner's medals; League Cup winner's medal annually 1966–70 and again in 1975; and, of course, the European Cup winner's medal of 1967 (and loser in 1970). All this and most Blades can't remember him at Bramall Lane.

Let me tell you some more about him. Put simply, there was a time when the footballing world was at his feet. Following the momentous European Cup final victory over Inter Milan in 1967 in Lisbon, Celtic were invited to the Bernabeu Stadium to play in Alfredo di Stefano's testimonial. In front of 134,000, Jimmy ran riot against the great Real Madrid side and left the pitch to a standing ovation. Another famous night saw him destroy the Leeds and England full-back Terry Cooper in a European Cup tie in front of 136,000 at Hampden. Victorious, Jock Stein, the Celtic manager, ran on and hugged Jimmy on the final whistle. Following the game in Spain, Real tried to sign him, then AC Milan, then Leeds, but his footballing ambitions were simple.

> I never wanted to leave Celtic. We won the League nine times in a row and played in Europe every year. Why should I play in England? It was hard for a team to win the League there.

Just to emphasise how much a celebrity this man was, two things were produced in his glory. Somebody wrote a song and, regrettably, Jimmy sang it and released a pop record. Although played in some Glasgow pub jukeboxes, it did not go platinum. Then—15 years before a few thousand thought it awfully fashionable and postmodern to carry inflatables to matches—there were dozens of wee Jinky ones: red-haired little blokes in a Celtic strip with hands on hips. But, after 310 League appearances plus dozens of Cup ties, Celtic no longer needed him and gave him a free transfer in June 1975. The day he got his P45 from one of the Celtic admin staff, he found a quiet corner and wept uncontrollably. Within a few months, he was at Bramall Lane—via California.

Offered a game by two Scottish Premier clubs, Jimmy sought new lands rather than face the unbearable—having to play against his beloved Celtic. Offered a short contract to boost the profile of the then brave new world of USA 'soccer', he turned down New York Cosmos in favour of San Jose Earthquakes. With this over, he needed a club and signed a two-year deal with United. How come?

> To be honest, I didn't know anything about Sheffield United. But my lawyer told me that Jimmy Sirrel had been a Celtic player so that helped things. Also, financially, it was a very good offer . . . I was well satisfied.

True, Sirrel had played four seasons in the mid to late '40s at Celtic and the side were in need of a hand. Accepting the challenge, Jimmy made his debut in November in a 2–1 defeat at Stoke. United played in a kit of all blue that day; a week later, a petition was passed around the Kop requesting the team never again wear such offensive attire. Anyway, after four games he was dropped. He returned sporadically in the remainder of an awful season, even forfeiting his lifelong number 7 shirt for a number 8 one. It just seemed to get worse. Not only did United almost beat the record for the lowest number of points in Division One, but Jimmy turned out in the 2–1 home defeat to Fourth Division Doncaster in the County Cup. Whither the Lions of Lisbon?

Following relegation, Jimmy played a few games in the Second Division and scored his second goal—which was not only his last for United, but also his last in professional football—in a 3–2 defeat at Charlton. Eventually given a free transfer, he spent a couple of weeks with his old Celtic team-mate, Tommy Gemmill, at Dundee before playing in Ireland with Shelbourne. A year at part-timers Elgin City ended in 1980 where it all began: Blantyre Celtic. Not that his leaving United helped matters. Weeks after Jimmy left, Sirrel left too. Cec Coldwell took charge for a few months before United appointed Harry Haslam, and the rest is history.

The original question asked was: What went wrong? If this question is now addressed specifically to Jimmy, the answer is complicated. The fact is Jimmy enjoyed life in Sheffield and the fans he met.

> Footballers will go anywhere, like it and settle. But my wife missed Glasgow; she'd go back home at the first excuse.

Living in High Green and enjoying the hospitality of The Bridge Inn adds a new dimension to his failure to set the city alight. He made friends, but they just happened to be in the wrong places: namely, pubs. This is where the genius of the man was troubled: there was a bit of self-destruction ever present. While not one to suffer those he considered fools too gladly, he enjoyed the crack offered by the camaraderie of drinking. To get the best out of this man required a perceptive manager. Celtic had this in Jock Stein; United at the time did not. This is probably the crux of the story.

Whenever Jimmy Johnstone's career is discussed in knowing football circles, two issues are inevitably raised: one is the relatively small number of Scotland international caps he won, considering a decade at the top at club level. The other is his legendary drinking bouts. Let's start with the caps, then work down to the bar stool.

Two reasons can be forwarded to explain the scarcity of international appearances. One is that vague footballing quality called 'attitude'; the other is the sectarian nature of Scottish football. In 1967 he was chosen for the national side ahead of his Rangers' equivalent, Willie Henderson, and was consequently barracked every time he approached the Rangers' end of Hampden. He never forgot this, and always played his heart out against Rangers. Henderson, meanwhile, got picked more times than Jimmy. But, as he told me, Celtic were his only love; he was never too bothered about Scotland.

Just to make matters worse, however, in 1968 he had a row with the national team's trainer when asked to be a linesman in a practice match. Jimmy's suggestion as to where to put the flag is, I believe, physically impossible. Still, he got picked by other Scotland managers and even scored the winner in a World Cup qualifier in Oslo in 1974. After the match, a cocktail of lager, blondes, Celts and Vikings meant front-page headlines for non-football reasons.

He never got to play in the World Cup. Maybe it was just as well. You know the plot: Scotland qualify; the nation gets delirious; Rod Stewart forgets he was born and bred in Archway, London, and joins the squad in proclaiming his Jacobite heritage. Stories appear of Glaswegian blokes nipping out for a paper and not returning for six weeks. Then the games begin and Scotland never get past the first round, losing to Costa Rica or Zaire; it's all over in seconds. It's called 'premature Jock-elation' and affects tens of thousands of men north of Hadrian's Wall. The only remedy is time and an understanding partner. The rest of Britain, cruelly, laughs.

When authority figures are mentioned in Scottish football, one man stands head and shoulders above the rest. This is Jock Stein, the Celtic manager from 1964 to 1978, and later manager of Scotland. There was a degree of similarity between the two (Stein was a former Lanarkshire miner); there was also mutual respect, Stein in fact stating in his memoirs that his greatest achievement in football was keeping Jimmy at the top of the game five years longer than he would have been, left to his own devices. Hearing this, Jimmy's reply was that such an accolade was the highlight of his career.

They had a soft spot for each other, but it could be stormy at times. In 1968, having been substituted, Jimmy ran off abusing the Celtic dugout. Stein chased him up the tunnel. The outcome is not known, but Jimmy was suspended by the club for a week. As long as Stein could keep an eye on the wee man, matters weren't too bad, but Jimmy's social life gave Stein sleepless nights. In pursuit of his player, Stein would phone well-known drinking haunts using a false accent and presumed name to track down his wayward star then inform him where to go, immediately.

Maybe there was a degree of mischief in Jimmy that Stein could not handle or just pretended he did not like. Before a vital European semi-final, Jimmy bewildered the Italian opposition in the adjacent dressing room by singing Beatles' songs, alone. Before the World Club Championship in Argentina in 1967, the somewhat paranoid Stein warned the squad of the hosts' devious tactics, which could include beautiful females sent to exhaust the team before the game. Breaking the ensuing silence, Jimmy announced his room number, should colleagues not fancy that sort of thing, then swerved to avoid a lunging Stein.

At other times, Stein had the better of him. A legendary fear of flying was not ideal, being in a team that was always in Europe. For one game, Stein promised that, should he do enough damage in the first leg in Glasgow, he wouldn't have to fly to the second. In an amazing performance, Jimmy made three goals in a 5–0 defeat of Red Star Belgrade and didn't go to Yugoslavia. Deep down, there was sincere mutual respect. When that goes, so, to an extent, does the ability of the genius footballer.

On top of all this footballing mythology, Jimmy was equally famous for his barroom tactics. Personally, I reckon he was a bit unlucky: whenever he had a drink, the world and his wife got to know. Rueful, Jimmy reflects.

> I always seemed to make the headlines for one thing or another, often for the wrong thing . . . letting down family and friends. It was usually drink-related, but usually just boisterous. Others did the same, but it was usually me that got caught!

One incident while with the Scotland squad saw him mix Scotch with water and end up in a creek without a paddle. Following a Home International against Wales, half the team evaded the manager (Willie Ormond) and sneaked out of the seaside hotel for a quiet drink—until 4 am. As they staggered home, a rowing boat proved too tempting, Jimmy got in, only for his promised fellow-crew to kick the boat out to sea. As they wept in mirth, Jimmy also saw the funny side of it and sang a rendition of 'Sailing'. Drifting into the Firth of Clyde, he then lost an oar. To his rescue went two of the finest flowers of Scotland, who requisitioned another boat only to capsize it in seconds. In all this commotion, two elderly native fishermen were quickly found to seek out the footballing journeyman, by now out of sight en route to Nova Scotia. When they found him, his response to their inquisitional anger was 'Just goin' to fish.' A few days later at Hampden, a 100,000 crowd sang choruses of 'What shall we do with a drunken sailor' at the embarrassed number 7. Scotland won 2–0. No player was disciplined: the manager stated they were in their own free leisure time!

This is the man United signed! A man who is synonymous with some of the great moments of British football and forever written into football folklore. Though Jimmy can laugh at those moments, his times in Sheffield were regretful and forgetful. Interviewed previously, he has stated that he cheated the Sheffield public by going through the motions and using his time here as one long drinking bout. At one time, he was probably bordering on alcoholism and, thanks to a 12-year-old Blade who thought he was being a good citizen by passing onto police a car registration plate that fell off when the vehicle reversed into a tree in his street, Jimmy got a drink-driving conviction. For some reason, the local papers did not make this headlines; fans heard about it anyway, by rumour.

The main problem at United during Jimmy's time there seemed to be at managerial level. The appointment of Jimmy Sirrel did not impress the playing staff, as Jimmy recalls.

> He was a funny, funny guy. There were endless games of first team versus reserves. I was usually in the reserves and we usually won! I didn't see eye to eye with him and the other players didn't respect him. A lot of them were mercenaries: don't get me wrong, they were all good lads and I got on well with them, but they all seemed just to be after making a few quid then gettin' away. I wasn't used to this. I'd played at Celtic with passion; at Sheffield it was a merry-go-round. They'd sit in the dressing room talking about who was after them: there was no loyalty. I'd no idea of a football club like this.

Regretting his move, the manager conveyed his feelings to the players.

> He would say to us in team-talks: 'I can always return to the house on the hill.' I think that was Notts County! No one knew for sure! You'd look round and see players looking the other way. There was also his trainer, a big fellah who everyone took the piss out of.

How can we forget his contemporaries, some of whom were probably the worst players ever in a United kit; or Peter Dornan, who left the club after only a month, preferring to read books in his native Ireland; or Bobby 'beer glass' Campbell, who, though uncreative on the pitch, had the good sense to sup the contents before breaking said receptacle over a bloke's head in a Huddersfield disco. Meanwhile, Blades turned up like fools to watch this lot get relegated on an average attendance of 23,500. The only consolation was across the city where Wednesday dropped into Division Three with only four victories all season and an average crowd of 11,200.

Yet, despite the turmoil at his workplace and the sad state of football in the city generally, Jimmy has some happy memories of his stay.

> There was great passion in that city, which I loved. They were lovely people and I want to thank them. They're passionate in Glasgow, but you've always got the Catholic–Protestant thing: soon as a player goes out, you're a target for someone actin' up and it puts a lot on your shoulders. In Sheffield, everyone was so friendly and relaxed—it was all new to me.

A rare shot of Jimmy Johnstone (second left) in a
Sheffield United shirt—showing his old form against a Fulham
side with George Best (far left) and Bobby Moore (far right).

There are just two games he remembers: one was a draw against Spurs, which saw Jimmy put in a great performance, and another match a year later when 28,700 turned up to watch a Second Division Fulham side containing Rodney Marsh, Bobby Moore and George Best.

> I ran riot against Spurs and the crowd loved me for it. Against Fulham, they'd all come for Bestie, but it was my show that day. I got the same reaction from the fans that I'd got at Celtic and I loved it.

Before he came to Sheffield, he took advice from his Rangers' rival on the wing, but good mate, Willie Henderson, who was at Wednesday.

> He told me it was a great place for football. He loved it there; he even got to turn the Christmas lights on.

Yet another little act of insensitivity by the City Council—inviting only a Wednesday player to flick the switch.

Various jobs followed football. One, short-lived, was the youth team coach at Celtic, but an argument and an admission from him that he was not managerial material put paid to that. An earlier enterprise saw the opening of the 'Double J' bar in Hamilton, but too many hangers-on with bouncing cheques and too much time for Jimmy on the wrong side of the bar ended that venture. At one time, he drove lorries, then dug channels for gas pipes, then moved into public relations. For a time, before Celtic games, he and Bobby Lennox were paid to chat with corporate sponsors.

Today, he does something similar for a refrigeration company owned by a Celtic director. Somehow you know he'll never be without work. For one thing, Celtic fans would always put something his way; for another, he's a good laugh—personable and genuine. He just cannot be forgotten. In the time I sat with him, two men left a wake in an adjacent pub room to ask for an autograph. How many of today's professionals will have people trying to buy them drinks over 20 years later when stumbled across one August Saturday lunchtime? How many, though, could ever combine boozing with such a high level of ability?

Precisely where this all began is difficult to pinpoint. Scotland, and Glasgow in particular, has an incredible drinking culture. Footballers are from the same culture that sustains such practices and only naturally some play and drink well. At Celtic, the fearsome four were Jimmy, Bobby Lennox, Willie O'Neill and Bobby Murdoch. They could drink for Scotland as well as represent the national side at football. How, though, is it possible to mix the two?

> As a footballer you can carry it off. You train all day, sweat it out. The problem, if you can call it that, is in being a well-paid player with too much free time. With time on your hands, you go to the boozer. It was like one long holiday time for me.

Being a Celtic hero meant too many people wanted to buy him a drink and chew the cud. Being genuinely friendly, he would talk football with them. Now, don't get me wrong here, part of the enjoyment of being a fan is laughing at the antics or misfortunes of players. Our tabloid press knows the principle that gossip is more readable than great literature, and knows what sells. But, in opposition to this, is the po-faced administration and police who run and control our national game and who lecture that footballers are role models who must live the lives of saints in order not to corrupt the young and impressionable. What crap! Implicit in this attitude is the belief that, hearing of misdemeanours, fans will go out and imitate them. But kids aren't as daft as some adults make out and can be detached, and even ironical, about what footballers do. Obsessed with its image, the game tries to stop or suppress wayward behaviour as if, somehow, we would all stop watching or turn to people more virtuous and exemplary. Okay, Jimmy will never join Trevor, Gary or Bob as overpaid Mr Nice-Guys mouthing platitudes presented as expertise, but that's TV's loss.

He had 18 months with United and it did not work out. In a nutshell, the problem seems to be that United signed a man who, having left the only club and life he ever knew, was a bit helpless without it. Furthermore, the managerial figure who knew how to handle him had let him go. With these foundations gone, United had a chap who was a bit lost and found a club adrift. Like most of his team-mates, he became a disconsolate worker, but a well-paid one, and the two-year contract meant he could live on his past and meanwhile enjoy himself. Although a football wonder, he enjoyed the crack and a drink. These are not mutually incompatible activities, but such a mix does need the respect of a manager who can permit so much, but also get the man to play for him. What a career; what a character. But, unfortunately for Blades, what a waste his time was in Sheffield.

Tapping and Trucking...
Terry Curran

Arguing, as they do, that 70p is too much for a mug of tea seems churlish to me. The café manager tells them that it includes a refill: in effect, the mug is 'bottomless'. When that doesn't work, he tells them to 'fuck off' and sup tea elsewhere. When sweet reason fails, what else needs to be said? Never worried about what people think about him, and knowing that he is giving value for money, the proprietor brings a philosophy he applied when a footballer to the equally critical world of truck drivers. What you see is what you get; take it or leave it, but don't ever say you were conned.

The trademark long flowing locks and moustache have gone, cut only a few weeks ago. Thicker round the waist and slower in the legs, this chap retains that mischievous twinkle in his eye and is mentally as sharp as ever. He played for 12 clubs, but was most famous for being the biggest name transfer across the city in Sheffield footballing history. Once, in 1979, he ran a derby match in front of 49,000; he now plays to potentially full houses of 60 diners drawn from truckers, travellers and tourists off the A1 in West Yorkshire. His name provokes mixed emotions among Sheffielders, but I always liked him for what he was: a maverick who could pull in crowds on his own and who never let an audience know what was coming next.

Migrating from the Scottish coalfields, Mr Curran Senior found employment in the pit at Kinsley, West Yorkshire. He married a local girl and they produced a family of eight boys; one came to be known as Terry. He was christened Edward and, as a child, was known as 'Ted'. However, early on in his career, a coach mispronounced 'Teddy' as 'Terry' and the name stuck—to the extent that his wife even calls him Terry. (As it happens, he has an elder brother whose real name is Terry.) Though Dad had no interest in football, Mum was a good runner, and her family included two rugby league internationals. A tough village saw little in the way of social life, except brawling, betting, beer drinking and whippet racing. Informal street football games briefly developed into an under-13 team, but Terry's school only played rugby league and Terry, ever the contrary, refused to play the game despite his family pedigree. As a consequence, he wasn't to play organised football until he was 16 when a local team was re-formed.

School was uneventful. Any ambitions Terry had lay solely in sport.

> I wanted to be a footballer or a jockey. I was only a little lad 'til I was 15 then I shot up.

In a village where gambling and greyhounds provided the main chance of a windfall, Terry's interest in the turf was a product of his mum.

> Every week I'd go down and put a three-tenner double and a tenner treble on for her. Me dad never gambled nor drank!

Leaving school, he found a variety of work, initially labouring on building sites, then in a textile mill. With money in his pocket and a loving family, he wanted for nothing and was easily pleased: he was teetotal and content. Only one thing ever perturbed him and that was when George Best appeared on the TV. Being a Manchester United fan was one thing, but this man—his style, his ability and his panache—touched something deep in young Terry. He saw something in him that he wanted to be.

His football abilities attracted various people at the age of 16. Playing for the village alongside his elder brother, Terry scored the consolation goal in a 17–1 defeat, and impressed scouts from Aston Villa and Blackburn. Both offered terms, but Dad said he was too young to leave home. Taking this in his stride, he carried on working then got a game for South Kirkby in the Yorkshire League. Games against Halifax Town Reserves and Doncaster Rovers Reserves prompted offers of full professional terms from both watching managers. On his way to sign for Halifax in the car with his dad and brother, he changed his mind.

> To this day I don't know why. We were close to Halifax when I said 'Stop! Turn round. I'm going to sign for Donny.' We drove down the A1 and I signed that day.

Doncaster were then in Division Four and managed by Maurice Setters. The 19-year-old Terry received £20 per week and lived in lodgings. As Terry was slightly built, the manager suggested he spend the close season on a building site. When Terry encountered incompetence, both site manager and football manager encountered the obstinacy of the new winger.

> We'd start at 7 am laying concrete floors in houses. Bloke I was with three times makes a complete bollocks of it and I have to dig it up. Third time it happens, gaffer comes long and tells me to dig it up again. I told him, 'You dig the cunt.' He sacked me. I phoned Maurice Setters expecting a bollocking, but he just laughed and said have a week off and report for training.

The wily ex-international knew he had a mercurial talent and knew he would not be with him long. What Setters was unaware of was the other side of football: namely, deceits by the more powerful.

After one season, Terry left Doncaster and joined Second Division Nottingham Forest under the managerial partnership of Brian Clough and Peter Taylor. The fee was £75,000 and his wages rose to £90 a week. Officially, this was a huge wage increase; unofficially, it was only a third more than he had received while at Doncaster. As Terry explains:

> Wherever I went, I got tapped up. What did I know at 19? I was advised to ask for a transfer, which I did, and refuse to sign any new contract, which I did. In return, I was promised that any money I was losing from an improved pay offer would be reimbursed on transfer and, until my contract ran out and the transfer went through, I met a bloke every week on the A1 who gave me £40 cash.

I won't name names. This happened—and it was the mid-1970s.

The young opinionated managerial figure of Brian Clough liked what he saw in Terry and, in return, his protégé has only good words for him.

> He excited me. You knew he was going somewhere. He was also a nice bloke. I lost two front teeth in a match at Fulham and on the way back he tells me to stay at his home and next day me and him and his wife and family all go out for Sunday lunch. Outside the restaurant, there's this tramp. He sees him and brings him in the restaurant and buys him dinner.

Possibly a mutual northern, working-class upbringing brought out the paternalism in Cloughie, who always ensured there were sufficient complimentary tickets for the Curran clan. It was his sidekick, Peter Taylor, with whom Terry fought, and the latter needed Cloughie to arbitrate a few times. Two incidents stand out.

> The team hadn't won for months and I'd just come back after a bad injury. An away draw and away win saw me play well when Taylor tells me I'm not getting stuck in. I told him, 'Don't start wi' that after the injury I've been through.' Cloughie came along and calmed me down. Then I find I'm dropped for the next match, home to Notts County. I watched 'em lose and afterwards I barged into his office and told him to shove his team up his arse. He said, 'Calm down; you'll be back in t'team soon.' As I leave, I banged the door so hard it fell off its hinges.

One senses few players could have done this with Clough and remain one of his favourites. The secret, according to Terry, was never to be scared of him, and if he told you to make a cup of tea to do it, because the next one to make tea was the one he had paid a million pounds for.

Relations with Peter Taylor continued to deteriorate. A pre-season tour of Germany saw a trip to a beer festival and the recently signed Kenny Burns vomiting then losing consciousness due to lager intake. Exonerating the new signing, Taylor instead blamed Kenny's new mates: in particular, Terry, who was the only one who did not drink! A row erupted in the beer tent, which ends with Cloughie telling Taylor to sit down.

On the pitch, the wing talents of John Robertson and Tony Woodcock were making it difficult to get a game, so Terry asked for a transfer every day for three weeks and, eventually, Tommy Docherty at nearby

Terry playing for United against Oxford in 1982.

Derby County took him for £75,000. A great team at the Baseball Ground included Charlie George and, in Terry's opinion, should have won the League, but instead, after only nine months, he was on his travels, this time to Southampton then managed by Lawrie McMenemy. When I ask why his stays at these clubs were short, he gets reflective.

> Why indeed? I ask myself that. What would've happened had I kept me mouth shut and stayed at Forest?

He cannot bring himself to speak a good word about Peter Taylor 25 years later, but he does reflect on the trouble he caused older men in his career.

> I'm calm off the pitch, but at five to three I changed. First to get it were the referees: first challenge and I'd be there shouting at him, 'You black bastard.' I'd get booked and I'd be thinkin' later, 'What did I say

that for?' The answer is: I don't know. It's something I've never been
able to account for.

Playing a match was for Terry a 90-minute adrenaline rush. He became
a performer on a stage, and good shows had to be contrasted with bad
ones.

> I was playing to all those people: you get such a kick out of it. Mak-
> ing mistakes? I made plenty of them . . . but the best players would
> make mistakes and not be frightened to do it again.

On his day, he was as good a winger as anybody in Britain. He was a
showman who had natural talent who did not have to train hard and
who livened up any dressing room and was a fans' favourite. Fast and
with an ability to make defenders look clumsy, he was also strong and
gave defenders a lot of lip as part of the wind–up that fans rarely see or
hear.

Even successful managers received his unsolicited advice. Terry recalls
when, at Everton, he came across a distraught youngster by the name
of Peter Reid who told him that Howard Kendall was about to sell him
to Burnley. The furious Terry burst into the manager's office and
demanded: 'What yu fuckin' doing? He's the best midfield player we've
got.' I asked him if Kendall changed his mind on account of this. His
reply: 'I know he fuckin' did!'

The youngster was not transferred and became the captain of a successful team. What else did Terry achieve?

> You check it out. Every team I went to was near the bottom of their
> division and, when I left, all were around the top. I always increased
> crowds. When Wednesday signed me, they were getting 11,000; when
> I left, they'd averaged 30,000. At Everton, crowds went from 12,000
> to 18,000 to 27,000 in my first six games there.

He attracted attention from the highest levels of English football. Some
excellent managers bought him and, while at United, both Manchester
United and Arsenal made bids before he left for Everton for £100,000.

Anyway, there's a bit of detail to be explained before we get to Everton. Let's return to Derby. No sooner had he made his mark than he
was bought by Southampton. He nearly went to play in the USA—
recommended to agents there by George Best—but that's another story.
But it could have been more lucrative.

> Looking back on my career, I wonder how many men got rich at my expense. Look how often I was sold. Let me tell you, in those days, many a player got robbed. Why was I allowed to leave so many clubs when the fans liked me and I was good in the dressing room? One club I found out later paid a fee, but then the chairman and manager who did the deal split £30,000 between 'em.

It was at Southampton that he had his first-ever drink in football—with Alan Ball, who took him for a pizza and introduced him to the English way of post-training recreation. He learned quickly. He also learned he did not like Lawrie McMenemy and was keen to return north. In March 1979, following a Cup replay played at Elland Road, he met the Sheffield Wednesday manager, Jack Charlton, in a Leeds nightclub. The pair talked and, a week later, Terry exchanged Division One for Division Three. He could have come to Bramall Lane: he told Harry Haslam he would keep the team in Division Two if he signed him. He didn't, and United got relegated. It all made for a supercharged 1979–80 Third Division and we all know what happened next.

For the outsiders, I'll explain. United were running away with the Division until a Sheffield derby at Hillsborough in front of 49,000 saw Wednesday win 4–0. The man Curran ran the match and United hardly won for the rest of the season. At the return fixture at Easter, 45,000 saw a 1–1 draw which included a goal scored by Terry, who received the ball at the corner flag, beat three defenders and chipped the goalie. Repeatedly shown on TV, it became a contender for Goal of the Season. Oh yes: Wednesday got promoted; United did not. In Terry, the Wednesday fans had a hero they have not had since. His personal fan club numbered around 400, and he cut a record 'Singing the Blues', which sold 3,000 copies. He was a cult. Blades called him something similar.

He caused a few commotions in his time at Wednesday. Some were in 'Sheffield's Ultimate Nitespot'.

> I was always in Josephine's. It was difficult sometimes, with United fans not appreciating me, but, if you turn up regularly, people tended to leave you alone. I know some wanted to fill me in, but they also understood I had a job to do. When they talked to me, they'd realise I wasn't a bad lad.

Many Blades 'spoke' to him when United played Wednesday. The long dark hair provoked predictable chants of 'Gypo' and 'Where's your caravan?'. He was accused of being and doing everything, and he replied by scoring against his accusers and milking the celebrations for all he could.

> Wherever I went, I got abuse. It lifted me. I loved all that. But I can't turn round and accuse you of being a wanker or shout 'bastard' back, but if I could run around and hold me hands out when I'd scored it was my way of saying 'fuck you'.

His antics while at Wednesday made national news and got him brought before the elderly in their blazers and ties at the FA. An egg thrown by Leeds fans never hit its intended target nor smashed. You know what happened next, but Terry might as well tell the tale.

> I threw it back and it smashed all over some poor bastard. It weren't him that lobbed it. Anyway, I went before the Football Association and got a reprimand. They didn't fine you for such things in them days.

Then he played a part in a riot at Oldham in 1980. A touchline fracas involving Terry and former Blade, Simon Stainrod, saw the latter prostrate.

> He tackled me. I went to get the ball for a throw-in and I grabbed it from him and he threw a punch that hit me in the chest. As he got up, I thought, I'll knee him in the knackers. Before I'd done it, he'd gone down. I got sent off five times in my time and four were by George Courtenay and he was the ref that match. Soon as I'm off, Stainrod's up and laughing. I hear a roar, look round and there's all hell goin' off at the visitors' end.

The 5,000 Sheffielders found tons of rubble at the back of their ter-racing and threw it on the pitch and brawled with police. The match was held up for 30 minutes and Jack Charlton, having pleaded for calm, walked away in tears. Days later, Terry faces both an FA panel and the Wednesday chairman. The former decided on a ludicrous punishment: for four home games, no Wednesday fan could stand on the terraces nor could they attend four away games. However, those that wanted to watched the next four away games anyway and all who wanted to watched home games as well: they simply bought tickets for Hills-borough's 26,000 seats. The club made extra money from the imposi-tion. Terry succeeded in ridiculing the ruling when he scored a crack-ing goal in front of the Wednesday Kop and ran behind the goal, sank to his knees and took the acclaim—from no one! The fans all laughed and the photo made the front page of *The Star*.

In the eyes of all Owls, he could do no wrong. One of his managers, however, could find faults, but, in pointing one of them out, was publicly mocked by Terry. While at Hillsborough, Jack Charlton insisted that every player had a responsibility to defend. Such insistence riled Terry and, one home game, when 5–0 ahead, Terry got the ball in the opponents' box and dribbled it back to his own goalkeeper, having beaten three rival players and bewildered all his team-mates. He then signalled to the manager that he was doing what was required of him. For some reason Jack was not amused.

Then, at the peak of his popularity, he did what few men have ever done in over a hundred years of professional football in Sheffield: he crossed the city. For the Owls, the move was an unforgivable betrayal; for Blades, it was a great way to humiliate their city rivals. But how could they accept a man who had done so much that peeved them? How did it all come about?

> Reg Brealey had been tapping me for months to join United. I was the only person in Sheffield who thought I could do it without causing problems. I was in a contract dispute with Wednesday and United's offer was very good, even if it meant dropping from Division One to Three.

The three-year deal included a £50,000 signing-on fee payable over the course of the contract. When he was close to signing, others jumped in. Newcastle and Everton made offers and Jack Charlton conceded their contract dispute and said he could have an £11,000 re-signing fee tax-free. But it was too late: a tribunal valued him at £100,000; Wednesday said he was worth five times as much, but the tribunal heard Terry ask that, if that was the case, why, with crowds of 30,000, did they pay him only £300 a week? A furious Wednesday demanded cash immediately from United, and Terry began his United career scoring in pre-season friendlies in Scotland.

The move to Bramall Lane lasted six months. He scored only three goals and made only 33 first-team appearances. United fans never took to him; he in turn played well only on a couple of occasions. When he was good, he was brilliant. Unfortunately, his best-ever performance, in a Cup match at Stoke, was his final one in a United shirt. The dressing room was not fully behind him. Though he and United's captain, Tony Kenworthy, became good mates, he never hit it off with United's goal-scoring hero, Keith Edwards. The crosses that produced goals were not acknowledged by the latter. Off the pitch, he ceased going to city-centre clubs. 'I got if from both sets of fans . . . it got dangerous.' Realising he had made a mistake, he asked for a move. Another factor played a part: he was signed by a chairman not a manager. He felt he had been forced on a man who was not that bothered about picking him. Following the Stoke game, he signed for Howard Kendall at Everton. Having breached his United contract deal, he saw only £10,000 of the signing-on fee.

The fans loved him at Everton and he had three happy years there. He won a Championship medal, but missed a season with a bad injury. A free transfer to Huddersfield followed, where he stayed for a season before Lawrie McMenemy signed him again while managing the ailing Sunderland. Rows with the manager resulted in him leaving soon after, effectively sacked on disciplinary grounds. After a couple of games with Grimsby, he packed the game in. The death of his father from cancer around the same time profoundly affected him. Losing interest in the game and much else, he tried a variety of jobs and found a niche in a pallet business.

The persistence of a fan of non-League Goole Town paid off, however, when, after a three-year absence, Terry agreed to turn out for them. Within weeks he was the manager, crowds were trebled, and the team went on a nine-match unbeaten run. Then Terry discovered those above him were playing silly buggers with the wages: to be precise, he was managing for no wage while his players were getting what he paid them plus backhanders. He walked out. He walked in at Mossley for a while in the Vauxhall Conference, but the travelling was too much, and the directors were not pleased when he interviewed for another club without telling them. Football today is a memory, and working six days a week from 5.30 am until last orders in the bar means he is never a spectator.

He bought the truck-stop next to the pallet yard about three years ago. It's now growing into a motel with a splendid function room and four acres of land to develop. He works with his wife and the kids are found in the adjacent house. He's not poor, but he is not wealthy either. As a Championship-winning Everton player in 1986, he was taking home a £400 basic with £200 win bonus. The modest signing-on fees were gobbled up by the tax office. Arthritis of the right knee limits his mobility. A pin remains a legacy of cruciate ligament damage and he cannot fully bend his left knee. Is he happy?

> . . . I'm pissed off. I work all day when I used to work for two hours. The work is all right: you get to talk to people, but it's basically trying to squeeze three or four quid out of lorry drivers. In truth, I'd love to be a football manager.

The one bad injury in his career, sustained when at Forest, cost him a lot. At the time, England Manager Don Revie was close to selecting him. When at Wednesday in Division Two, he believes he was England standard. One match at the time reflected his genius and his nemesis. A 3–0 away victory at Luton saw him in devastating form, and the game was featured on Match of the Day. Unfortunately, Jimmy Hill also chose to focus on an incident where Terry was visibly throwing coins back at home fans. This was not the behaviour the England selectors wanted.

His dream of being a footballer having been achieved, he contemplates what might have been and wishes he could still be managing. His playboy days in Josephine's are long gone; the reality today is fat men in overalls grumbling over the price of a cuppa. Football chat is still afforded by Sheffield fans travelling north, who occasionally drop in to reminisce and stuff themselves. The grub's good value and so is Terry, who then, as now, is never short on opinions and was never cowed by big names in football—be they players or managers. He has an admirable spirit. A crowd-pleaser and teaser, he packed them in; he got fans excited and he got them singing. His move to United was a disaster in the circumstances. Had he played at Bramall Lane and not Hillsborough, United may well have been promoted in place of Wednesday. It's history now, and so is Terry. It would take a Blade with a heart of stone not to like this former tormentor.

Cheers and Booze...
Billy Whitehurst

There has never been a shortage of working-class men in South Yorkshire who aspire to the status of being 'hard'. What this actually means
and how it is expressed is subject to contest through gossip, challenges
and, ultimately, punches. The term has been applied to men on account
of their propensity to use violence against peers or their ability to with-
stand such violence and various other knocks life can offer. In this era,
the term is too readily used in professional football. All teams are presumed to have a 'hard' man, but this covers everything from the midfield ball-winner to the cynical tackler; from the robust centre-half or
centre-forward to the scuffler, who, when the inevitable 'handbags'
occurs, is always in the middle, safe in the knowledge that no one throws
a punch in such a fracas.

One man who put the fear of God into defenders throughout the

1980s and early '90s also did the same to contemporaries in the various pit villages from where he originated. He remains today a man to avoid taking liberties with, as he manages a pub only yards from Bramall Lane. Despising cheats and incapable of being intimidated, this big man's single-mindedness cost him money and status in the game, but his name produces a smile in those who watched him or played alongside him; and stories about him will be retold long after those concerning most of his playing colleagues.

He loves the pit village that raised him. His parents still live there, and he visits frequently. Devastated by the mid-1980s pit closure, the place is just picking itself up, but drug-taking and crime is a tempting option for the sons and daughters of the unwanted and dispossessed. A hard but what Billy terms a 'tremendous' upbringing produced a tough lad. Dad worked on the coalface of the pit and Mum was a school cleaner. Four older brothers no doubt kept Billy in his place and offered protection to the youngest of them, their one sister.

Knowing the physical conditions of pit life, the old man vowed not to allow his sons to follow in his footsteps. Thus, from an early age, Billy had to raise his ambitions beyond the pit and pit village. Recognition that he possessed something beyond his peers came with selection for the under-11 Don and Dearne team. He played for the next four years for the region's finest at left-back, but is modest in reflecting on his selection.

> At that age, it was more about strength than ability. I was a big lad until 11 then, between 12 and 16, stopped growing; then at 18, I find meself at 6' 1½".

Knowing truancy would result in a belting from his dad, he attended school diligently. Being the best fighter in the school meant that school was quite pleasant! Aware that he'd bred a scrapper, the old man had him boxing training for four years at Hickleton Pit gymnasium. The training he loved; the sparring was a different matter.

> I didn't like it . . . kept gettin' me nose smashed! It happened a few times. I thought, 'Fuck that for a game' . . . and it's the hardest training going.

His admiration for boxers and their fitness is tinged with a degree of regret around his fitness at the top level of football.

> I never got to the maximum level of fitness 'cause I was always out on the fuckin' pop. Some years, I did a bit on the punchbag in pre-season training—it was knackering, I was breathing through me arse after a few minutes.

When not brawling in pub car parks, Billy was learning to become a bricklayer. Saturdays saw him playing for Hickleton Colliery in the Doncaster Senior League. The manager saw something in the 17-year-old and moved him to centre-forward, and the rest is history. The first to notice the big lad was Keith Mincher, the manager of Retford Town in the Midland League. They met in unusual circumstances.

> I was in the Five Acres nightclub after a match with Hickleton. It stood at the junction of five pit villages, so it was always a bit of a cauldron. I'd had an argument with this bloke who'd come at me with a big spanner. I'd got it off him and done him over the head and then his kneecap and fucked off. When he was in hospital, I learned that he'd paid a couple of blokes to 'do' me. So, weeks later, I'm in the pub in Thurnscoe with me wife when in walks Keith and Tom Clark (Retford's assistant manager). Keith had a busted nose and Tom's got a long crombie coat on. Keith comes up to me and from behind said, 'Billy Whitehurst?' and taps me on the shoulder. I was gonna smack him, but instead I said, 'Who wants to know?' He said, 'Keith Mincher—Retford Town.' I thought, 'Thank fuck for that . . .'

Over a few beers, he signed for Retford and took home £15 for playing a match and training twice a week. A year later, he moved to another Midland League team called Mexborough, where Harry Lee signed him in unusual circumstances—but, inevitably, it involves a pub.

> I was bricklaying and me and me labourer finished early so went to a pub called The Station. As I'm drinking, the landlord gave me a beer mat that Harry Lee had left asking me to play and telling me that I can train when I want.

At £25 a week, this was a better deal and less travelling. Selected after only ten games for a Midland Select XI, he scored in a friendly against Nottingham Forest. A watching scout from Hull City asked Harry Lee if he could have Billy for a trial match at Notts County. Here begins another story.

> I went to Meadow Lane with Harry Lee, but he'd been drinking all day and was half-pissed. I thought this was it: the big time. I played and

scored. In the bar after, Hull's manager, Mike Smith, and the scout had a chat. Mike Smith says to me, 'Come and have another reserve game.' Harry Lee says, 'Sup up, get your bag, we're off.' He says to Smith, 'You've seen him once . . . there's a lot more interested in him.' Hull signed me next day.

Guess where he signed? Correct—and it was called The Cecil.

Hitherto, football had given him a maximum income of £25 a week. Bricklaying brought in £140 a week. Hull City paid Mexborough £2,500 and offered a basic £250 a week plus bonuses. Unfortunately, he now had to work for his money.

I was a brickie on the Council, which means you've never really worked in your life! I'd been five years with the Council, which meant at 7.30 I'd be on the job, but then I'd go to me mum and dad's for breakfast, then do a few jobs till half-ten, then go to the bookie's, watch a few races, then clock off.

Sounds to me like the ideal preparation for becoming a professional footballer, but Billy had to put some graft in. For a start, because of a driving ban, he had to hitchhike daily from Doncaster to Hull and back and then get fit.

The first two years were horrendous: it's a big step from the Midland League to professional. I'd gone from playing for Mexborough Tuesday night and bricklaying to playing Third Division football the following Saturday.

The realisation that he had much to learn, along with the assistance of a model pro—whom Billy considers the biggest influence on his career—pulled the big young lad through.

My touch was crap . . . my second touch was always a tackle. Now, your first touch is paramount in football and I was knackered at the time, which doesn't help. Chris Chilton who was a centre-forward at Hull got me three bollards and he'd drill balls at me and, as he did, he'd shout 'Left' or 'Right' or 'Kill'. Me touch got better.

Another unusual training technique at Hull also involved the issue of touch, but it was Billy's fist and forehead that did the talking. One player, a Welsh International, kept going for him in training. One bad tackle too many saw the assailant unconscious and the educational process complete. 'It was the best thing that ever happened to that cunt.'

Good things were not happening at Hull, however. Relegated to Division Four, they sacked the manager and appointed Colin Appleton, who in turn was followed by Brian Horton, who in 1985 sold Billy to First Division Newcastle, then under Willie McFaul. At £230,000, Billy was at the time the Geordies' record signing, and in return Billy was on £350 a week. It all started well, but he left within a year after only 28 games. He made the cardinal sin at the time of insulting the fans up there. Today, of course, you can call them everything and your reward is a place on the board, but things were different then.

> We were playin' Bradford in the League Cup and we'd lost 2–0 down there and we're winning 1–0 with 15 minutes to go and I'm pulled off. As I walk, one of the fans gobs on me. I've cracked. I walk back onto the pitch and give 'em that [the two-fingered salute from both hands held high] . . . I'm not taking that crap. Next day, McFaul gets me in the office saying I'll never play for the club again and you can't do that up here. It was a reaction: the majority of fans up there were brilliant. Anyway, as I'm sat there, the phone rings and it's Oxford United asking him if he'd let me go there.

Then in Division One, a fee of £175,000 took Billy to Robert Maxwell's team managed by Maurice Evans. The threat of him returning to Newcastle panicked McFaul and they even paid him to leave!

> I talked all day with Maurice Evans and I wanted a £25,000 signing-on fee; he insisted on half of that. I said to him, 'Give Willie a ring.' He did. Now Willie's tapped Paul Goddard up that day and I hear Maurice saying to Willie: 'He wants £25,000; can you help?' In the end, he puts me on the phone and I says to Willie, 'I'll see you tomorrow at training.' He says, 'No fucking way: give me Maurice back.' They agreed that Newcastle would pay the other twelve and a half so as I wouldn't go back!

Leaving a team that contained Peter Beardsley and a youngster by the name of Paul Gascoigne, Billy teamed up with John Aldridge and was on £900 a week. The assistant manager at Oxford was the avuncular ex-pro Ray Graydon, who was soon to feel Billy's wrath. Undecided whether to put the newcomer on in place of a struggling forward, he made Billy peel off his tracksuit twice and then failed to make the swap. The furious Billy complained. The squeaky-clean Graydon, unaccustomed to backchat, told him what to do and was promptly chinned in the dugout. The crowd and team were blissfully unaware of events as Billy immediately decided to shower and then told his inquisitive manager he was off for a pint.

Forty games and four goals later, he was on his way to Second Division Reading. Ian Branfoot paid £120,000 for a player who was in a rut and hated everything about Oxford.

> Training even got me down and I've always loved training. I didn't even enjoy waking up. I put meself on the transfer list.

Training two greyhound dogs, he sought solace in the Oxford greyhound stadium. Dog racing was more exciting for him than football at the time, and maybe the crowd knew it.

> They'd boo me in the warm-up . . . shout 'You fat bastard'. It was water off a duck's back, 'cause I'd tell them to fuck off back. I weren't fat . . . the kit was too small.

They had a more generous cut of kit at Reading and the crowd took to him. In his few months' stay, he came runner-up in the Player of the Year poll and found the best drinking squad of players of any club he has ever played at. The manager went public, stating that Billy was the best signing he ever made. Then it went wrong when Billy lost his driving licence again for drink-driving. There were two reasons why he left Reading: one concerns the silly demands of the manager; the other had to do with a nightclub brawl. Let's allow Billy to explain the first scenario.

> I'd kept me house outside Oxford and, after away games, our coach would drive within ten miles of where I lived, but Branfoot won't let people get off. So I have to go 30 miles to Reading, get a train to Oxford then a taxi 20 miles home when me wife could have picked me up at the motorway. Anyway, one match I thought, fuck this, and jumped off anyway. He couldn't do anything.

Then a pre-season tour of the north-east took precedence over a possible transfer and events on the tour cost him a good move.

> All the gear's on the coach and we're about to go when Branfoot tells me Ron Atkinson at West Brom wants me. He doesn't want me to leave Reading and all I want to do is go on the tour so it's left in the air. In a Sunderland nightclub we get brawling with bouncers and I get arrested and charged with ABH on him and sexual assault on some bird.

The tabloids loved the story. Big Ron and Alan Clarke at Barnsley didn't, and their interest in Billy ended. In court, Billy was fined for assaulting the bouncer and the sexual assault never got to hearing stage: the 'victim' was the bouncer's girlfriend and the claim was a fabrication, but the tabloids don't print that.

Banned from every nightclub in Sunderland, it was somewhat ironic that Sunderland signed him in 1989 for £100,000. Their manager, Dennis Smith, no doubt saw in Billy a mirror image of himself as a player and the three-and-a-half-month stay resulted in 17 appearances, three goals and regrets.

> I loved it there: I was the supporters' Player of the Month twice, but Sunderland wanted Tony Norman from Hull. But they'd only let him go if I'd go back to Hull to appease the fans. I couldn't see a future at Sunderland if he was so willing to let me go for a goalkeeper.

Now in Division Two under Eddie Gray, Billy lasted 21 games before Harry Bassett brought him to Bramall Lane in January 1990 for £30,000. The manager probably remembered the big lad from his Wimbledon days.

> I always played well against Wimbledon. They were always blood-and-thunder matches. Harry called me Conan the Barbarian.

Bought as a cover player for the Tony Agana–Brian Deane partnership, the move was the best thing that happened to Billy. In Harry he found as good a manager as he had ever known and who was a straight-talker like him. He could do something few managers could: namely, keep players happy who were not getting a regular game which, as Billy points out, is not easy. He also found Harry understanding in times of bother.

> I need two and a half grand quickly. Harry signs a cheque and gives it to me telling me to give it back when I'd got it. Weeks later, I give him £2,400, so I owed him a hundred quid. At a PFA dinner in Doncaster with a few mates, we got Harry on our table: they're well happy and lovin' it, then I gets £100 out and gives it to him, so we're quits now. One of my mates clocked it and in the bogs asked me what it was about. I told him it was payment so Harry would sit with us!

The instructions the manager issued to his signing, though not sophisticated, were understood by the recipient.

> When I was sub, he'd usually say as I went on, 'Go and cause some bollocks.' We played a friendly in France against Auxerre: they're lead-ing, and start pissing about passing the ball everywhere and Harry's getting angry. He says to me, 'Go on and splatter some cunt,' so I did their goalkeeper first ball. We lost, but, as Harry said, at least we'd done something.

Harry once asked a favour of Billy after the big man had left United. Attending a match at the Lane as a spectator, Billy observed Brian Deane getting rough treatment from a well-known centre-half and 'hard man'.

> Harry said, 'Do me a favour and threaten him at half-time: stand in the players' tunnel.' When half-time comes, ✻✻✻✻✻ ✻✻✻✻✻ sees me and says, 'All right Billy?' I said to him, 'Don't all right me' and 'Kick Deansy once more and I'm gonna twat you after the match.' He stood there with his gob open, saying, 'I haven't touched him.'

United won that game 1–0.

A year earlier, Billy, wearing a United shirt, had trotted onto the pitch as a substitute, along with a certain Vinnie Jones. And it was Vinnie who did the wind-up this time. As Billy was standing in close prox-imity to his marker, Vinnie said to the opposing defender—the same player who was to needle Deano a year later: 'Go on then, call him a fat bastard now he's stood next to you.' The defender was speechless and Billy played the part of insulted footballer beautifully.

Billy's desire to win, however, gained him the wrath of team-mates in training.

> I can't play a friendly and I weren't good enough to turn it on and off. I couldn't not put me foot in.

It was Mark Morris who had the unenviable task of marking him in training games and who would nurse black eyes, thick lips and moan to Billy about taking matches too seriously. As Billy recalls, 'Harry would sit in the corner giggling at events.'

In numerous narratives from numerous sources, Billy's off-the-pitch punching is legendary. His victims included officers of the British Army and the hooligan element of Sheffield Wednesday. The former, in the shape of two sergeants, suffered black eyes when finding the United squad in their base for one of Harry Bassett's fitness and team-building exercises. When they had opined rather loudly in the officers' bar that all professional footballers were homosexuals, Billy told them to finish their drinks and, on his own, took the pair outside and wasted them.

A few months later, one of the Owls' top lads was prostrate outside a Sheffield bar, courtesy of Billy, having taken up Billy's one-to-one offer. Their match at Coventry postponed, 30 Owls decided to wander around town. Also out were the United squad. Finding themselves in the same bar, words were exchanged and a bottle was thrown at the players. Offering the lot out, Billy then knocked the main challenger out with one punch. To his credit, the Owl never told inquisitive police who his assailant was and Billy, when questioned by police, did not divulge details of his opponent.

Inevitably, when on a pre-season tour to Spain, there was some horse-play. It started on an aeroplane and ended with Billy facing the beak. Eight of the team, accompanied by the physio Derek French, were having a laugh at the expense of the absent Harry. David Barnes, a capable mimic, took a felt-tip pen and imitated a Bassett team-talk using the video screen as a tactics board. Joke over, he then realised the pen marks wouldn't rub off. The stewardess wasn't too pleased and, when Billy suggested she get some 'Jif' and a cloth, got angrier. The captain appeared and supported his cabin staff. Next thing, the West Midlands police boarded the plane and eight players were arrested. The wily Frenchie avoided arrest apparently by hiding behind a newspaper. Locked up for eight hours, the suspects were told that they had caused damage to the tune of £10,000. The incident made one of the 'Bong' headlines on News at Ten.

The incident served to highlight a boardroom power struggle. The man who thought he was chairman, Paul Woolhouse, phoned the players in custody to tell them they were not going on the holiday. The man who was *de facto* boss, Reg Brealey, overruled him and said they could go. Most of the charges were dropped and just Barnesy and Billy faced court. At 9 am on the day, Reg Brealey turned up in Birmingham to support them with character references, and some deal was done whereby money was paid and the matter sorted. Billy got his own revenge on Paul Woolhouse at the club Christmas dinner in Josephine's nightclub when a fiercely thrown roast potato splattered his neck. The culprit was never found.

For a man his size, he was an excellent trainer and he wasn't that fat! His fat-to-muscle body ratio was the second lowest of all the players when at Bramall Lane and he could keep up with the best on long-distance running. So when Blades christened him 'Billy Tightshirt' and visiting Leeds fans sang 'Ninety pies an hour' and 'Have you ever seen your dick?', they were misinformed and even plain wrong. And I, for one, believe Billy's version of events. One could perhaps say, kindly, that he was built more for comfort than speed.

Moving on quickly to the next topic . . . ah, yes: Billy's attempts to become a defender. For one first-team game, Billy played at centre-half in a 1–0 United victory. Harry spoke in the press about a possible new lease of life for him and, a few days later, played him at centre-half in the reserves at Liverpool. He tried to mark two youngsters called McManaman and Fowler. They lost 5–0 and he was back up-front on Saturday.

The new lease of life came elsewhere: initially at Stoke where Alan Ball took him on loan in November 1990, but an injury saw the deal fall through. A few months later, Billy Bremner signed him for Doncaster. His departure was quick and quiet—'I just got me boots and shot the crow'—but he kept in touch with Harry and the squad for years afterwards. Following 22 games for Donny, Dario Gradi took him to Crewe and then followed a one-season contract with Northern Ireland club Glentoran, who flew him over for games.

He had a bit further to fly for his next pay-packet when South China FC of Hong Kong gave him £600 a week plus expenses and accommodation for the family. His year there culminated in a cup final in front of 50,000, but no renewal of contract. Another Hong Kong team stepped in and explained why he was not retained and offered their own deal.

> They said to me that the manager at South China told them I drink too much. They said you can drink all you want for our club as long as you play.

This was too good to be true. Unfortunately, after one game, he did his right cartilage and, post-operation, on his first game back, did the left cartilage.

Next stop was the familiar surrounds of a pit village. Returning from Hong Kong football afforded the chance of moving into a managerial capacity. An old mate was Ronnie Glavin who was managing Frickley Athletic in the Unibond League. He became Glavin's assistant while still playing, and was on the subs' bench for an FA Cup tie against Skelmersdale. This was when Billy decided to defend his manager.

> Ronnie complains to their dugout and all he gets is a 'Fuck off' from one of them. So I went over and stuck the nut on him. He's lying there and then all the players pile in. Later, one of theirs gets sent off and,

as he goes down the tunnel, calls me a 'Yorkshire bastard', so I dropped him as well. Ronnie afterwards said to me that maybe I wasn't cut out to be assistant manager.

Months later, Ronnie went to Emley and the new manager was Billy. He only lasted a few months, leaving with frustration at a situation where wages were not paid on time, if ever.

A new form of management then came his way: he became a pub landlord in his home village. Doing well, with a packed house and plenty of after-hours drinking, he lost his licence when police opposed his renewal. Why?

They said that Thurnscoe was a volatile area and they didn't want me in it!

This was strange, considering that the one man who could control a volatile pub was Billy, and his boozer did not see a minute's grief.

The pub he now manages outside Bramall Lane is packed three nights a week and every match day. Volatile situations are dealt with by Billy and the place has become a regular haunt for many current players. Now managing eight staff, he has learned the hard way that trust can be broken and those to whom he has given leeway have at times ripped him off. His karaoke nights are famous and Billy is a legend with a microphone— or, if he isn't, nobody has had the guts to tell him. I met him in the pub the morning after the night before the big night. Did he sing?

Only about 30 times! Imagine getting paid to sing, you know, for doing what you like . . . like being a footballer, really.

He rarely plays now. Three games for a pub team managed by a former United team-mate were all he managed this year. He was dropped, in a way, and in a manner he had never experienced before in all his career.

He rang me and said, 'Come up for the team photo session: don't bring your boots, but look good for the photo.'

Although throughout his career he picked up many drinking injuries and, from the age of 25, smoked 20 a day, he doesn't carry any injury as a football legacy. Neither is he rich from all his years in the game.

I would have been if I'd looked after it! We're comfortable. The house I live in is mine and I'm manager of a pub.

The 'we' is a reference to his wife and kids. He met his wife when she was 17, and she has seen it all and travelled everywhere with him.

> She deserves a medal the size of a bin lid. I couldn't have picked any-one better.

He can attribute his physical appearance to her diligence. About five years ago, a fight outside a pub saw his opponent bite the end of his nose off. Billy went to hospital while Julie, with the aid of car head-lights, found the piece of nose in the pub car park. Wrapping it in ice cubes, she presented it to the surgeon who managed to sew it back on. The only listener is me; there is no audience to impress; the facts are presented calmly and without comment; and the past is not dwelt upon. This is truly a hard man. Thankfully, he's also happy, although he misses the crack with the lads that the game always provided. But he's got plenty of crack available at the pub and he runs legendary trips to racecourses both for regulars and his old football mates.

What the game lost as a player, it gained as a fan. Although he fol-lowed United as a kid, he was too busy playing to attend regularly. Now he's a regular Blade both home and away and admits to never having been caught up in football so much than he has since he stopped play-ing. In hindsight, he realises he could have got more from the game, but that was not his style.

> If you speak your mind, you're not well liked. If I felt something, I'd say it. If I'd counted to ten I would have remained in the game longer.

But he played liked he lived and he had no time for cheats.

> I never stayed down looking to get a man booked. If I went down, there was something wrong. The World Cup was diabolical with blokes rolling over three times when they'd been touched. It's cheating and it spoils the game.

Sent off six times, he remembers that the two men who were his most difficult opponents—Hansen and Lawrenson of Liverpool—were men who never talked or fought with their opponents. Others remember Billy for his habit of stroking their foreheads and murmuring, 'You're sweating . . . I know you're scared.' One who spat on him during a reserve game found Billy waiting for him in full kit outside the dressing room. Another international-level defender was told to leave the post-match players' bar and fight outside. He didn't.

> Looking back, it was petty and stupid . . . but they were players who were supposed to be hard, and one's gobbing on me and the other's trying to get me sent off.

As Billy saw it, most of his disputes were about injustice. Even managerial staff were not immune to having his hand grip their throats. One who suffered this ignominy was a former United manager.

> I was playing in this pre-season friendly a few years back and I'm up against an 18-year-old. From the touchline all I can hear is ✳✳✳✳✳ ✳✳✳✳✳ telling this kid 'Kick him' and 'Hit him hard'. I said to the kid, 'Play your own game and ignore that bastard', and at half-time I went in their dressing room, got the big-mouth by the throat and said, 'Don't tell other people to do what you're not capable of.'

His time at Bramall Lane was short—less than a year—yet he seems part of United's 1990s history. His old manager Harry speaks warmly of him and remembers him rounding on a young team-mate who was moaning about something trivial on a club holiday. Billy told him he didn't know he was born and should be grateful that he got for nothing what thousands would give their right arm for. He silenced the party and shamed the affluent but dissatisfied player. Billy spoke from the heart and spoke up for those he grew up with.

Some readers will disapprove of Billy; some might be uncomfortable with the idea of such a larger-than-life, sometimes aggressive, character. But be wary of condemning those who are quick to respond physically. Such men win battles and allow those of us who are inept and cowardly to sit on fences. Billy was uncompromising and, to Blades, was on the side of virtue when in a United shirt. In opposition colours, of course, fans' attitude towards him was different. It must be remembered that he came from an environment where hardness was valued and the car park decided who won the argument. Such communities are largely finished now and the legacy of manual labour and pit life replaced by economic devastation and an entrepreneurial drug culture in the young, which does not respect camaraderie, fair play or fist-fights.

Backroom Boys

The history of football is a sad voyage from beauty to duty. When the sport became an industry, the beauty that blossoms from the joy of play got torn out by its very roots. In this *fin de siècle* world, professional football condemns all that is useless, and useless means not profitable.

(Eduardo Galeano, *Football in Sun and Shadow*: 2)

Stars and Stripes...
John Greaves

A new chap bought the club yesterday.

In the changing room at Bramall Lane at 10 am on Saturday morning, life goes on much the same. The physio Frenchie enters singing 'Old MacDonald bought a club', then reassures first-teamers that, within a week under the new regime, they will be out on their arse. He departs without provoking a response, people having grown to ignore him. Elsewhere sit six white mice, sometimes called juniors, suffering ridicule from first-teamers reassuring them that the task they have been given—to attend a match that afternoon and write a dossier on each player—will ensure they look completely stupid.

A football club is rife with hierarchies. At the pinnacle stands a rich man—thicker around the waist and usually older than the manager and coaching staff—surrounded with men of similar age and attitude, but less money. Then comes the team boss and his sidekicks: a sort of inner cabinet. Then come the players, demarcated into first-teamers, reserves and juniors. Throughout this structure, however, one man at Bramall Lane serves the various echelons equally, eating with the directors on overnight stays, party to every dressing-room drama, and yet not above making tea for the laundry girls. Indispensable to the club, the man who held this role between 1989 and 1997 was known to all as 'Greavsey' and his job title was 'the kit man'.

What is there to say about football kits? For one thing, ex-players are always associated in the fans' mind with one particular design. Think of Bob Hatton, or Keith Edwards, or Bobby Booker. Until recently appropriated as a fashion garment, the football kit, like the game, was always considered a privileged male item. Such kit brought heartbreak to schoolboys whose football obsession centred on wanting to be precise. You see, at the time, Subbuteo teams included Sunderland and Southampton, but not United. The solution was to buy them and then try, with Airfix brush and paint, to change red socks into white. The correct kit mattered. Across the decades, the game and its associated colours and kit paraphernalia has provided for tens of thousands of boys the first occasion when they cared about their appearance. Football also accessed the realms of technology, provoking in-depth discussions about 'correct' designer football boots and studs, which the discerning carried in designer shoulder bags.

The game as played by adults provided boys with sounds and smells to which they aspired. Remember wanting to be able to kick the ball with such power with thick thighs so as to be able to make *that* noise: the chunk of the shot resulting from the ripple of the plastic-coated ball striking plastic netting? Remember wanting limbs glistening with embrocation combined with the ability to spit? Thousands watched, then participated, as they grew older in male locker-room rituals. The aroma of the dressing room would resound with the sound of the football bouncing, studs clunking on concrete and sellotape stretching around shinpads. The package was complete with the squeal of nylon shorts rubbing as one went from walk to jog to sprint.

Part of playing good was looking good, and over the past three decades every Sunday morning a thousand dreams were begun. Usually the same number of dreams were shattered 90 minutes later, the pain compounded by the reluctant, but democratic, practice of each player having to carry home then wash the entire team kit every twelve weeks. By the end of the year, the kits had often shrunk, faded or were, via some biological process, the cause of at least 24 inflated nipples.

In a footballing world obsessed by appearances and ideas of correct style, the man who controls access to the rather expensive gear can be powerful or is at least worth being polite to. What is true for local leagues applies to Bramall Lane. Like all good quartermasters, Greavsey doesn't give much away easily. Showing me around his office ('Aladdin's cave') he explains one of his main problems is interpreting what the manager actually said in contrast to what some people think he said.

> There's always people comin' down here tryin' to ponce gear. I won't gi' owt away. They're always givin' it 'Harry said this' and 'Harry said that'. I go to see 'im missen and usually find out Harry's said fuck all. So they can all bollocks.

One suspects, on first impressions, that, if not kit man, Greavsey would drive buses or be a park-keeper. Truth is, he's not the monster some might think, but God help anyone who enters his room, packed as it is with new kit and boots and, oddly enough, 24 packs of lager and bitter. Only him and a trusted apprentice go in here, which means few ever see the photo of Mel Rees over the door. Noticing my interest, he explains.

> Whenever I'm down—and it isn't very often—or some o' t'players start moaning about owt, I tell 'em, 'Look at 'im and then tell me what your problems are.'

Having been in his pocket for a day and a half, I know he's all heart. On the wall of the dressing room is a memo from the boss to all players which warns that any discarded kit found after training would be retrieved, identified and the culprit fined £1. Furthermore, players are reminded that all equipment is the club's and, should it go missing, the cost would be deducted from their salary. How much has Greavsey collected so far? He smiles.

> A couple o' players got a warning from me. I informed 'em of what I'd 'ave to do. Thing is: boss'll be expectin' fifty quid or more probably, but I ain't collected a penny yet.

Maybe it's just as well. The gaffer would only blow it buying a couple of non-League players.

The kit man has neither job description, set hours or a contract. His competence, I suppose, is reflected in not being particularly noticed either in training or on match day. Working to his own method and check-lists, the smooth running of match day is dependent on him. Not that he seeks acclaim. Like any public event involving star performers, a huge number of hours are put in by unsung workers who never receive the praise they deserve. This week, for instance, despite being in daily at 9 am, Greavsey did not get home until 10.30 pm three nights in a row: an under-21 game, the reserves, then a Coca-Cola Cup game all required his services. Tomorrow's Sunday match at Huddersfield means his only time off this week is Saturday afternoon. Between you and me, he didn't go shopping, but, in the company of six first-teamers, went to Hills-borough to watch the team he followed for years. Mention it quietly, but he's actually a closet Manchester United fan.

I'll try and extricate him from this. Born in Mexborough, he could easily have followed Leeds or Wednesday. Taken to Old Trafford at the age of 14, he followed the Manchester club for the next six years. Meanwhile, he played for Denaby United and Mexborough in the County Senior League. Daytimes were spent plastering and the rest of the time bringing up two lads.

Then it all changed: invited in his mid thirties to run a boys' team, he realised there was so much he didn't know about the game. To edu-cate himself, he did two things: one was watch local professional clubs training when supposedly supervising building site progress. The sec-ond was enrolling on a coaching course. He won his badge at the same time as ex-Blade Colin Morris and the pair were examined by Keith Mincher, United's youth team manager who Greavsey knew from their attending the same school. With this newly won football knowledge, Greavsey was managing Mexborough Main Street in 1988 and spend-ing summers coaching football in the USA (he still has his own schools out there).

One day, his side played the United youth team and, still wanting to know more about technique, he asked Keith Mincher if he could watch coaching sessions. Beginning with the under-14 team, one day he was asked to lead the warm-ups and he subsequently coached the school-boy trialists during the school holidays. Volunteering to be both kit and transport manager for an under-16 tour of Brittany, he came to the notice of a few people higher up. Nevertheless, he had plans of his own. With the two lads grown up, he briefly emigrated to coach football full-time in the US, but various circumstances brought him back home and back to the club that had become his second home. He busied himself and showed an eagerness to help out, and jobs were soon found.

Initially, Harry Bassett paid his expenses and sent him scouting. Then he accompanied the under-16s when playing the national School of Excellence. Soon after, Keith Mincher asked him what the future held. Aged 40, mortgage paid, kids grown up, he didn't fancy a life plastering, but what was the alternative? Mincher suggested a job as United's kit man. The response?

> Me stomach raced. I wo' like a kid player being offered a big move. I can't describe it even now. He told me the idea would have to go to the board of directors. I had to wait. It wo' unbearable.

The directors gave the plan the knock-back. Fortunately, it wasn't the end of the road.

> Harry pulled me in and said, 'Fuck it! Keep comin' and do the job anyway, 'cause I'll get what I want in my own time.'

Having found his man, Harry found the money. For eight years, Greavsey held the job. 'I never treated it as a job. For me it was like one long holiday.'

There has not been anyone in the history of the club employed in such a role before. There were various chaps over the decades known to all as the 'dressing-room man' who would bang nails in boots and run the bath, but that was a Saturday job only. For away games, humping the kit around was the job of an 'A'-teamer, the 'A' team's coach and the twelfth man. The youngster had the task of ensuring the best players got the best kit, i.e. the one without the holes in. When training, United, like other clubs, used old pairs of shorts and those thick woolly polo necks you see in old pictures. Mind you, United were a little bit trendy because 'SUFC' was stitched onto the left breast as far back as the 1920s. It can only be presumed that the club washed the kit.

Becoming one of Harry Bassett's original inner circle with Geoff Mulgan, Derek French, Keith Mincher and John Dungworth, Greavsey's new job proper began at Hillsborough in the Zenith-Data tie in 1989. The beginning was inauspicious.

> I got a pair of pliers and a big bag of studs from Suggs [a Sheffield sports shop] and got stuck in. From then on, we always had things to hand.

His job, in short, was dealing with anything the various levels of United players want. For what reward?

> Put it this way: three days' building work would beat it. But it's worth
> a lot in other ways. I go all over t'world and stay in top hotels; me
> drinks are on t'club slate and I wouldn't change it for anything.

His only gaffer was the manager. Their dialogue was frequent and he
rated Harry as a mate. Not that he was above getting a flea in his ear.
Once Greavsey made representation on behalf of three large reserve team
players who complained their shirts were too small. The boss's reply
had cruel logic.

> He suggested the way to wear the best kit was to earn the right to it
> by geddin' in t'first team.

When I spent a couple of days with Greavsey in 1995, United had
more players, and hence more kit, than at any time in their history. With
40 professionals, 20 juniors and 10 staff, the kit for each consisted of
the following: towels, 'slips' (Mark's & Spencer's undies), t-shirts, sweatshirts, 'wet gear' (waterproof tops), tracksuits, socks, shorts, bibs, boots
and trainers. Quite a bit, eh? Oh yes, all 40 professionals have three sets
of this training kit! Then there's the small matter of the four under-16
teams and the School of Excellence. For the first time in the club's history, not one of these teams was playing in hand-me-downs. Fortunately, the shirts are not made-to-measure.

> Above the age of 16, we buy man-size for all of 'em. A few have an
> XXL shirt. Shorts are all 36–38. Mind you, Blakey wants a size 40 for
> his big arse. Avec [the kit sponsors] are working on it for us.

Towels and slips are communal and socks are all the same size. Every
day all this needs collecting, washing, sorting and putting into appropriate places. Two laundry ladies slave over the three washing machines
and two dryers. When it's done, it's then placed in plastic trays numbered 1 to 40. Each player has a number and all his kit has his number
written in it. Each day he comes to fetch it or, if he's a first-teamer,
someone (an apprentice) fetches it for him and puts it out on a peg each
morning awaiting his arrival.

As well as kit man, Greavsey sometimes coached junior aspirants; for
many, he was the first line of management. Their footballing ability has
to match their ability to serve their elders and betters. All juniors serve
two to three players by preparing their kit or cleaning their boots. The
professionals tell them how they like it. And if they don't get it as specified? 'They get a bollocking.' Those that get it right might get a few

quid each week from their superiors: recompense, I suppose, for picking up brushes on which some cruel star has felt-tipped 'scrub' and 'does it hurt?'.

Football's a strange world. Under this system, a 17-year-old who might be the ball-winning midfielder on Saturday could be cleaning his teammates' boots on Monday. Young footballers have to do as they're told, but in some cases shouldn't need to be told, particularly when Greavsey leads by example.

> If a player wants ice for an injury, I'm not gonna say, 'That's not kit, someone else fetch it.'

Similarly, if he sees some muck in any part of the bowels of the South Stand, he would do his bit. 'It's like yer house: you've got to keep it clean.'

The lack of job definition means a couple of thousand Swedes, followers of Brakke FC, believe he's got a double-barrelled surname. A pre-season tour match against some no-hopers saw him, aged 41, selected as centre-forward alongside Brian Deane! The joker in the squad—David Barnes—doctored the team sheet so the Tannoy announcement stated that, up-front, was 'Johnnie Nine-Jobs'. He scored a goal that day in the 9–1 victory, as well as collecting soiled slips.

Although the lowest-paid adult in the match-day dressing room, he has always been a valued and popular character with everyone at the Lane. Considering himself a fully paid-up member of the squad, when they were in for Sunday morning training, he came in as well. 'It'd be wrong not to . . . I'm part o t'team.'

In a sense he is, but not averse to mocking them. With his mate Frenchie, the two produced comments which they turned into dressing-room posters. Following five successive defeats, one read 'This is no time for wimps' and was signed 'The Jolly-Up Brothers'. When they finally won a match, the players were greeted next morning with a balloon-and-bunting welcome courtesy of the same two and a message 'Thanks for 21 days of continuous training' (Harry had had them in every day until they learned how to win a match).

In times of stress, he loosened the prohibitions on entry to certain rooms normally in the compass of his empire. In 1991, the squad came in 16 successive Sundays until they won a match. Some came in especially early for tea and toast with Greavsey. Some juniors would call in for a chat; some were homesick; some had other problems. He would either attempt to put them right or told others of the problem. On the day the juniors' contracts were up, the kettle was always on the boil.

> A few are kept, but many aren't wanted. They usually leave the room where they've been told, run out onto t'ground, cry their eyes out, then some come and have a cup o tea wi' me.

Not a man to pull rank, the one player who tried it on with Greavsey nearly got hospitalised.

> Before an away game he told me what he wanted packin'. It wo' unusual, 'cause he didn't want his Nikes. I asked him specifically; he said no. Twenty minutes before kick-off, he realises he's brought wrong boots for t'conditions, so he says to me in front of all t'players and t'gaffer, 'Where's me Nikes?' and starts 'avin a go at me. Anyway, Vinnie [Jones] got old of 'im by 'is throat and told 'im he was out of order. On t'way home we all had a can of beer and that wo' that.

Allowed a weekend to watch Greavsey in action, I made the initial mistake of looking for the big wicker basket I thought the kit travelled in. I was 15 years out of date. For away games, kit travels in three metal skips on wheels. One contains the match-day kit; one is full of boots; the other is full of spares. The choice of away kit is decided first by home-team colours and then by the manager.

> A lot of it's confidence and feelgood. He'll say to 'em what d' yu fancy playin' in? And if they got a good result before, they'll wear it again.

The kit is individually wrapped in the club's maroon towels by Greavsey the day before the match. Players' boots are wrapped together with individually chosen shinpads and the spare kit skip contains match balls. Here lies a story.

> You go anywhere, you'll find they give t'opposition bad balls to warm up wi'. We're obliged to give 'em three and I know I give away teams who come here crap balls. So when we go away, I keep a good one just for our goalie to warm up wi'.

There's other baggage on top of this. A bag of balls, spare towels, and, of course, the ghettoblaster. Fortunately, the physios and coach driver pitch in to carry the stuff. Some players help out, but not all. 'Some won't lift a finger: you'll be surprised who'll just walk past.' If such away games sound a daunting task, think of the pre-season tours of Norway.

'We move house for two weeks, we tek seven skips and it's a fuckin' nightmare.'

On the day United played away at Huddersfield, Greavsey was first in and last out. By 9.15 am, he's doing his daily six laps of the Bramall Lane pitch. Showered and tracksuited, and with the skips aboard the coach, the first stop was breakfast in a posh hotel and then he and Dennis Circuit (physio for the day) departed on the coach to sort out their various luggage before the players arrived an hour later. This is Greavsey's big moment. With meticulous care, the kit is laid out just how each player wants it (long sleeves or short, optional Lycra shorts). Shirts are hung with numbers facing out, and—nice touch, this—the shorts are laid on top of all the other kit and folded so the United club crest stares at each player as he enters. The procedure takes 40 minutes.

The artwork is shattered, though, when United's version of Laurel and Hardy—Wally Downes (team coach) and Derek French (physio)— enter the room acclaiming a Freddie McGregor classic on Radio One by attempting a reggae dance in unison. Such attention-seeking behaviour is ignored as the players enter moments later. I'm not sure the players notice the subtlety of the shorts. Sometimes Greavsey must feel like a pastry chef in a pie stall. Within 15 minutes all are changed and undergoing some form of stretching; one plays 'keep it up' with Greavsey. Then, following the pitch warm-up, some players undergo their first kit change—replacing their undershirts. Then out they go for the real thing, looking very fetching in their blue and yellow, 100% polyester, made-in-Morocco Blades shirts. With Avec emblazoned on the shirt's left breast, the word 'Ward's' appropriately enough across the belly and the Endsleigh League insignia on each sleeve, we might do well to reflect on what it is exactly that we the fans are supporting.

Thousands of people in the city of Sheffield woke up one day, realised they were Blades and have followed things red and white and had various degrees of antipathy to things blue and white ever since. Quite why United are red and Wednesday are blue has no great logic. In fact, the first-ever United team wore white shirts and what were described as 'blue knickers'. Years before, The Wednesday played in blue and white hoops. By 1890, however, United had red and white stripes and Wednesday the same kit in blue and white; no one knows why. Possibly it was the association of United with the city that decided it. The only reliable historian in this field is Denis Clarebrough, who posits the following hypothesis.

Firstly, the first football match ever mentioned in the city in 1793 was when Sheffield played Norton, and Sheffield played in red. Secondly, when Sheffield FC, the world's first football club, was founded in 1857, they played in 'scarlet' and white, possibly out of respect to their predecessors. Thirdly, the Sheffield & Hallamshire FA played in red out of respect to Sheffield FC. So, when United were formed with the aim of being the city's representative side, they might, you would guess, try to follow the same colour code. Certainly, the club badge reflected the city's heritage. Originally, shirts sported the crossed arrows and sheaves of wheat that was the badge of the Sheffield & Hallamshire FA. Then, by 1891, that design was moderated by adding the initials 'SUFC' in the four quarters of the badge, accompanied by the arrows and sheaf with a lion holding a shield! This lasted a year, and, despite wearing a badge when playing at Wembley in 1925 and 1936, the team did not sport one weekly again until 1968 when the club got permission to wear the city's coat of arms.

Then as football left tradition for modernity in the 1970s, the kit changed drastically. Until then, it was pretty simple. United was, from 1895, a team that wore red and white stripes and Wednesday blue and white ones. The shorts were black and the only notable design changes occurred in the sock region which changed over the decades from red to red and black to white, red and black. Then came commerce, and in 1974, for the first time in the club's history, the shirts became advertising vehicles: the word 'Umbro' appeared between the stripes. A year later, a new deal saw Admiral advertise. The same company, a year later, again managed to abominate the shirts by adding open-necked white collars. By 1978, a new design had replaced the Sheffield crest, Designed by manager Jimmy Sirrel, the Yorkshire Rose sat above the two swords, representing a local history of sorts.

Then the players' shirts made them into high-speed sandwich boards. Between 1979 and 1982, Hobott were the kit manufacturers and allowed various businesses to put their names across the shirts. Initially, it was a department store called 'Cantor's'; then car dealers—Bentley's, Crabtree & Nicholl and Renault—superseded in 1982 by Simmonds cutting tools, in turn replaced by Laver's wood yard from 1984 until 1995, when Ward's brewery splashed its name over the midriffs. Meanwhile, depending on the season, between 1979 and 1984, the red stripes got thicker and thinner, the socks changed colour from white to black, to red to black and red, and the badge moved from the left breast to the middle to the left breast again.

Away strips were far simpler in the past. When United played at Southampton or Sunderland or anywhere with red shirts, they changed into white shirts, black shorts, white socks. Occasional discrepancies occurred such as white shorts away from home with the usual home shirt, but nothing too breathtaking. For sartorial historians, there have been a few rushes of blood over the years. At Newcastle away in 1968, United played in orange; at Stoke in 1975, all blue. Solid red shirts were worn at Doncaster in 1979 and at Fulham in 1981.

Then it all went daft. By 1978, we've got a yellow kit with black 'Admiral' Vs; by 1983, it's yellow shirts with red collar and cuffs; the early '80s saw the awful banana yellow and brown (burgundy?) stripes; and by 1989 we've got the unforgettable electric glow-worm (with red cuffs). By 1992, we trot out in jade, no less. When—as in 1989–90—the club turn out in nine different combinations of kit in 30 away games, what does one sing? 'Come on you red, white, black, sometimes yellow, sometimes green or is it jade wizards?' Tradition is tampered with quite unforgivably. In the early '90s, we had blue tracksuits, and the club crest even had the Yorkshire Rose coloured red. The badge went monochrome when United played at Sunderland a few years back. Why? I don't know. Lost? So am I.

Anyway, I digress. It's now kick-off and Greavsey takes his place on the bench with a little bag of tricks: studs, captain's armband, laces, marker pens for the manager's flipchart team-talk, gumshield and thermal gloves. Content to shout encouragement at the team and abuse at the referee, his only other task while the game is under way is acknowledging the goals. After the second goal, he, Wally and Frenchie stand in a row and, in unison, strike a pose impersonating a golfing fairway drive. This could catch on. Half-time requires him to provide a couple of clean t-shirts and help out with leg rubs.

Then, 45 minutes later, the procedure employed at two o' clock is reversed. First comes the now-compulsory post-match warm-down, which requires for some a clean pair of socks and sweatshirts all round. Then, after half an hour of busy kit-gathering, he's back on the team coach, can of lager in hand, ready for the task of watching a Scandinavian film on the coach video screen, which seems to be giving hints on relaxation techniques, but why is everyone in the film naked? Back home, the skips are unloaded, the boots are put back in their place and the kit sorted out for laundry. Finishing at 7.15, he can now meet Marcia, his girlfriend, and put his feet up until tomorrow's 9 am start and night match at Preston with the reserves.

An unusual accolade that Greavsey holds is that of being, in 1995, the only kit man ever sent off by a referee in the history of the British game. Losing 1–0 at Sunderland, United then went 2–0 down to a goal that was clearly offside. The linesman close to the dugout received a variety of advice from Wally, Frenchie and Greavsey, but chose to remember the Yorkshire accent above the southern ones. What he heard was meant to be educational, but it was not the sort of thing taught in teacher-training college. The linesman told the referee who then told Greavsey to sit in the stand and gave him a red card. On a charge of 'foul and abusive language', Greavsey was fined £250 by the FA and banished from the touchline.

A few things stand out in this incident. First, the referee was from Doncaster and had met Greavsey in an earlier life when he had booked him when he played in a local amateur league! Secondly, when taking up a seat in the stand after being 'sent off', he was ejected from his seat by a steward who told him it belonged to Peter Reid, the Sunderland manager. Then, to finish on a happy note, Harry paid his fine for him!

When Harry left, Greavsey stayed on—he had nowhere else to go. He stayed until November 1997 and left for reasons he finds hard to articulate. No criticism will ever cross his lips with regard to Harry's successor, Howard Kendall. He got on well with him, but the new regime at a higher level did not suit him. While he did get a pay increase, he also got new tasks to do and found that the spirit generated at the club by Harry was no longer there.

> I no longer felt part of it. I was now an outsider. I'd travel to the training ground with some of the new staff and they wouldn't lift a finger to help me get stuff out. One bloke in particular started to make me job difficult.

Uncertain of his future, he rang Harry. 'He talked me out of leaving months before; he told me he'd got nothing for me at Forest.'

Becoming moody and not sleeping well, he took Harry's later advice and jacked the job in. The day after he left, the phone rang and it was Howard Kendall, by now managing Everton, who had only just learned of his departure. Staying in a hotel before the Everton game at Leeds, Howard told him to get there as quickly as he could to sing the 'Toe-Tap' ditty to the Everton squad. He couldn't make it, but the invitation reveals the impression Greavsey left on Kendall when, at a drunken players' outing, all involved had to sing a song or pay money into a pot. A 15-minute narrative accompanied by hand and feet movements amused Kendall immensely and it became a much-requested party piece. Football, eh?

Anyway, the departure. What happened?

> I went to see Charles Green and Mike McDonald and said I've had enough and I've done me time and it'd be better for all concerned for me to go. They agreed and said, 'Sort out some money with the accountant.' I left wi' about two months' money.

Ever diligent, he did what needed to be done first.

> It wo' Friday afternoon and United was off to Norwich. I'd packed all t'kit and I said a quiet goodbye to the players.

And the board?

> Nobody came down to say goodbye or thanks. I got me cheque and bawled me eyes out in me office then drove home sobbing.

Six months' coaching football in Florida ended when he returned in May of this year to accept an invitation from Harry to attend a Forest match. Offered his old job back with Harry's new club, he accepted and made his Premiership debut for his new team in August 1998. A couple of days after we met again in 1998, he phoned me to ask if I could mention a few things on his behalf. Pleased to oblige. On behalf of Greavsey, a big thank-you to Derek Dooley for everything he ever did for him while at United. Furthermore, it should be noted that, following his departure from United, the players contacted him and invited him to join their Christmas piss-up. They also had a whip-round and gave him a leaving present of a few hundred pounds.

A new beginning with an old boss is what the future holds. Just maybe, in this instance, there will be a happy ending for a bloke who made a lot of people at Bramall Lane laugh and who received little financial reward for the hours he put in.

Crops and Shares...
Glenn Nortcliff

There are two things a reader will not find in any edition of the 1990s *Sheffield United Yearbooks* published by the club. One is evidence of mud on the kit of any United player photographed in action. The other is any mention of the groundsman and his staff. These people, however, unlike the mud, are visible every home game and prod the pitch back into shape at half-time. On the day I met them in January 1997, they were performing this routine as the electronic scoreboard and Tannoy announcements informed spectators of the club's share rating on the FTSE Index.

Other kinds of footsies, however, are the concern of the same chaps who, for years, have ensured that the best efforts of the police horses standing watching the match were put to better use on the car park flowerbeds. Just maybe, in the image-led marketing world professional with which football clubs now concern themselves, it is inevitable that essential personnel are overlooked when publishing glossy club brochures. People like Glenn and the gang do not make the club instant profits; they merely make the pitch playable, the game a fairer contest and spare the fans possible ridicule from rivals about the state of the ground. It also saves the breath of whinging visiting managers, keen to attribute any defeat to the state of the pitch. An important task, then, you'll agree. So, in search of the—presumably—camera-shy, I presented myself at the ground early on Saturday morning.

I honestly expected to meet a bloke called Tom, Dick or Harry of the age and appearance of Reg Holdsworth, for whom decadence was touching 30 mph on a seated lawnmower. I was wrong. The club does not have a seated mower and the head groundsman is all of 28 years of age and wears trainers, a tracksuit and the club overcoat. His staff of three assistants and two YTSs are even younger and have a sense of humour—something traditionally perceived by many as lacking in those who tend grass for a living. The one assumption that was not shattered is that Bramall Lane has had a groundsman since the day it was built and will need one to its dying day.

The Lane was originally a cricket ground, and, when football caught on, whoever had the job had two pitches to tend. A few past grounds-men were formerly cricketers whose tasks would also include odd jobs around the place and, as early as the 1920s, they were given an assistant. Their background, however, was probably nothing like Glenn's.

Arriving ten years ago on a YTS placement, Glenn (from the Arbour-thorne estate) was appointed head groundsman at the age of 20, thereby becoming the youngest man ever to hold the title for a professional football club. Two years' part-time study and day release at the Lane got him a City and Guilds in horticulture and a permanent job with United. Soon after, his boss left and the job fell in his lap. Choosing such a career on the rationale that 'I didn't want to work indoors', Glenn has since then attained both the respect of other groundsmen and a decent income 'Forest recently advertised for a head groundsman and offered £16,500 . . . that's quite good.' For those interested, the career perks include a one-day course in how to spray chemicals, the chance to pose around on a mini-tractor and the freedom to take a penalty in front of the Kop any time you want.

There'll be a few hundred of you reading this who can admit to having been on the Bramall Lane pitch. Now, not all of you will want to explain the full circumstances, of course, but let's just say some fans of Liverpool, Manchester United or Birmingham still remember you and so do the ex-players of Leicester and Walsall. For those too young to realise what I'm on about, ask that 30-something Blade: your uncle, brother (or even dad).

Thousands of others have encroached on the hallowed turf in another form of ritualised celebration, because at one time the club did not mind end-of-season pitch invasions. The last home game, from 1970–84, always saw thousands of Blades on it who would chase the players off, try to pinch their shirts and then run a lap of honour and, generally, throw themselves around like their heroes did. Inevitably, the police decided such fun had to end. The final home game of the 1984–85 season saw 150 officers and 14 mounted police patrol the perimeter of the terraces to prevent those among the 8,000 crowd risk indulging in the carnival-esque. Such restrictions continued until thousands swamped such efforts at control in 1989 when United beat Swansea and went up from the old Third Division. In recent years, the last away games have seen similar incursions; one, at Wimbledon in 1991, involved a Blades' trapeze troupe display, which resulted in a crossbar being broken and the unforgettable disgusted announcement over the PA system of 'Very clever . . . well thank you very much.'

Today, trespassing onto the pitch, even in joy, is a criminal offence and will lead to arrest, a criminal record and, no doubt, a life ban from the ground.

What is interesting is that the football authorities like it when people whose connection to the game is tenuous, to say the least, take to the pitch. Initially, in the early 1970s, it was the police and their dogs entertaining the pre-match crowd with a show. Later came marching female majorettes as football attempted to Americanise itself as a 'leisure spectacle'. Concomitantly, there were five-a-side matches played before games and at half-time between supporters' clubs, and long-legged lovelies promoting this or that product as part of the match sponsorship. Then, thanks to Sky TV, we got gigantic inflatable sumo wrestling and the dancing, cheering, smiling all-female Sky Strikers (Cor!). In fact, over the last decade, other sporting professionals have performed on it—rugby league, floodlit cricket and boxing. Billy Graham's preached and Bruce Springsteen's bulged and sweated. It does nothing for the pitch and is only a headache for the ground staff, but it brings in money and that's what matters.

Mid-morning on match day, I'm standing in the six-yard box and Glenn's checking the nets. Considering the season's half over and it's winter, the pitch is in an amazingly good condition: the centre circle and six-yard boxes show barely a blemish. The nets are put up and the pitch is watered by sprinklers and, by midday, a waiting game begins. No one needs the ground staff, so it's coffee and chat until the flags are placed in their holes an hour before kick-off and finally the nets are re-checked following the players' kick-about. Here's something that'll surprise you: a pair of nets, would you believe, costs £250 and a set of goalposts a mere £1,000. Today, the former are red; the latter are aluminium. Over the years, the nets have gone from white with wide space to white fine mesh to their present colour and fine mesh status. At one time, they were hung over two stanchions then, from the 1980s, draped over hoops. In recent years, they are stretched and attached to two poles. It's a bit different to pub football: the biggest and fattest did not force the littlest bloke's thighs round his ears as he hoisted him up to put the nets on the hooks—Glenn used stepladders. Furthermore, there are no wedding-ring fingers hanging off the crossbar as a consequence of vain attempts to jump and hook, as there must be on various recreation grounds in the region.

With kick-off approaching, it's into the bottom corner of the South Stand to watch the match. After only four minutes of play, the first divot is quietly commented on. Yet the bigger divs wearing red and white are watched in silence. The big moment comes at half-time with the chance to wander across the pitch occasionally prodding it with a mini-pitchfork. Such a procedure was begun in the early 1980s, and it would seem that this is the only time the club sees fit to let the fans look at the ground staff. Such people always used to remind me of characters from the L.S. Lowry paintings: stooped, and a bit miserable-looking. At one time, there was double the number of prodders, but now the maintenance staff have other demarcated duties. For 15 minutes, blemishes and divots are pitchfork-prodded and training-shoe-stamped on in the hope that turf tears will knit. A similar procedure is repeated for 30 minutes at the end and the pitch rolled, occasionally straight after or within 24 hours.

Having tended the turf all week, all year round, it must be disheartening to watch a lot of over-fit young men hurl themselves around it with metal-studded boots. In fact, one of Glenn's former bosses was so annoyed when players ignored his advice to keep off it after torrential rain and shortly before kick-off that he walked out of the gate and was never seen again! Some players are notorious for their part in this destruction.

Vinnie Jones once slid in and ripped about 10 yards of turf. You just sit there thinkin', 'Fuckin' hell.' Goalkeepers are a fuckin' pain: all that marking out they do which they're not supposed to.

The players, some of whom call the ground staff 'the gardeners', have little contact with the men who prepare their stage.

They don't particularly praise or moan. Some might say for a joke that t'pitch is crap. Mind you, a few of 'em start being nice when they want seeds for their lawns.

Some who do talk might as well have kept quiet. One of the four team managers Glenn has served suggested curing an icy pitch by pouring hot water over it. His second-in-command recommended the floodlights be turned on for a few hours to thaw it out. Such opinions are suffered with good grace and a straight face.

The groundsman never knows precisely what the work hours will be each week, owing to the nature of cup competition and the demands of televised football. Summer is the busiest time. Three days a week are taken up with cutting and rolling the pitch, while others weed the car park and terracing. Winter means Mondays and Tuesdays are taken up with divoting and rolling and Wednesdays reserved for 'pickin' out dead bits and spiking'. Procedures all depend on fixtures and training. Furthermore, the groundsman's job is more than watering and mowing.

People think it's easy . . . but, if they didn't know what they were doin', they'd kill t'pitch wi' fertiliser. It's a mixture of course work and experience: you've got to know what to do in various circumstances.

One Premier League club recently hired a former landscape gardener who fed the pitch by hand from a wheelbarrow instead of using a spreader and can now look at the hundreds of visible lush green curves.

That word 'training' so crucial to the football world is not one of Glenn's favourites. In doing precisely that on his pitch, the players put weight on it and compact it. Ultimately, this is how it gets destroyed. It also interrupts his schedules, because there's no knowing who will hang around for extra practice. One procedure particularly annoys.

That where they stand in a circle knockin' t'ball about with one in t'middle trying to get it. That causes a lot of damage. I've told 'em to move around the pitch every half-hour. They're just startin' to listen.

One day, a session involved 150 corners taken from one position. It did not do the turf there much good, but the team did score a few subsequently from such set-pieces so it was, as Glenn concedes, worthwhile.

Employed with a contract, he is subject to the authority of both team and club management. What the former requests, he does.

> Howard Kendall asked for a lot of water to stop t'ball bobbling on a dry pitch. Dave Bassett sometimes asked for the grass to be kept long to slow t'ball down or for it to be watered to make it heavy.

Bassett also reduced the width to facilitate the long-throw tactic and to support his favoured defensive system of full-backs tucking into the centre-backs so as not to get stretched. While Glenn's expertise and opinion is occasionally sought by the team's manager, it is the manager who decides when players train on the pitch. Should Glenn require materials and equipment, he needs authorisation from the chief executive (in former times the managing director). In the recent past, it was a disheartening job when firms would not send his orders because the club had not paid the bill for 18 months.

In turn he, too, has to manage people. Two of his staff are sent daily to divot the training ground and, when the new training centre is under way, two will be posted there permanently. Occasionally in the past, he has had to pull rank for staff misdemeanours.

> . . . comin' to work late, not pullin' their weight and technical things like not checkin' t'oil on machines or not watering t'pitch or using too much feed on it . . .

Thankfully, the current lot seem a competent bunch. They occasionally play matches in the gym against other backroom staff, and all but one is a true Blade. As part of their job, they receive two free season tickets. Until recently, they could also travel on the supporters' club coaches to away games free. Such perks, however, depend on the club management; since the departure of Harry Bassett, no crates of lager, footwear, Christmas turkey or end-of-year pay bonuses have been seen.

All football fans comment on the state and aesthetics of pitches. I, for one, always envied those clubs who had small strips of contrasting grass shades and thought Coventry in the late '70s were quite flash with their concentric circle pattern. United fans were never to see such designs (okay, Bramall Lane did have a concentric mowed centre-circle for a pre-season match in the mid-'70s) and are not likely to in future. Glenn's preference is for 17-foot bays, which require six one-way mows. A full mow of the pitch takes one man walking about six hours. But it's not all a question of leg work. Keeping a good pitch is a combination of age-old gardening methods and state-of-the-art technology. When nature intervenes, only brute force can compete: for example, snow that has settled can only be cleared by an eight-foot-wide brush tied to the back of the tractor; and heavy rain requires a barrel-spiker punching thousands of holes in the pitch. In recent years, however, university-trained specialists and consultants have arrived annually to re-seed the surface using a cocktail of 90% rye grass and 10% 'creeping red fescue' with a special mix along the wing which grows with little sunlight due to the South Stand shadow. A worm would find five inches of sand, a foot and a half of soil and then clay, and on the way have to negotiate an irrigation system laid initially in 1940, improved on in 1975 and made super-effective nearly 20 years later.

Installed in 1993 at a cost of £200,000, the undersoil heating system makes the pitch playable all year round and the ground staff's life easier. A boiler adjacent to the equipment room pumps hot water into the 14 miles of inch-diameter plastic piping 16 inches below the pitch. It's almost idiot-proof, because a sensor turns it on whenever the temperature drops under 3°C. I say 'almost', because a few years back a night temperature of −7°C caused the thing to overheat and trip out and a home game had to be postponed.

But not all technology has proved itself. A new top pitch and irrigation system installed in 1990 at a cost of £60,000 involved 14 sprinklers popping up to wet the pitch but, because of the potholes they created, they were taken away. Today there are 12 sprinklers on the pitch periphery, but the middle of it is served by two sprinklers attached to hosepipes dragged on by the groundsmen. If a match is postponed tomorrow, it won't be because the pitch is unfit; it will be because the terracing, seats and surrounding streets are considered unsafe. When the most recent postponement occurred, it was a Christmas fixture against Wolves: the pitch was perfect, but the surrounding streets had a couple of inches of snow. Yet, strangely, a year earlier, the Cup fixture against Villa, scheduled to be broadcast live on TV, involved the club hiring two JCB excavators to clear surrounding streets, requesting 150 volunteers to sweep snow from the stands in return for free entry and the ground staff working nine solid hours so the game could be played. The six-figure TV fee was duly paid.

What with the irrigation and heating systems, and the fact that the reserve team have played elsewhere for a few years now, means that the groundsman's job is a luxury compared to that of his predecessors. No longer do 32 hessian tarpaulins need to be laid across the pitch in winter, and no longer will we ever see muddy matches. Like so much of professional football, what was once the task of the unqualified but dedicated has become professionalised. Groundsmen now have an institute and a monthly magazine. Football League groundsmen meet annually for lectures and question-and-answer sessions.

In the rapidly changing world of football, the only thing left that has not been altered in the last ten years is the pitch itself. For many, the pitch is part of their personal geography and the most visible and material representation of what the club is. So much so that, in the past decade, around a dozen deceased Blades a year choose to have their remains scattered around the pitch. Such private and often very moving moments involve Glenn. Initially, the cremated ones' ashes were scattered around the centre but, even in death, some apparently caused damage to the turf! Today, Blades' final resting place is under a clod of turf cut by Glenn close to the touchline. While not likely to be the quietest repose, such a procedure makes the surviving family happy who will hope, like we all do, that the grass is greener on the other side.

The words of St Paul, often recited at religious burials, is sadly inapplicable to the current state of football. 'As you sow, so shall you reap,' says the minister. What this implies is a celebration that says your reward will be equal to whatever good or effort you put into life or a pursuit. This is not necessarily the case in football. Many of those who made four- or five-figure profits from United's stock market flotation had no emotional or historical connection whatsoever with the club. Expect to see their smiling faces in the next yearbook. As the game itself threatens to become a scheduled interruption in marketing affairs, give some praise to those who hoe, mow and mend. Similar to a shareholder, the groundsmen invests and wants to see a dividend. His investment is physical and emotional, made up of his time and dedication. The return he seeks is a good pitch and, through this, he gives a good account of himself and the club. Perhaps the next yearbook might consider recognising the groundsman and his staff, whose performance is one of anticipating nature and is measured visibly and critically by tens of thousands—not the end result of the unknown vagaries of world financial markets.

Sold Out...
Andy Daykin

After 20 years, the trademark trimmed beard has given way to a clean shave in what marketing people might call 're-branding'. The charm and chat remain, and the bronzed features that people in marketing seem to have been born with is the product of a family fortnight in Florida. Now back home, he faces the reality of finding new employment after the football club he served so well for 16 years told him to leave a month ago.

On the afternoon we meet outside his former place of work, we go off on a seven-hour tour which includes two pubs, a computer firm and his family home. Generous in his opinions and in buying pints, the shaving of the beard is, he admits, symptomatic of a new start. What concerns me is how this man is the symptom of the way a football club can waste the talents of dedicated and capable servants without apparent rationale. But this man is not a team manager nor footballer: ironically, in this day and age, he's more important than most of the first-team players because he held the position of commercial manager. He played the role well and is going to be a hard act to follow.

Innovation and business acumen runs in Andy's family. Grandad invented a concoction he named 'Pecto' to relieve coughs and his son became a wholesale pharmacist. A middle-class upbringing in Sheffield's Nether Edge district led to the schoolboy Andy aspiring to become a PE teacher. A teacher spotted some ambition in Andy, and advised him well.

> He said, 'What's gonna happen when you're 40 when you can't keep up physically with the rest of 'em? You're avaricious; you need money . . . you won't get it in teaching.'

A degree in business studies occupied four years before the young graduate found a job in Sheffield's Spear & Jackson tool-makers as 'Sales and Commercial Co-ordinator' in 1976. Paid £3,500 to 'give out pens to sales reps', the upstart in him began telling them how to do their jobs. Torn down a strip, he decided to become a salesman. His rise was rapid: regional manager, then distribution network manager and, in 1978, export manager, which involved the 28-year-old visiting 13 countries in three weeks and learning a few tricks which would doubtless be of great benefit when employed in the world of football.

> After South America, I put in my expenses correct to the penny. The marketing director calls me in. He said my claim was £300 too low. That was a lot of money in the late seventies. He said, 'Try again.' When he did the same trip, he'd invented an extra £300 for himself. So I had to do the same, so he's not made to look a liar.

Made redundant in 1982 when the company merged, he saw an advert for a marketing executive to work in a 'small business in the leisure industry'. The advert added that knowledge of the engineering industry would be an advantage. The latter specification made sense because the small business was Sheffield United FC and the local industry was considered the paramount one to tap for money.

A London-based recruitment consultant handled the interviews. Asked which team he supported, he responded with 'Sheffield United', whom he had followed since childhood. Showing him a copy of *The Sun*, which contained an article about a chap called Reg Brealey and his development proposals for Bramall Lane, the consultant explained that the new job was to market this dream. Driving a van for the family business to keep him ticking over, he was finally called to Bramall Lane and faced an interview panel of Reg Brealey and Dick Chester, then company executive. Chester was cynical about Andy's football loyalties, but changed his mind when the interviewee answered every question about United correctly. He accepted the job in August 1982. The early days were not easy, because United already had a commercial manager in the shape of Derek Dooley who did not see the purpose of a marketing executive. Looking back, Andy considers that Derek was probably right at the time.

> I didn't know what I was doing; neither did Reg Brealey, but I didn't worry 'cause it was my team I was working for.

What Andy could do was calm the chairman's excesses. New to football, the chairman had big ideas which were a bit far-fetched. He wanted to fly celebrity United fans into towns and do leaflet drops from aeroplanes days before away games and use the local media to inform locals that the 'Blades were coming'.

> Luckily it never happened! With some ideas he was years ahead of his time. He was like that, though: always having ten ideas. Out of them one would work and could make him a fortune.

A serious heart attack struck Derek Dooley in 1982. Instructed by Dick Chester, Andy took over his job and became the most successful fundraiser in the club's history. On his return, Derek became a director and Andy commercial manager. The pair became and remain great mates.

The game was about to take off commercially and Reg Brealey was taking the club places. First stop was Brunei in 1983 to meet the Sultan and a United juniors side played his Select XI to commemorate the opening of a stadium. Not yet 30 years of age, Andy was presenting the team to the richest man in the world. The following year, United were in China via Hong Kong, Tokyo and Sarawak. The club's sponsors, Simmonds Cutting Tools (a deal negotiated by Andy), had begun trading links with the Far East and promoted their product through the newly promoted United. A paying audience of 100,000 and a TV audience of 200 million watched the Blades. Two years later, the team toured the USA in a schedule arranged by Andy and ex-Blade and Tulsa resident Alan Woodward. Another tour took in Abu Dhabi and Dubai.

Mates and memories of tours and good times remain by the score. The players were a large part of his social life for 16 years. In his younger days, he was part of their safaris to Josephine's and in Vinnie Jones he

Cheers: Andy finds Sky TV presenter
Anna Walker in exuberant mood.

found one of the nicest people he had encountered in caring for other people. The hard man would always pick Andy first when the squad played volleyball or head tennis. In return for such kindness, Andy once struck Vinnie, and lived to tell the tale after the latter had thrown him fully suited into a hotel pool.

In United's archives, the name 'Daykin' once appeared on the team line-up after he had played half a game for United against the Jersey national side. A four-man card school the night before (which included Andy) had ended in a disagreement and two players in hospital. Cometh the hour, cometh the man, and his first touch saw him skip past three before being dumped on his backside by a big bugger much to the hilarity of his new-found team-mates.

Hilarity and absurdity were part and parcel of one particular era. He was once dismissed from his job by the team manager in a Sheffield night-club. A recently sold United player was a good mate, and, in his absence, the manager who sold him began to pour forth a drunken tirade about him in front of the squad. Andy answered back.

It was the least I could do. Anyway, ✶✶✶✶✶ went apeshit; told me there and then I was sacked. He couldn't sack me: that wasn't his job! He couldn't remember any of it next morning.

On the downside, he had tasks to do which were his responsibility, but not pleasant. Fortunately, he had to dismiss only two people in 16 years for having their hands in the till.

By the time he departed, he had a personal assistant and a department to look after. And, because of the dominance of finance in football post-1990, in a sense everything at Bramall Lane was related to what the commercial side were doing. Initially and single-handedly he bought goods for the souvenir shop, sought sponsors, ran the lottery and produced the match programme. Match days saw him on the pitch taking penalties with mascots and handing out cheques to winners of draws and generally being there and about and everyone's mate. Years later, he would have staff to do these tasks for him while he concerned himself more with brochures for corporate clients and six-figure sponsorship deals.

Older fans will remember that commerce and marketing in football was once a question of Golden Goal tickets, Bovril and Wagon-Wheels, match programmes and season tickets. Then, in the early 1970s, the club opened a souvenir shop in a terraced house on the corner of John Street. Opened by the mini-skirted, white-booted blonde babe and lead singer of Pickety Witch, the ribbon was cut and money poured in. Today, the shop approximates a small supermarket and is found under the 'Arnold Laver Stand'. Is this success down to the commercial manager?

> Not really . . . it builds itself . . . people buy things. That said, it survives on replica team shirts.

When in the ground, fans can sit and read the match programme and, when the team trots out, read the logos on the team shirts. Andy had a hand in both. The match programme has changed radically over the past 16 years. A sloppy publisher and writing credits for various people had provided for a chaotic document and poor delivery schedules. In the mid-1980s, Andy appointed a new editor and negotiated a new printing deal. Sources of information available to fans were expanded with the introduction of the 24-hour club-call phone-line and later a United page was set up on the Internet. As for the shirts, Andy got a few deals in his time: one in the early 1990s with Avec was worth three times the previous deal. Shirts sell, and the biggest seller was the luminous yellow away strip of the early 1990s seasons which sold over 20,000. That product remains Andy's pride and joy.

The commercial activities that have been manifest in British football over the past 20 years have their origins in the sporting experiences of the USA. It is no coincidence that Andy returned from a week's fact-finding in the mid–1980s full of enthusiasm for what he had seen. Awarded a bursary from Rothman's Tobacco, he spent a week at the Kansas Chiefs American football franchise. One lesson he learned was that the US did not have all the answers: for example, they could not fill a stadium on match day because the game was televised. Furthermore, any financial gain from sponsorship went towards the cost of advertising the next fixture. In Britain, the media are expected by clubs to do the same task for free. What he did like, and copied on returning, was the concept of group sales, i.e. targeting a group, be it boy scouts or a factory, and offering them a deal and maybe a chance to play a five-a-side on the pitch before kick-off.

Many of his innovative ideas fell on deaf ears. Such inertia would cause many to seek new employment. Why didn't Andy?

> Because the job became my life. You forget you're an employee and become part of the club. It was like going home, not going to work. I was a Blade and all I ever wanted to do was work for United.

The job never had specified hours. Over time, he received pay increments and, with these, security of employment. The job could ruin a social life when a quiet drink was made impossible by inquisitive Blades wanting to know the inside story on this and that. As the presumed source of match tickets, he found many mates in times of scarcity! The long hours he now regrets.

> Six days a week meant I've missed some of the life of my two boys . . . but I let it happen.

Andy's presence at all away games when board members were notably absent always impressed me.

> I didn't have to go to any away games if I didn't want to. But I supported the club and I considered that you had to be seen supporting the club. I loved going to games.

At times, his duties were way beyond his job description. When mobs of Blades gathered in the car park baying for the dismissal of managers or chairmen, he went out with them as they addressed their critics. Consequently, abuse came his way as fans assumed he was part of their regime. When I ask who was his boss, the answer is that it depended on who owned the club! For 13 years, this was Reg Brealey; then, following him, matters were not so clear-cut. In recent times, the executives of the club (of which Andy was one) reported to in the main non-executive board of directors. But, too frequently since 1992, nobody was certain who owned the club or who reported to whom.

Sheffield United now exists as an FC and PLC; the flotation was reported to have brought in £11 million to the club to reduce debts and buy players. But why the team's two leading goalscorers were sold in the first month of 1998 was never explained to fans or investors or even the team manager who left soon after. Such sales cost the club promotion, which ultimately cost the club millions. It was not an action of men who love football; it was an action of men who love balance sheets. If confirmation of this opinion was needed, it came when the chief executive addressed a shareholders' meeting and told them that, if growing potatoes on the Bramall Lane pitch could bring a greater financial return, he would happily plant the seeds. Maybe this is an appropriate time to ask who are the most important people at a football club. This vague question requires clarification, so I take it step by step. How important are shareholders?

> Right now, no individual owns the club. There is a major shareholder, but the club is really owned by major financial institutions like Commercial Union.

At flotation in 1996, Sheffield United FC was valued at £28 million with shares valued at 65p each. As we speak, the shares are worth 29p and the club is worth half of what it was floated for. Not exactly a good business deal there, then, but no one can pin that one on Andy. Neither can they blame him for the revolt that has been ongoing now for about two years involving the 200 original shareholders. Offered £3,000 for their share, plus ten years of free season tickets, they refused and reminded the new chairman that their shares gave them free football in perpetuity.

How important are season ticket holders?

> They're the be-all and end-all. You should do everything to sell them. Say you break your leg and don't come for the next three home games, you might not come again! If you've a season ticket, you'll come and watch even if the team's shit. The danger is you stop going and enjoy not going.

The turnstile-paying fan is worth little to big clubs today. It's hard to accept, I know, but only about a third of match-day income at Bramall

Lane comes from the cash-paying punter. The big money is from the variety of schemes that have grown up in the last 18 years.

Take, for example, the Executive Club, begun in 1981. This officially demarcated fandom into an élite section, physically differentiated from the rest and with privileges. Membership, which was costly, produced a car-parking space, cushioned seat and private pre- and post-match bar and refreshments. Now 450-strong, there is obviously demand for such forms of spectating. Then came corporate boxes. United were one of the last 'big' clubs to install them, but, with the construction of the John Street Stand in 1996, 31 became available. Only four remained unsold last year. At this new executive level, match-day corporate hospitality caters for 850 people, which meant a new duty for Andy: 'box hopping'—ensuring that those who paid well get well looked after. But what is it that the club is selling in such deals? Taking his time to answer, the quiet reply is: 'Sheffield United . . . and me! It's important that I come out of it with people happy.'

The first-ever sponsored match at Bramall Lane occurred in August 1975. The philosophy of match sponsorship is simple in the eyes of Andy: 'make everybody happy'. By the mid-1990s, sponsors would pay around £5,000, depending on the opposition and, in return, 30 people were guests of the club. Associate sponsors paid less and fewer of them were allowed in and a poorer fare was offered for their bellies. On the day, sponsors were met by Andy, taken on a tour of the ground, given good seats and allowed as much booze and grub as they could eat before and after the match. Free food and beer? Surely in Sheffield there would be no profits for the club at the end of the day? I was wrong!

> You'd be staggered as to how little people drink and eat. The average bar bill is about £10 a head.

Mugs!

At one time, match-day sponsors wanted in-your-face advertising. At one time, fans endured pre-match and half-time entertainment in the shape of flotillas of new cars or beach ball pushes with glamorous young ladies or giant inflatable sumo wrestlers. Now sponsorship is generally more low-key and is about branding and strategic hoarding around the pitch, with an eye not so much on the match-going fan, but the TV viewer.

Others want to use the ground for purposes other than money-spinning. It was Andy who dealt with requests to marry on the pitch or to dispose of deceased Blades' ashes. That Bramall Lane was packed to the rafters on a few occasions was also down to Andy. For a week in 1984, the evangelical proselytisings of Billy Graham brought in tens of thousands from all over Britain. Later years saw the ground bounce to the sounds of Bruce Springsteen and the pitch get ruined by fans urinating on it! Then there was Errol Graham winning boxing championships . . . then it all stopped. The Council would no longer grant a music or entertainment licence to Bramall Lane while they had their own Don Valley Stadium gathering dust.

For those who attend Bramall Lane only for football, what you have to pay to enter will be a subject you have already discussed. Between 1982 and 1992, admission costs rose about 400%. Who decided what to charge? The answer is that the decision on charges is ultimately made by the board of directors, the commercial manager having given quotes to the company director who will be seeking maximum revenue. If maximum returns could be achieved by lowering prices, Andy assures me the club would do it.

> Economists call it 'inelastic demand'. It's like cigarettes: put the prices up, people will still pay for them. Football is grossly over-priced but, compared to other clubs, United are not expensive. You do have the opportunity to rip people off in football. You sell the game for what you can get for it; it's like selling a house.

Or is it? For all the market-speak about clients and product loyalty, football is beyond simple product placement. Loyalty remains even when the product is awful, and true fans do not seek the product elsewhere, even if it is better. Fans, in a sense, are marketing fodder.

One idea of Andy's, implemented only a few weeks ago, is the introduction of classical music over the PA system. Years ago, when he mooted this, no one on the board swallowed it. As I write, the day before United ran out to a classical piece which segued into the theme tune for TV series 'The Professionals' the moment the players were visible. On top of this, fans have to endure trashy pop tunes whenever the team scores and at the end of a victory. Maybe I'm showing my age, but the sooner football does away with this nonsense, the better. But I doubt it will, because the authorities are trying to destroy spontaneity. Having imposed all-seater stadiums which ensure a sanitised regimented space and which facilitate the photographing of all therein, the next step is to destroy the spontaneity of chants that may contain unflattering messages to the directors or are considered inappropriate to some middle-class family ideal.

Some punters, however, have started to vote with their feet. Only five years or so ago, United were the eleventh-best supported team in England. Now the gates position them around twentieth. Boardroom turmoil? Poor football? Who knows what else made fans disappear? While marketing people can tell me that the game has never been so popular and talk of new target audiences, I remain sceptical and await the day the game loses its fashion and the bubble created by corporate sponsorship bursts. It might be sooner rather than later. Fortunately, Sheffield does not have the same new middle classes as London, which make for such nouveau-chic fandom as found at some Premier League grounds.

Gates being what they are, a few questions remain: namely, are crowd attendances ever fiddled? And where does the money go? Surely, crowd figures are massaged to reduce the amount declared for tax? A moment's thought gives the following measured answer.

> I might have come into the club at the end of that . . . but I can assure you in my time there is no such thing as a director's turnstile for their pockets. Mind you, in recent years we lied about attendances—but actually raised them! You count all members of schemes who don't enter the turnstile as if they had all turned up, which they won't do.

But why do this and who did it? The answer was certain men more senior than Andy and the reason was probably to make investors think the club could attract more people than it actually did. And where does all this income go?

> Players' wages. Many believe footballers are grossly overpaid and that's what the commercial department are working for—to pay them.

This fact of life will make commerce more significant in the game and make the role of the commercial department even more crucial to clubs. Yet the biggest money-making venture that Andy provided came once again from the pockets of fans as they gambled on the 'Blades Revival Scheme'. Begun in the mid-1980s, the scheme was similar to that at other clubs who had exploited a loophole in the law on licensing. Enabling a weekly payout of £1,000 and an annual £20,000 prize, the scheme was sold to fans via huge publicity and the hiring of a Sheffield nightclub for two nights. Over 4,000 fans attended the presentation and learned from Andy of the financial sacrifice in Sheffield terms: 'Two and a half pints of beer a week'. It had, 12 years later, a membership of 2,500 and brought the club an annual profit of £150,000, which went towards the cost of buying new players.

The best deal that did not ask fans to contribute came typically enough from a Sheffield brewery. A four-year deal three years ago took a year to negotiate and brought United—alongside Sunderland whom the brewery also sponsored—the most lucrative sponsorship deal in Division One at £300,000 per annum. Should you enter the souvenir shop, the best-selling item that Andy provided was the 'Blades on Tour' t-shirt from the mid-1980s. The idea was borrowed from a rugby club t-shirt, the front of the shirt being a caricature of a bloke wearing hobnailed boots holding a full pint pot. On the back was the fixture list for the season. The most original item, Andy felt, was the commissioned painting of Bramall Lane by Sheffield primitivist Joe Scarborough. Selling at £50 each, all 500 limited-edition prints went like hot cakes.

Other objects Andy takes responsibility for include 'Captain Blade', the gonk that minces around before every home game waving to the crowd. Why do clubs feel that all teams need one of these? Before him came the inflatable swords from the time of the inflatables fashion, circa 1989. Then came his parting shot when 1998 saw the whole of the John Street Stand converted into the 'Family Enclosure', and the return of another version of the luminous lime-green shirts which was the best-selling 'away' strip in the history of Umbro's production.

His job required him to market concepts that were not of his making. Thus he inherited the task of reinventing Sheffield United as 'The Family Club', an idea that originated with chairman Reg Brealey. This is where Andy and I part. The daft cliché was begun in 1981 and has accompanied every item of club literature ever since. With this comes a market-driven philosophy that the ideal football audience are families and with this the concept that the match-day experience should be akin to a family gathering. This pisses me off no end. Firstly, United are not a family club and why should we celebrate 'the family', anyway? Secondly, if clubs were not so greedy, young fans could be let in half-price. But no: they have to pay money to join schemes just to enter the match. Thus casual young fans are victimised because they cannot get reduced entry without joining a scheme. Finally, the 'family' ideology gives police the excuse to impose any morality they wish, particularly on the young working-class men who constitute the majority of the footballing audience and to whom the label of 'hooligan' is so easily applied. Now, thanks to this family ideal, fans are arrested for using a swear-word, be it in jest, hate or by way of commentary, and those that are boisterous in their singing and goal celebrations are subject to surveillance every match and their mug-shots and identity are held on police 'football intelligence' databases. I'm on a losing wicket, though, with Andy.

> Football's no longer a game for groups of blokes who go and have
> five pints then come in and stand together.

Groups of blokes, though, are still the backbone of the game at Bramall Lane.

What is football at the top level today? To me, it is a game over-obsessed with profits, forever seeking sponsorship, exorbitantly priced and involved in the manipulation of shares. It is a game where contracts seem to mean little, where fans are ceaselessly exploited and, thanks to media investments, it is promoted with ridiculous hyperbole. The people who sustained the game for a century are now not wanted; the ideal fan will be the one who watches the game at home on the pay-per-view TV channel selecting a variety of camera angles and, inevitably, in future, virtual reality techniques.

The irony, in a sense, in this scenario is that a man who diligently worked for the club he supported and who made millions for them is out of work because the personal image of a man higher than him at Bramall Lane and the revelation of certain truths could be detrimental to the club, and implicitly this could affect investments and share prices and sponsors. The game he fed for so long has now bit him. Now a mere spectator at the match, does he look back with any regrets?

> Not pushing myself harder in the eyes of the board. Over the years,
> I should have said I want a reward commensurate with service . . .
> maybe a place on the board and a serious role in the club. I did a good
> job for 16 years.

In truth, he did, and was recognised by his peers when three years ago he was elected to be chair of the Football Commercial Managers' Association. Offers came his way from other clubs, but he turned them down—he was a Blade.

Arriving at work a month ago, he was given an hour to clear his office. As we talk, two men are performing his old tasks. The club's longest-serving full-time employee of 16 years is now relieved of his job. Now aged 44 and unemployed, how does he feel?

> Shit. Many people have been nice to me. It hasn't hit home yet. I'm
> not bitter towards the club so much as to one individual. I still speak

daily to some players and people down there. It's like a wife you're still trying to convince not to leave.

Condolences have come from the world of football and marketing. One day, however, the calls of commiseration will dry up.

I know . . . something's gone out of my life. This is my divorce and what pisses me off is I don't know why. I haven't done a thing wrong.

Former players and managers of United are still mates. At his home, he took four calls in two hours from ex-Blades. I was impressed.

His dismissal has nothing to do with marketing ability and everything to do with indiscretion. The full story will probably become public knowledge via a court of law. Thus the club loses a servant and capable employee. And another local connection is severed to be replaced by faceless men who did not know where Bramall Lane was a few months ago, but who are now drawing a good wage. Personally, I think Andy is irreplaceable.

Mr Chairman

Professional football does everything to castrate that energy of happiness, but it survives in spite of all the spites. And maybe that's why football never stops being astonishing.

(Eduardo Galeano, *Football in Sun and Shadow*: 204)

Steak and Veg...
Reg Brealey

The story of the gingerbread man tells of an ambitious biscuit boy who ran from the baker's oven and, after many trials, tribulations and taunts, is eventually, while attempting to cross a river, eaten by a fox who was pretending to assist him. It was a terrible deception inflicted upon a boastful naïveté. Just maybe there is a lesson in life for all of us there. And, for those who get involved in the higher echelons of football club ownership, there's surely something in the parable to heed. Anyway, that's by the by, because the reason I mention the story is that the man with whom I'm sitting has just rewritten it and, having changed the words somewhat for educational purposes, now has a publisher and hopes to make a lot of money.

Aged 60, the dignified, but ever-bemused-looking chap with the thick-lens spectacles tells me further how the profits could then be used to invest in the local school of which he is governor. Over a drink in the social club of Dr Marten's League side Grantham Town (known as 'The Gingerbread Men'), the same man tells me of his version of a 16-year involvement with Sheffield United which saw a mass of controversies, the full details of which few people ever knew. Furthermore, the mystery of his nickname known to the players and officials at Bramall Lane is explained to me: 'Steak and Veg' rhymes with Reg and it all had something to do with Harry Bassett and Cockney rhyming a decade or so ago.

The Cockney contingent have long gone. Where Reg came from is more interesting. From what Reg knows, the Brealey clan were Nordic and arrived in Lincolnshire from Hatfield in Hertfordshire in the 1940s. Without prompting, he explains where 'the arrogance' comes from: namely, a distant relative by the name of John Brealey who was at one time a fabulously wealthy cotton trader who owned vast tracts of land in central London, particularly Whitehall. Over a century or so ago, the government took the land to build the Home Office and Foreign Office, but offered only a pittance in return. The money remained in chancery for generations until it ended with one of the female line who married out and the lucky chap got a wife and a fortune. What this leads to is Reg telling me that, being the middle child of seven, born to a farmer's daughter from Derbyshire and a civil servant in the Ministry of Agriculture, he is from solid rural working-class origins. Rather surprisingly, I thought, he used the Marxist term 'proletariat' to define his origin.

He played football as a lad and followed a team from a distance. His loyalties then and even now are with Aston Villa. His idol was Trevor Ford, to whom he wrote when at Villa and who duly sent his autograph. In exchange for such returns comes lifelong fandom. Football enthusiasm was initially a product of collecting Turf cigarette cards.

> Any youngster who collected these believed they could be the next Billy Liddell or Tom Finney. I was an inside-right, but I would never have made the grade. My problem was the ball: if it wasn't highly dubbed to stop water getting into it, I could never shift it more than 15 feet!

The proudest moment of a footballing career that centred on the village team was winning a trophy and having his winner's medal presented to him by the great Tommy Lawton, who told him he would make the grade one day.

With hindsight, he made the grade all right, but not on a football pitch. Meanwhile, there were a few grades he did not make. Failing his eleven–plus meant no place at the local grammar school. He went to a secondary modern and left school at 16, the day after he went to the labour exchange not knowing what to do for the rest of his life.

> There were two jobs. One was errand boy in the Co-op; the other was office boy in a construction firm. The first job meant one bus ride; the other two. They phoned the Co-op and the manager was too busy to talk, so I took the second job.

From office boy he became the owner of the firm and made his personal fortune. Attached to the manager, he qualified to become a quantity surveyor. Preferring to be a big fish in a small pond, he moved to a company whose managing director had no children and who took the young Reg under his wing for five years. His sudden death was followed a few years later by the death of his successor and Reg found himself at a very young age in charge of the company.

His obvious financial acumen brought him to the attention of local businessmen, one of whom was the chairman of Lincoln City. Facing financial difficulties in 1976, the latter contacted Reg with a view to building a new board of directors and with a view to Reg becoming financial director. Accepting, Reg re-capitalised the club and the same season, under manager Graham Taylor, Lincoln were promoted. The big-thinking manager wanted a new stand and a set-up to emulate what Bobby Robson had achieved at Ipswich. Reg was all for it and had arranged the finance, but was outvoted by a board afraid of losing control. Soon after, the manager left and Reg, similarly seeing no future, left too.

Before long, he got to meet the chairman of Sheffield United FC, John Hassall, through Dick Chester who, formerly at Lincoln City, was now club secretary at Bramall Lane. Facing financial difficulties, Chester suggested to his chair that he had a chat with Reg, who, in June 1980, was invited to become finance director. Two significant things happened. He was invited to watch United play at Grimsby Town in May 1980, and the new director was stunned by a 5,000 Blade following who remained in the ground 30 minutes after losing 4–0 singing their hearts out. Then, weeks after being asked, he produced a financial assessment for Hassall.

> It was a 30-page document as to why the club was going nowhere and I argued it stemmed from various policies: selling young talent to stay afloat and particularly the selling of Sheffield-born players. I fin-

ished it saying remove Haslam and Peters immediately or you'll end up in Division Four. John Hassall threw it back across the table saying he'd never read such rubbish in all his life. But that was my opinion and it was prophetic.

Not long after, United were relegated—to Division Four—and Hassall walked out on the club. The club was £1 million in debt and made an annual trading loss of £725,000. The vice-chair, Albert Bramhall, was ill and, a few months later, died. Asked by other directors to be acting chair, Reg became the full-time chairman on the Bramhall's death. Aiming to emulate what he did at Lincoln, he attempted to re-capitalise the club and launched a share issue. He underwrote the launch and was left owning 90% of them! He wishes to stress one thing: he never wanted to be chairman of United; the job came to him by accident and he remained in it because he was the majority shareholder.

It wasn't a bad arrangement, really. He was the chair and the club gained a millionaire. But how wealthy is he? This provokes a mini-lecture on paper millionaires: shares by the tens of millions, maybe, but cash is different. It's a bit beyond me, but the gist of it, as far as I can see, is that he was rich. Hotels in the USA, Lincolnshire, restaurants in the Mediterranean and London, a construction company, two Piston aeroplanes and a helicopter which he flew himself made him rich in anyone's language. Once chairman of 24 companies simultaneously, Reg tells me it's all over now. However, such wealth inspires envy and legal proceedings.

I used to get sued every bloody week by some bastard. I fight my battles . . . I win some, I lose some. Thank goodness it's all come to an end.

Having established that he maintains he was once wealthy, I am now intrigued about his religious motivation. He was, after all, a member of the Church of England General Synod (a sort of parliament for Protestants involved in doctrine and policy), a position that has to be earned. Chapel and Sunday school as a boy made such an impression that he went on to become a chorister until his late twenties. Serving on the local church council, he became vicar's warden of the parish church. From there, he was eventually elected to the General Synod and served for a decade. Armed with such background knowledge, it is appropriate at this point to address two issues that Reg brought to Sheffield United: the campaign for 'family values' and his highly political clash with the local Labour authority over plans to develop Bramall Lane. Before questioning him specifically on these issues, a reader needs to be introduced to the events. Allow me to tell a few stories.

In the 1980s, with gates declining and debts growing, having just taken over as chairman, Reg Brealey inherited a club with financial problems. As an astute businessman, he could imagine what might be possible financially if only the damaging image of some fans did not obstruct his projects that could otherwise 'rescue' the club (and his pockets). Thus Reg Brealey set about producing, promoting and marketing United as 'The Family Club'. What followed over the years was a concerted publicity effort to promote the new image, which involved photographs and clichés in merchandising brochures describing United as both 'The Caring Club' and 'The Friendly Club'. To encourage the attendance of the young— and their accompanying parents—the chairman, in his first season, periodically gave away tickets and allowed reductions on child admission with an adult ticket. There was more to his scheme than profit: in 1982 he outlined his intentions in *The Star* (10 August), explaining that 'The Family Club' was crucial to the club's publicity, because 'the family is still the most important unit in our nation'. He added:

> We live in difficult times, and Sheffield as much as any city: perhaps more that most. Families are under pressure. There is the recession, unemployment and the associated social problems. We see football as a great safety valve, and making our Club the Family Club is, I feel, a contribution we can make.

The new Brealey-inspired plans to alter the face of Bramall Lane, which accompanied this ideology, were on a grandiose scale. In March 1981, he sought planning permission from the Council to demolish the Shoreham End Kop and utilise the land behind it to build an 11,000-seat stand with private luxury boxes and, behind this, a shopping complex, 150-bedroom hotel, restaurant and wine bar, sports complex, running track, conference centre and car park. The scheme would cost £5 million, but would be financed by a London-based development company called Land Assets and would provide 600 new jobs. However, in September, city councillors declared the plans unacceptable. A stumbling block was the proposed shopping centre, which councillors feared would have a serious impact on town-centre trade. Also, the area was designated as a 'Housing Action Area' by the Council and the scheme conflicted with their plans to serve the district. The councillors also wanted an alternative way of financing the project.

The following July, a new scheme costing £20 million was submitted to the Council with Brealey announcing, 'This time we've got it right' (*The Star*, 30 July 1982). The plan again proposed an all-seat Kop end, hotel, restaurant, sports centre, running track and, in addition, a trade warehouse, residential accommodation and, bizarrely, a plan to bring back cricket matches to Bramall Lane. The proposal was again rejected by the Council, however, and finally dropped when an appeal to the Department of Environment failed. The refusal by the Council was considered political by United supporters. The Tory capitalist was not being allowed to develop facilities for which the Socialist Council had their own plans. It was also believed to be related to football loyalties and, in Blades' eyes, the Council were Wednesdayites.

Although furious at the time with the Council's refusal, Brealey contained his outbursts. Nearly ten years later, on resigning the chair, he cleared his mind when, in an interview in *The Star*, he said of the Labour Council:

> They delight in destroying jobs and enterprises, in killing companies and then masquerading concern. Their maladministration is unbelievable. We wanted the Local Authority on our side in the creation of this complex but they fought us instead of supporting us. We were building to cater for the greatest need of the next 50 years, the leisure demands of the city. I was warned by friends that, at the last minute, they would turn us down because their ideology differs from our own private enterprise spirit. We were sold down the river. I offered to resign as chairman in the belief that I was the political problem supporting a party different from the one in power in Sheffield (article by Tony Pritchett, 'The Day the Dream Died', *The Star*, 3 January 1991).

In the face of political opposition, he decided to leave the club, as there was little in it for him financially. He had, on becoming chairman in 1982, announced he would review his position after five years. In 1982, he launched a share issue worth £1.2 million, but ended up buying 75% himself, and a club losing £2,000 a day when becoming chairman. In response, he injected £1.5 million into the club and, alongside other directors, had, by 1990, put £3.5 million into club funds. It was in December 1987 that Brealey became disenchanted with the club and announced his decision to sell his shares. Following Tottenham Hotspur's initiative, he planned to make the club a publicly quoted company, believing that major companies could be interested in taking shares. A financial broker was quoted in *The Star* (10 April), saying

> . . . several major companies [were] prepared to take a 50% interest in clubs with which they have some geographical link. The rest of the shares would go to supporters, giving them an added interest in their club.

This scheme had come to nothing a year later; no one had made an offer. Interviewed by Tony Pritchett, Brealey explained:

> . . . the situation is that those people who did show an interest wanted to know all about planning permission and development. Football and the progress of the club seemed a secondary consideration and so the talks stopped (*The Star*, 20 December 1988).

This might seem a sanctimonious statement, considering that Brealey himself had been seeking planning permission for development of the ground, and inability to provide funds for players in 1985–86 was responsible for a dismal season. The shares were on sale for two years, but no buyer appeared. Furthermore, Reg tells me that the profits from his proposal would have been ploughed back into the club.

His financial ambitions for his football club were a decade ahead of the times. His personal financial dealings, however, were the subject of immediate scrutiny. Despite winning 'Share of the Year' in 1978 on the stock exchange and being a candidate again two years later, Blades fans generally (without fully knowing why) believed the chairman was 'shady' in his dealings: an opinion that gained some credence when he was investigated in 1989 by the stock exchange and arrested by Fraud Squad officers on suspicion of 'insider dealing'—making use of privileged information about a company before trading in its shares—centred around shares in an Indian-based company of which he was chairman. Facing Crown Court in London in 1990 on charges under the Company Securities Act 1985, he was acquitted.

A month later he was arrested in India and questioned on allegations of breaching currency exchange regulations. The issue concerned his chairmanship of the world's largest jute-producing factory, which employed 18,000 people. Accused of not paying £2.5 million in pensions and not paying wages for six weeks, Brealey claimed the event was a vendetta against him by a former employee—a company secretary—whom he had sacked. A week later, *Star* readers learned from Tony Pritchett how, having been released from custody, he was helping a 'barefooted street doctor treating paupers and beggars in Calcutta'. In 1988, he had become the chairman of a jute-producing company called Titaghur. However, in 1990, the London stock exchange cancelled its share listings, stating there was insufficient financial information about the accounts. The Crown Court judge dismissed the charges after only two days and awarded him costs.

A few days later, readers learned that, when he arrived in India, he had planned to modernise the factories and give 20% of voting shares to a workers' trust. This, however, had not materialised and, by March 1993, the company had a trading loss of £4.2 million (*The Star*, 29 April). Faced with accusations of failing to match employer pension contributions in the mills, an arrest warrant was issued against all directors by an Indian court, but no extradition order presented. In April 1994, disturbances at the jute mills saw mobs rampaging and managers beaten and the temporary closure of the mills. The problems were, in his opinion, due to the inconsistency of suppliers (*The Star*, 24 April). Meanwhile, an organisation called the South Asia Support Group passed leaflets around the city publicising how an assembly-line worker at the jute mill died of starvation—although no such person was ever identified—and that his family held the chairman responsible.

At the same time, he yet again attempted to extricate himself from another liability: the chairmanship of United. However, a few dramas had unfolded in these years which made the football world watch with interest and then laugh at the farce that developed.

In August 1989, Reg was quoted as speaking of 'the most expensive love affair man can imagine' in a message to Blades Revival Club members explaining how he joined the board to do a job as finance director then 'fell in love' with the club. The lovers parted soon after when, in March 1990, the club was 'sold' to Mr Sam Hashimi, an Iraqi-born businessman apparently prepared to pay £6.25 million for his shares. National tabloids pictured Hashimi wearing a United scarf laughing with team manager Dave Bassett and pledging a million pounds towards players. Sam would not deny rumours that he was only a broker in the deal, but would not reveal who the person was who had put up the money because 'they are people who like their privacy protected'. On the same day, a front-page story told how Mr Brealey had been prohibited by law from selling shares and assets after an injunction was served on him by the Midland Bank and then cancelled a few weeks later.

Four days later, Paul Woolhouse a Sheffield-born property developer and chairman of a company involved in metal, computers and property and, from 1987, the club's second-biggest shareholder, made an 'unconditional offer' to Mr Brealey to buy his 63% shareholding. Sam Hashimi, meanwhile, claimed his deal was 'watertight' (*The Star*, 10

March), and referred to Reg Brealey as his 'dear friend' (*The Star*, 12 March). Two days later, Mr Brealey appeared to respond to this when saying, 'There is no alternative but to support the man I supported in the first place.' It would seem that he had backtracked on his statement when, in June, Paul Woolhouse became the club chairman, paying only half of what Hashimi was publicly offering.

While the dispute was ongoing, Mr Woolhouse and four other directors requested that Hashimi stay away from the home match against Manchester United in the FA Cup quarter-final or risk being turned away. The group declared their scepticism (somewhat sanctimonious, as it turned out) about his bid 'until his personal and financial credentials have been established beyond doubt'. His non-appearance prevented a showdown for the awaiting TV cameras and journalists. Later in the month, he was again publicly informed that he would not be welcome at the ground.

Meanwhile, Hashimi arranged a meeting with Reg Brealey's brother, Len, in a Sheffield hotel. *The Star* got wind of this and interrupted, to the annoyance of both parties. When questioned, neither would specify the nature of their discussion. In June, Hashimi demanded compensation from his 'dear friend' if his bid failed. Hashimi, meanwhile, showed the press a signed contract entitling him to the shares. The club's senior director, Dick Wragg (vice-president of the Football League and FA) demanded Brealey call a board meeting to enlighten them on what was going on. The board at this point could read in the papers about another local businessman negotiating with Brealey about buying the club: a claim that the named man promptly denied the next day!

The courtroom, however, was to become a familiar surrounding for Mr Brealey. In June 1992, he lost a legal dispute with Paul Woolhouse, then sued him over breach of contract regarding payment of shares. In 1992, possibly forgetting his 'love affair' with United, Mr Brealey became a director of Chesterfield FC (12 miles south of Sheffield). Len Brealey then brought a High Court writ against the club for alleged debts of £¾ million owed to his brother. Mr Woolhouse, meanwhile, agreed to pay the Brealey family's Gibraltar-based company ELSE (1982) Ltd in instalments for the club's shares, which the Brealey family would reclaim if he defaulted. By August 1992, Woolhouse's arrears were £300,000, so another agreement was negotiated with Len Brealey; this not only reduced the total price, but actually loaned Woolhouse money! Even this did not work.

In October, Len Brealey began High Court proceedings to reclaim United's shares with a view to selling them to a new buyer. Six weeks later, Woolhouse's assets were frozen by the High Court, due to an injunction taken out by five companies. The musical chairs continued when another director, Alan Laver, took over as temporary chairman of the club. The affair got shabbier: the managing director, Derek Dooley, known to favour a different bid to the one ostensibly in power, was banned from travelling with the team by Woolhouse. The reason was that ELSE (1982) had approached him to be chairman if they won the impending court case. The club then suffered the ignominy of a transfer embargo, when in October 1992 United were barred by the Premier League from signing new players because they had failed to pay Leeds United £25,000 owed to them for the loan of two players.

Soon after, Woolhouse's problems got worse: his wife left him and was threatening to freeze his assets during the divorce wrangle. (Another irony: 'The Family Club' almost financially ruined by the institution of marriage.) Trouble also came from a Belgian company to whom Woolhouse had mortgaged his company. In late 1992, they claimed he was using company money to pay for United's shares. In October, Woolhouse stepped down 'temporarily' as chairman of the club and became a director and 'chief executive', thereby removing Derek Dooley from the job and permitting himself to be paid a salary of £100,000 per year.

In December 1992, another High Court hearing began on the subject of who owned the club. Unusual personal details were revealed when the Court heard how, during a row with Len Brealey, Woolhouse had threatened to publicise the rumour that Reg was a homosexual with a flat and 'friend' in Bangkok. This produced a counter-claim that Woolhouse's wife had left him because he was having a homosexual affair with his accountant. Mr Woolhouse denied making the threats, stating that a former player had contacted the *News of the World* telling them of Brealey's secret sexuality and illegal cash-in-hand payments to players. Then, to cap it all, a High Court judge told Woolhouse he was a liar regarding information he had given Len Brealey about the *News of the World*. The Court ruled that the shares should return to the Brealey family, whose immediate response was to demand an extraordinary general meeting of shareholders to force Woolhouse out and then to sell the shares.

Meanwhile, at the club, long-serving director Alan Laver considered resignation, demanding repayment of his £¾ million loan to the club. Len Brealey then announced his plan to get rid of the current board and replace them with Derek Dooley as chairman and two new faces: a Sheffield car dealer turned business entrepreneur and a Scarborough property developer. Len Brealey also went public and told of how £44,000 had gone from the club to Woolhouse in wages and expenses since March (*The Star*, 7 April). No doubt at the end of his tether, Len Brealey, in April, handed various documents to the South Yorkshire Police Fraud Squad.

Two days after the court hearing, Woolhouse was relieved of his position as United's chief executive. The situation was eased somewhat at the annual general meeting in May, when both Woolhouse and another director (Michael Wragg) lost their seats, while Steve Hinchliffe perhaps pre-empted his loss of face by resigning beforehand. Woolhouse left with two years' annual pay. A few weeks later, a recently appointed director, Kevin McCabe, quit (having held the position for five weeks!), leaving a board of only four men: Arnold Laver, Len Brealey, Bernard Proctor and the recently exiled and now returned managing director, Derek Dooley. Dooley was chairman until June 20th when, lo and behold, Reg Brealey resigned his position at Chesterfield FC and returned as chairman, apparently at the invitation of the new board!

What fascinated shareholders at the AGM was the obvious antagonism between the Brealey brothers. It was apparent in the meeting that Len did not want his brother to return to the club for some reason. Observers realised that there was no love lost between the two. But Reg was back, and John Plant, the owner of a local fruit company, was invited by Brealey onto the board. Fans learned he was a United fan for over 30 years and for him it was a dream come true, etc., etc. (*The Star*, 2 July). Such was his love of United that he was the second-biggest shareholder of nearby Chesterfield FC and had been the commercial director for five years!

Meanwhile, Paul Woolhouse was back in the familiar surroundings of the High Court, being pursued for money by five companies to the tune of £1 million and being threatened with jail for contempt of court (July 19th). Steve Hinchliffe was meanwhile preparing to sue Len Brealey for libel regarding allegations of irregularities in a takeover of a Sheffield company of which he was chairman. The legal profession loved Sheffield United.

Amid all this rancour, £6,500 in cash from match ticket sales was revealed to be missing from Mr Woolhouse's office. Weeks later, he began a life as a fugitive. Since February 1994, Mr Woolhouse's whereabouts have been known to very few people. He is arrestable on sight and of great interest to Interpol.

The returning chairman in the pre-season sold Brian Deane, United's best player and top goalscorer, for £2.7 million to Leeds United while the manager was on holiday. Sold on his casting vote (directors Dooley, Laver and Proctor threatened to resign over the transfer at the next board meeting), the sale provoked a storm of protest among the fans, which manifested itself in an immediate protest in the car park followed by dozens of letters to the *Green 'Un* and outcry on Radio Sheffield's post-match 'Praise and Grumble' phone-in. To complicate matters, two directors, Dooley and Proctor, said in *The Star* (13 July) that there had been no financial pressure to sell Deane. Brealey's reply was that it cleared debts.

When Harry Bassett returned from holiday, he was informed that only £1 million was available to purchase someone to replace Deane. Fans could only watch as this reprehensible saga unfolded and were left to deduct that millions of pounds had entered the club's coffers: they could not see any financial crisis. During the 1993–94 season, United spent only £1 million on players—the lowest sum spent by a then Premier League club. As a result, they were relegated. Yet fans believed there was money around. A record sale of season tickets had netted £1.5 million before a ball was kicked. Added to this was money raised from the

A wanted man: Paul Woolhouse.

sale of top scorer Brian Deane for £2.7 million. Added to this was the £1 million trading profit the club made in the year. With £1 million due to the club from Sky TV's transmission of matches, Sheffield United was, seemingly, in a very healthy financial state. All of this sounds good, but the extent of indebtedness, Reg tells me, 'soaked it up like blotting paper'.

Off-the-pitch controversy was never far away. It reappeared in a fusion of the old and new in 1993 when the Titaghur group paid £2 million for a 16,000-acre estate on the Knoydart Peninsular on the west of Scotland. The aim was a project called 'Back to Basics', which was to take young offenders from local authority care and give them fresh air and, possibly, instil in them a philosophy of self-help and responsibility. By April 1995, a national newspaper could reveal that nine employees had not been paid for two months (*Independent on Sunday*, 30 April). The 50 residents of the island formed an association to buy Brealey out; in response he called them 'nasty, selfish buggers' who wanted their island to remain as a sporting estate as opposed to an outdoor centre for deprived children. The estate was reported to have lost £345,000 in its first year of operation. A few weeks after all this, but catalysed by the sale of Brian Deane, 120 Blades met in the Sheffield Trades and Labour Social Club just outside the city centre, heeding a call from a group of six men who were calling themselves BIFA (Blades Independent Fans' Association). Within ten weeks, BIFA had 1,700 members.

BIFA displayed a form of spontaneous collectivism and agitation, of which Sheffield has a long history, although never before expressed around football. But in a city decimated by the past 15 years by world recession, with little industry remaining and one of the country's highest levels of unemployment, there was little left to fight for. In this environment, BIFA became the largest 'non-political' gathering in the city for ten years and the largest independent fans' association in Britain. With the chairman trying to dismiss them as malcontents and agitators and the club disowning them, BIFA had to create an identity distinct from the club they loved and followed, and so invented their own insignia, albeit in the club's colours.

BIFA decided to take their protest to a more public level and targeted the match. Insisting on 'peaceful' and 'fun' protest, they would take no part in any form of threats of violence or criminal damage. One form of direct action was for fans to hold up cards at the match. Distributed free in surrounding streets, the first 'Red Card Day' saw 8,000 referees' red cards with the word 'Go!' raised shortly after kick-off, intended to show the chairman that they wanted him 'sent off'. The next home game saw a similar number of green cards with the words 'Sack the board!' on them, held aloft for one minute as the match kicked off.

While BIFA wanted well-organised strength in numbers, others partook of spontaneous bouts of anger. The 50 who protested in the car park after a match in February 1994 attracted the attention of 70 police officers and eight mounted police. Even more police arrived when in October more fans gathered to chant 'Where's the money gone?' The other source of their agitation was the state of the Bramall Lane ground. With the John Street Stand demolished, the proposed replacement had not been built. Match-day atmosphere was poor, and aesthetically the club looked third-rate. Why, fans asked, would the chairman not build what had been promised?

In the battle for hearts and minds, the chairman had the ear of the local newspaper and could produce his own brochure. After 42 editions, between 1981 and 1985, *Blades News*, a publication inspired by Brealey and given free to fans, containing a variety of news and events, was not seen again until a special issue appeared in November 1994. In this one-off, diagrams and details were given detailing the proposed John Street Stand development, and here the chairman was allowed to explain his thoughts on BIFA. According to him, this organisation was involved in 'anti-Blade behaviour' which 'may well be the ruin of the club'. Furthermore, Reg blamed such people for the delay in building the new stand, arguing that their activities worry money-lenders: '. . . snide, cynical comments do nothing other than spread despondency and despair'. Furthermore, the current predicament was not of his making:

> I feel aggrieved at having to pick up the pieces of a diabolical mess and being criticised for doing it having left it so sound, financially and management-wise.

Further details were revealed. It transpired that Dave Bassett's talk about no money being available for players was a game the two of them played. And, if BIFA were under the umbrella of the official supporters' club, he would visit them anywhere, anytime. Earlier, the chairman had told Tony Pritchett in an interview that 'The official supporters club is the proper vehicle for such matters' (*The Star*, 3 November 1994). Another vehicle at his disposal to present his case was the electronic scoreboard at Bramall Lane, which he used both to announce the intention to build the new stand and to announce the sale of his majority shareholding in January 1995.

In pursuit of getting their views heard, BIFA members sent dozens of letters weekly to the *Green 'Un* letters page in the (usually) vain hope of having them published. Then, a publicity officer was appointed at Bramall Lane in November 1994, and, in response, BIFA encouraged all members to phone him about anything! The club established a dialogue of sorts, when five BIFA members met with Derek Dooley. Admitting that there was a lack of communication between club and fans, he refused their request to see the trading accounts. Unable to give any precise details about the proposed new stand, he had to admit that he had no idea what the chairman's intentions were, nor could he say there and then whether BIFA could be accepted as a bona fide representative organisation of the supporters in further discussion. The fans' protests provoked comments from manager, Harry Bassett. He spoke of the 'poxy' atmosphere on match days and questioned whether the protesters wanted to see United lose their games. But the protests were always against the board, not him, and the following game the fans were more vocal in encouraging the team.

A variety of potential buyers were identified by both BIFA and the local media. A brief mention was given to a Sheffield estate agent who was prepared to invest a six-figure fee of his own if a consortium would join him. Unable to find sufficient takers, this plan came to nothing. A consortium was attempted in November 1994 by a lifelong fan and owner of an engineering firm, but this too came to nothing. Then the familiar figure of Stephen Hinchliffe reappeared, only to articulate what we, the supporters, believed should happen:

> My belief is that Sheffield United should be owned by Blades fans. I don't see the point in some outsider who in one breath wants to buy Manchester City and in the next breath Sheffield United (*The Star*, 15 November 1994).

He promised to obtain enough votes to call an extraordinary general meeting, but failed to do so. His critical comments had doubtless been aimed at a prospective buyer who was to become the chairman in 1995: Mike McDonald.

In April 1994, McDonald was believed to have offered Brealey £2.7 million in cash; Brealey refused. Meanwhile, McDonald publicly sent his best wishes to BIFA. This Manchester-born-and-bred scrap merchant turned business entrepreneur had, in 1993, tried to buy two other

Premier League clubs, and in 1994 tried to buy his beloved Manchester City. When that avenue was no longer open, he looked elsewhere, and Sheffield United was available. He in turn told *The Star* of his intentions: 'we have certain plans and ideas that we plan to bring over from the States'. Without naming who else was involved in the takeover, it was revealed how the proposal for Sheffield United was strictly a business deal. He admitted that the consortium had selected a shortlist of three clubs 'which we believe we can run with', and United had been the lucky winner (15 November 1994). The prolonged arrival of McDonald in late September 1995 coincided with the club's being unable or unwilling to pay the players' wages the following month. By the middle of October, the current (or was it former?) chairman and the intended (or was it new?) one were still sorting out the legal aspects of ownership and, on the first day of November, the manager was told to abandon his plans to sign two players because no one knew for certain who owned the club!

A contract for the new stand was signed with a building company, who were invited onto the pitch, along with a member of the Supporters' Club, before the final match of the 1993–94 season. The first day of construction was declared as being June 6th and completion would be 32 weeks later, i.e. January. On TV and in the local press, the chairman told fans of the impending start on the new stand. In October, regional TV news showed him declaring that work would begin 'soon'; the *Blades News* special stated likewise in January 1995. At the annual general meeting he specified 31st January 1995 and, in June 1995, he had shuffled the start date to August 12th. In response, BIFA organised a march to the building site to watch the first day of building and found it deserted.

Months earlier, in December 1994 a shareholders' meeting saw the press excluded for the first time in the club's history on the excuse that an item in the accounts was sub judice. The meeting revealed an end-of-year operating profit of £½ million, and the overall club debts had been reduced from £5 million to £3 million, with assets in the players (as estimated by the manager) of £6.2 million. In September of the following year, a BBC radio journalist was barred from the ground by Brealey for reporting stories about the players not being paid. Unwilling to play along with this situation, the team manager held post-match press conferences with the reporter in the club car park!

What this saga also produced was a cynicism towards representatives of the local press. Believing that the man who for 25 years had written

about United's affairs was a stooge of the chairman, Blades ridiculed
him in the fanzine and sent him letters of criticism. Throughout the
reign of Reg Brealey, *The Star*'s Tony Pritchett tried to play down the
social differences between chairman and fans. Pritchett had, on meeting Brealey in 1981, offered to be his 'football consultant', for a salary.
Despite Brealey's naïveté about football, which Pritchett had recognised,
the chairman did not take him on in such a role. There were instead
various 'profiles' on the chairman over the years. After Brealey had stood
on the terracing at a match, Pritchett later wrote—under a small headline, 'Kop that! Chairman joins Fans'— of how . . .

> Mr Brealey stood anonymously for a time but was then recognised.
> One fan said 'It was great to see the Chairman among the youngsters.
> He really is one of us, he knows how we think and feel about the team'
> (*The Star*, 4 February 1985).

Certainly, he continued to fawn over him with clichéd epithets: 'a gen-
erous, easygoing despot' and 'man of the people image' (*Green 'Un*, 23
June), later describing him (28 December) as a 'media-loving extrovert'
and later 'admired, even loved, by tens of thousands of supporters to
whom, despite all his millions, he was just "Reg"' (4 January 1991).

An unexpected Christmas present came the chairman's way in 1994
when six BIFA members and two of their children called at his home
on Christmas Eve with 900 BIFA-produced cards bearing a variety of
messages. Inviting the callers in, he argued his position and took their
gifts. The card had a cartoon of Reg Brealey manipulating a tiny figure of Tony Pritchett as he sat on the chairman's knee. The journalist
was apparently none too pleased with the depiction, and reports in *The
Star* spoke of abusive messages in the cards, which infuriated BIFA members who had meticulously censored any abuse.

If he was to leave, the chairman obviously wanted a return on his
investment. He was believed to want £3.5 million, although he had
paid only £1.4 million for the shares in 1981. Claiming he wanted only
his capital investment back (*The Star*, 28 November 1994), the price
he asked for would provide him with a 450% profit. The fans considered his asking price vastly over-inflated. They asked why, only four
years earlier, he was content with the £2.75 million offered by Paul
Woolhouse at a time when the club were in Division One with a centre-
forward and all the attendance money from Sky TV. The fans believed
that the club had money. The club shop had made a profit of £800,000
in the 1993–94 season. Money from Sky TV and the sale of Brian Deane

meant that somebody had money somewhere. Season ticket sales, even when relegated, numbered 8,500, despite crowds declining by 6,000 per match. The 1993–94 season had resulted in £6 million in gate receipts and wages of £3 million. The Blades Revival Scheme would bring in around £200,000 and the club were the eleventh-best-supported team in English football and had the tenth-best operating profit for a football club that season. Regardless of what the fans said or uncovered, the deal with McDonald was finalised in November 1995 and Reg departed.

Now that this background has been explained, readers will hopefully be in a better position to understand the questions and answers that follow.

One of Reg's first innovations at Bramall Lane was to appoint a chaplain to the club. He then wrote to every club chairman in the Football League urging them to do likewise. Over 50 clubs made similar appointments. With this in mind, I ask whether the chance of entering the Kingdom of Heaven as a rich man was akin to a camel passing through the eye of a needle. In reply, Reg gives me a little sermon about how religion and family values underpinned his task as chairman.

> Mine were true socialist values. You can't grow up in a working-class family and say you're a right-wing Tory. You grow up and look at the political arena and find the political avenues which allow you to express certain values. At that time, the socialists could not accept such values; they had lost their way. You could say these things with the Tories.

He speaks well. I was reminded of the time he addressed the massed ranks of Blades in 1986 in a Sheffield nightclub during a public meeting that was to reveal the Blades Revival Scheme. The chairman spoke in religious tones of 'a revival of faith, hope, courage . . . a new spirit is running your club'. Telling listeners how he would be £5,000 a week better off if the money he invested in United had been put into money markets, he asked all listeners to join the scheme and 'Share with me the onslaught of pain.' He had obviously spoken in public before, and now I realise where the practice had come from. The audience was very different, but they shared something in that they were true believers.

Few of his brethren at Bramall Lane would share his politics, however. As treasurer of the local Tory constituency party, he met Margaret Thatcher a few times. While telling me that for 26 years he chaired the governors at his former school, I learn the following.

> My family have given over a million to that school in my time and it's now got the status of College of Technology. When I was a pupil there,

> nearby were two grammar schools. My school got nothing. If I were
> a socialist, I would give all to that school at the expense of the other
> two. Tory values say 'build on strength'.

I'm not in a position to argue with that, so I try a different theme.
For all the talk about 'the family', and its patronage at Bramall Lane,
why did the fans never see Reg's family?

> My children were at boarding school. They would come occasionally
> to football. My wife did come to games, but she is a modest woman
> who did not want to be in the press.

Right. So did he feel the refusal for the planning permission was a political matter? Reg tells me the full story. David Blunkett was the leader
of the Labour Council and Reg, in hindsight, thinks he made the mistake of appointing the former director of planning from the Council
to help his cause. Only later did he find out that this chap and Blunkett
once had a big fall-out from which they had never since recovered. A
friendly councillor phoned him one night and told him that he would
never get his way in Sheffield, saying that the Labour Party would rather
keep the unemployed in their predicament than accept funds from Tories
aimed at alleviating the plight. As for the man who led the Council who
refused his scheme?

> He was a bloody awful councillor but a hell of a good education min-
> ister . . . the best in my lifetime.

The new John Street Stand is much higher than his proposed scheme,
but one of the reasons his was refused was because it would block sunlight on nearby houses.

It wasn't just elected members that Reg fought with locally. He also
took on those who thought they could do what they want even though
no one had ever voted for them—the police. His thoughts on the subject of hooligans were aired on a radio programme in 1983. He explained
how he did not like the word 'hooligan', preferring 'ruffians', as 'hooligans' was a term too often applied to all supporters when visiting a club.
He was, furthermore, happy with the behaviour of his club's supporters,
adding that they had 'got a dozen', like all other clubs, who would 'make
a mess of things', and considered that crowd disorders were nowhere
near the magnitude they were blown up to be. He also questioned the
evidence that hooligans kept people away from the game. Furthermore,
he considered there to be too many police in the ground and younger

policemen, who looked like they were looking for trouble, would receive taunts, their presence being tantamount to saying 'You dare and I am here' ('Hallam Forum', 22 November 1983, Radio Hallam).

To his credit, in my opinion, the chairman was not happy with the way police treated his football fans. In 1990, filmed in his office as part of the BBC 2 documentary 'United', watching police pass the club car park he commented that they did not consider their task worthwhile unless they had arrested a dozen people each match. The following day, the managing director, Derek Dooley, answering journalists' questions, told *The Star* that Mr Brealey was speaking in a personal capacity and that the club had an excellent relationship with the police.

So he was never super-critical of Blade support and he alone of all football club chairmen challenged the police right to decide how many officers should be present at matches. At the time (remember the club was in debt), he had to foot a very substantial police bill which was decided by the police alone. This meant that the more police that were present, the deeper into the red the club went. Ironically, the police's right to do this received strong support from local socialist politicians—who might have been expected to oppose an unnecessary authoritarian presence. However, in this case I believe it was a situation of locals and Labour versus an outsider and a Tory. In this instance, the outsider and Tory was an establishment figure who, for once, failed to exaggerate the issues.

In late 1983, Brealey challenged the South Yorkshire Police Authority's legal right to charge for policing at football matches, arguing that, since the club had not requested policing, no contract existed between them. Besides, he argued, the issue was a public order matter, and therefore policing should be free. He also claimed he could quote figures to show that the costs in South Yorkshire were higher than anywhere else in the country. In response, the police threatened to close the Bramall Lane ground if they considered it to be inadequately policed, and a game scheduled for 30th January 1984 was under threat of having to be played behind closed doors.

An impasse followed and, by June 1985, United were in debt to the Police Authority to the tune of some £122,000. The matter went to the High Court in February 1986, with Brealey telling how he proposed employing a lone police spotter to watch for trouble. This officer would alert others on stand-by outside the ground, and the club would only pay for police called into the enclosure. This somewhat bizarre proposal was, unsurprisingly, rejected. After a hearing lasting a week, Brealey lost the case and the club was ordered to pay £71,500 to the police for their presence at the ground. The judge stated that police duty at the match constituted 'special police services' within the meaning of the 1964 Police Act, and added: 'If the police attend in order to enable the match to take place, then I consider a request to be implied.' Brealey decided against an appeal to the House of Lords, and was left with a £400,000 debt to the Council and legal fees. He tells me now:

> Peter Wright [the then Chief Constable of South Yorkshire] was excellent, a nice man. He said to me, 'I can't allow you to play football matches without policing the ground.' Yet the law stated that police were only in the ground at my invitation. I told him, 'I don't want your police in the ground!'

Reg also insisted on the perimeter fences being removed, following an incident in 1981 when a fan lost a finger, having got his wedding ring caught on the fence when attempting to enter the pitch. Believing fencing treated people like animals, Reg wanted them pulled down, but the police would not allow him to do this. He reflects:

> Had I had my way, fans would not have invaded the pitch and the tragedies of Bradford and Hillsborough would not have happened.

Listening to the accounts of his battles with the local great and good, I ask a question I had not prepared: namely, was he ever the subject of a vendetta? He thinks he was, and one that was from a disgruntled local businessman and a young police officer who knew him. It happened at the height of the boardroom turmoil in 1994 and he believes it was instigated by someone who wanted him out. It began in the boardroom and ended in a police station.

> I would, every game, have a drink before kick-off and one at half-time. I would have some food and leave two hours or so later, well below the limit. On this occasion, I was enticed to drink champagne by a certain individual who poured me another glass and, when it got knocked over, poured me another. He was trying to plug me with liquor. I didn't want it and left it. On leaving and getting into my car, I saw a woman with a baby the car park in a car which had broken down. The husband had gone to fetch some tools and the social club had refused her entry. The temperature was freezing. I took her into the club as my guest and sat her down and, inside, I got chatting to fans. One fan was the worse for drink and, half an hour later, when I'm going home, I offered him a lift. I noticed a police car following me. It fol-

lowed me on and off for 20 minutes and, after I had dropped off the supporter, he then stopped me. He wanted to breathalyse me. I refused to do it without a witness: I didn't trust him. He said, 'I can arrest you.' I said, 'Let's do it at the station.' I was taken there and found to be negative.

Adamant this was a prearranged set-up, Reg divulges who the man was and adds that he was part of BIFA, adding his own interpretation of this acronym, as told to him by one sympathetic Unitedite who explained that, in his opinion, BIFA stood for 'Bunch of Interfering Fucking Activists'.

Well, we're here now. So, before I go any further on BIFA, I'll now ask what dozens of Blades have always wanted to know: namely, was Tony Pritchett on the Brealey payroll?

We had an agreement. I would never deceive him, nor him me. He gave me the back page of *The Star* every day and I would tell him who we were buying or selling. I gave him stories first that were accurate and even sensitive.

As for money?

Not a single penny was ever given . . . nor did he ever ask for a penny. What he did have was total access to dressing room, boardroom, offices, in fact everywhere. I gave him that which no other club ever gave its local reporter.

I think that closes the matter.

Let's talk football. As someone relatively new to the game in 1980, what did he reckon to his fellow chairmen? The answer is that, while some were easier company than others, all were ultimately to remain at a distance.

They were acquaintance. In football you don't have friends because you've got to beat their club and even employ sharp practice when trying to buy or sell a player to or from them.

Describing himself as a 'telephonic chairman', he recognises that he was probably quite a unique figure in football, in that one-third of his life is spent abroad and therefore much of his football business was done over the phone or delegated. For this he thanks Derek Dooley, in whom he found the most honest man he has ever dealt with.

Being a chairman, however, meant that what would have been a small news item became a headline. What would possibly have been of no interest to the press was of interest when a football chairman was involved. Then he mentions the case of Titaghur in India and tells me simply:

> I employ 18,000 people and I'm in England. The company's spread over six townships. There are 120,000 company dependants. There are three shifts a day and I'm the only company chairman. I don't know what's going on in India nor do I know what all my employees are up to. But because I was chairman of a high-profile football club, I'm in the papers.

His time in a Calcutta jail totalled three hours. He was alleged to have given an Indian £2 million, but this sounds implausible and Reg merely adds, 'Business in India is a minefield.'

He tells me he kept well out of transfer deals. In his 15 years, he remembers only being present at the signing of four players, one of whom was Terry Curran.

> Ian Porterfield said, 'I want him; get him for me.' So I talked to some newspaper people to ask him if he wanted to leave Wednesday. Somebody got back to me and said he would and was out of contract and if he signed it would go to a tribunal.

The longevity of the contract he gave to Porterfield (i.e. 10 years) was surely a naïve move? 'Absolutely,' Reg agrees, then tells me what he wanted from Porterfield.

> I said, 'give me a team of Sheffielders,.' Ian said, 'I can't give more than 50%.' Credit where it's due: his teams did contain half of the players born in Sheffield.

It was a policy Reg asked of his later managers. 'I knew that a Blade man was twice as good and would play for nothing.' As chairman, he had to get rid of two managers. The first to go after six years still troubled Reg six years later when he sued for unfair dismissal, which cost the club £90,000 and was, according to Reg, an unusual legal precedent. 'I never sacked him. He drove out of the car park himself . . . but I liked him.' Two years after him came the departure of Billy McEwan, which hurt Reg and brought him to tears—'I hated losing him'—but he was in a minority of one when the board discussed Billy's future.

Then came Harry Bassett, the mention of whom provokes Reg into an imitation of the Londoner which involves a snarl, a cockney accent and swinging his head from side to side: 'Effing this . . . effing that . . . all this crap'. This is the Reg the Synod never saw, and it throws me for a moment, but I'm pleased he did this. I take it as proof that he's not giving me a controlled performance of PR bullshit. Why did their relationship, so good at the beginning, turn sour? Harry tells a joke about Reg. He was the most honest chairman he has dealt with in his time in football, the punch line being: 'He told me on the first day there's no fuckin' money and he kept his word.' I think Reg was going to go off on a tangent about Harry, because he began: 'He tells a story . . .', and then didn't tell me anymore bar the vague but significant admission that, no, the pair of them no longer exchanged Christmas cards. Things deteriorated between them when Reg tried to sell the club in 1991 to Paul Woolhouse: 'Harry was good; like all of us, the right man for the time.' Harry was being courted by the latter to be manager/director, and, when the deal fell through, relations between manager and Reg became strained.

> I always had an arm's-length relationship with managers. The closest I got was to Ian Porterfield because he was a family man with children of similar age to mine at the time.

Anyway, now we're into the ownership saga and the chat gets onto Paul Woolhouse. The story I now hear is that, when Reg returned to pick up the pieces in 1991, he found a situation he describes as horrendous.

> The club were pariahs in the hotel industry—unpaid bills; no coach company wanted to take us—unpaid bills. There were no postage stamps. The only way out was to sell Brian Deane.

The sale was forced through by Reg. According to him, Harry would not have sold him.

> He was the only goalscorer at the club and we shouldn't have sold him, but unless we did we were bust. Deane had been promised his release by Paul Woolhouse—ask him. I honoured that promise and it suited me to do so.

So where did the transfer money go?

> The first tranche of the transfer came by telegraph from the Football League—it was 50% plus VAT: £1.6 million. From that we paid all the bills and reduced our number of creditors from 400 to 50. Ninety per

cent of the telephone calls to Bramall Lane stopped; the morale of the office staff trebled.

Now let's look back a few years. When Reg tried to sell the club in 1989, up popped Sam Hashimi, who was a front, because the real funding was from the Mayor of Jeddah, Saudi Arabia. 'At that time he was investing in England in as big way.' However, the Mayor was not impressed by the publicity Sam generated and, alarmed at all the fuss in the national newspapers, pulled out of any business relationship with Sam.[9] So where did Sam come from? 'He just appeared via my broker and said he wanted to buy a big club.' Was Sam a stalking horse to flush out the ambitions of Woolhouse?

> He [Woolhouse] was talking about 'no way are we having the club owned by an Arab'. But I knew nothing would come of the Hashimi offer. Then it was up to Paul to make his offer.

The pair agreed on a price; it was £3 million. The buyer was to pay Reg £300,000 out of his own pocket up-front and the rest in instalments. As a security, Reg had checked Woolhouse's accounts over the previous two years and found an annual turnover of £800,000, but how much came via shady deals with a variety of other victims he will never know. So, what went wrong with the sale of the club to Woolhouse?

> He did not pay what he had to. He put £300,000 down and then had to give me more, but what he was giving me was stolen from the club—he was paying me out of my own money! I had to go back, but if I hadn't I don't know what would have become of the club.

In the ensuing court case, Reg had to pay Woolhouse a sum of money, but he got the club back from him. Woolhouse had to forfeit everything as he broke the contract. What Reg got lumbered with was a club he did not want, no realistic buyer and a fan group that targeted him, believing he was the root of all the club's troubles.

---

9. In 1998, Sam Hashimi, formerly a married man and father of two, became Samantha Kane after extensive surgery to turn him into a woman. Making national tabloid news, 'Sam' explained that the Gulf War and the stock market collapse known as 'Black Friday' had destroyed him financially and hence ruined his intentions of buying Sheffield United.

> Sure, I got the club back, but my brother had sold our 76% share-holding to 51% and when I returned there was a board of directors who were not of my choosing. They were foreign to my way of thinking.

One man on the board, Stephen Hinchliffe, offered to buy Reg out. According to Reg, the two of them shook hands on a £3.5 million deal and a promise of cash on the nail next day at 2 pm. Where was the exchange done?

> It wasn't. He'd pissed off to Spain on holiday for three weeks. He was the joker in the pack.

Who was the ace? 'There was none.'

Next in line was Mike McDonald, a Manchester-based businessman who presented problems of another nature.

> The fans were calling for my name and telling me to get my act together, but the negotiations with Mike took over a year. He had to do two flotations to raise the money.

When the two shook hands on the deal, the price was £2.75 million, which Reg considers a give-away. The deal also came with a proviso.

> I had signed a contract on the pitch before a match to build the new stand. The fans never gave me credit for that. Anyway, part of the sale deal was that the price was deliberately low because the new chairman had to build the stand: it was in the contract. I didn't have to do that. I could have sold the club for £4 million instead. And I would add that Mike carried out every commitment and undertaking. Bramall Lane is magnificent today.

After 15 years of being the chairman plus the protracted negotiations to sell, which he estimates took around 18 months in all, he left the club he joined when they were in the pits and which he had at one time taken to the top.

> It was a brutal ending. You have to accept the club is never yours; it's always theirs [the fans']. It's the only thing many of them have in their lives.

The BIFA campaign, though not enjoyable for him, does not seem to have had a damaging effect on this man. I asked about the Christmas card affair. He responds by laughing and then telling me a story.

I think half a dozen came with several hundred cards. I met them at
the door and invited them in, and in fact we had a drink and a good
laugh. I took their 'gift' and then the family started to open a few. But
some had messages which were . . . well, my 10-year-old daughter
was opening them and I decided it wasn't suitable.

The memory provokes a chortle and, taking hold of a large envelope
I had brought, Reg gets his pen out and writes down the message as
he recalls it from the one card that stands out most. The envelope I take
home now has on it: 'Dere Redge - plese fuck of'. Possibly he inter-
preted the standard of literacy as indicative of the level of sophistica-
tion of his critics. He then adds that he has kept a handful of the cards
'which I will treasure all my life'.

A few months after leaving Bramall Lane, he returned to watch a match
and considered that he was 'snubbed' by certain board members. Hurt,
he vowed never to return. Then, a few weeks ago, when United were
drawn against Darlington, he attended to watch the latter—whom he
has or had a financial interest in—as the guest of Mike McDonald. This
time he felt he was received extremely well and the men who snubbed
him were no longer there.

How he came to be associated with Darlington is worth explaining,
because one would think that what he went through at Sheffield United

would put him off investing in football for the rest of his life. But there's no predicting this chap. What about the 'love affair' with United? How could you go to other clubs at a later date? The answer is that, shortly after leaving United in 1989, a mate who was the chairman at Chesterfield FC offered him an invitation.

> Being a football compulsive he thought I'd miss the game. I joined them for a little while, which was nice. It was just a few moments of fun.

More fun was later available at Darlington FC in 1996, an involvement he attributes to his old manager at Bramall Lane, Billy McEwan.

> He contacted me when the club couldn't pay the wages. He said, 'Can you help?' I do. This is the procedure: you save the club from bankruptcy and pay all their debts. I then find a buyer who builds them a new stand.

I then annoy him by informing of the latest edition of the football magazine *When Saturday Comes*. Their survey of every club in Britain involved them asking representatives of each club what they considered the 'crucial act of last season'. The reply from one chap who's the editor of the Darlington fanzine states: 'The departure of Chairman Reg Brealey. The man should not run a jumble sale, let alone a football club.' I point this out to Reg, who loses a bit of his cool in his reply.

> I do all that for them and then they say ban me from football? I think I know who it is who's saying that. We sued him for defamation and he settled out of court.

This has riled him, and so I receive the full offensive.

> I find a man to put on the board; I buy shares in the club; sorted it all out; paid their bills; and a £750,000 grant; find a new buyer who gives them a new stand; and take the team to Wembley for a play-off for the first time in their 100 years. Nobody knows what I did for them.

Then came rumours of an involvement with Scottish side St Mirren.

> The club was in a poor financial state. A Scottish friend suggested I become a shareholder; the directors all sign an agreement. My signing took the pressure off the club in the face of the bank and their creditors. One individual then said, 'I can do it—alone.' So I said, 'Do it.'

Now, as we sit in the social club of Grantham Town FC, it is reasonable to ask what precisely is Reg doing here?

> I was invited to the club by a friend who told me that the club was in a state. I looked at the situation and realised it was in turmoil. I told him the job had to be done properly or the club would close. I wrote a financial programme and, having read it, he realises he hasn't got the finance to do it. I then appoint people to manage the plan and they carry it out.

The team on whose premises we have our chat are going places. A new ground, which was used by the Turkish national side for the Euro '96 tournament and later by both Japan and Ajax, contains sponsorship deals that Blades would recognise. The team shirts have 'Ward's' brewery emblazoned on them; the lounge bar has the name of the main sponsors; the programme publicises club open days and sponsorship deals with clothes shops and others. Then, of course, comes 'the family' enclosure and a warning about the consequences of using bad language here. And the name of the club chaplain appears in the inside page. One name conspicuous by its absence is that of Reg Brealey, who wears the regulation club tie and whose Jaguar is parked pride of place in the first bay of the car park. An enigmatic involvement, no doubt, and one that accords with his statement: 'I shall never be a director or chairman of a football club again' (*The Star*, 6 February 1998).

The happiest days at United were, not surprisingly, those that saw the team promoted from the Fourth to the Premier Division. Then I learn that he never watched the whole 90 minutes of a match!

> I'd have a drink then walk around the outside of the ground. I'd watch the stewards and turnstile operators letting their mates in cheap! But I wouldn't inform on them. Then I might watch some of the game from the roof galley or even inspect the toilets in the stand, then a half-time chat with the directors and say something about the referees or 'tough game', or whatever they wanted to hear in football.

Not only did he not see a full game, he also considers he lost a fortune for his involvement. To stress the point, Reg makes a calculation on the envelope which explains how the £3.5 million he invested could have made him 10% interest per annum if left in a bank, which means he has lost £5.5 million in interest alone over a 15–year period.

The boardroom nonsense cost him in more ways than financially. He no longer speaks to his brother Len. Could it be said that Sheffield United cost him the friendship of a brother?

> The circumstances surrounding the matter should never have arisen,
> but it would be wrong to blame the club. I pushed him to the level of
> his financial incompetence. That cost me dearly and our relationship.

How did he see his role at Bramall Lane?

> I came in as a 'foreigner'. I decided my role was to be the foreigner.
> A 'hands-off' distant relationship was best. All my directors were local
> men. I insisted on that: you get no credit for that from your critics; in
> fact, you get remembered for what you didn't achieve. Look at it today:
> it isn't a local board anymore.

But I'm still intrigued as to why a 'foreigner' would want any involvement in something that he had hitherto had no interest in. The reply
brought in the sense of duty again.

> Perhaps the lesson I learned in football was that I shouldn't step in
> too soon. I could, of course, have let the club go broke, twice . . . but
> I was the difference between whether many a man lost his job or not.

So why all the hostility wherever you seem to appear in football?

> You do some things that other buggers cannot do and that annoys
> people.

He has learned a few lessons from football: namely, that the fans who
shout 'you walk on water' will, when they see fit, seek to drown the
same man.

> Those fans who saw the years of decline and then the re-emergence
> of United were sympathetic. But, after a number of years, the younger
> fans who had known nothing but success could not cope with failure.
> That is a lesson every chairman must recognise: that each club has
> a generation of new fans and with them comes a change in attitude.

According to him, the BIFA visit on Christmas Eve contained very
young delegates—the generation who did not know failure. 'They never
gave me credit; they just condemned me for failure.' Then, a sermon,
albeit a small one. Claiming to work 16 hours a day, seven days a week,
he divides society into two: 'those who make contributions to society
and those who live like fleas on a dog's back'. As he sees it, many people
were parasites upon him; they waited until he stepped in and then they

got aboard and profited from his success. So much for certain directors, but what about the fans? 'They got their new stand: objective
achieved. I wish them well.'

Are we likely to see Reg Brealey reappear in football in the near future?
'There are many more challenges in life.' So, what is the future? A pause
is followed by a parable. He remembers being advised as a youngster by
the bishop at his Confirmation who said: 'Aim at the highest and walk by
faith and not by sight and never fear changing course.' He chuckles as
he claims that he followed this advice, but if he saw the man today would
probably squeeze his throat for what such faith got him into.

> I'd never regret anything in my life. I take all they throw at me in my
> stride.

So speaks the gingerbread man who, guided by faith, has crossed many
rivers, but has yet to stumble upon the fox.

Epilogue

THERE WOULD SEEM LITTLE NEED, in this day and age, for TV soap opera scriptwriters when there are institutions such as Sheffield United. It would seem evident from what preceded this epilogue that football clubs can provide dramas that prove that age-old adage that truth is stranger than fiction. While many of these accounts have a unique Sheffield United 'angle', one suspects that similar scenarios take place in football the world over. In which case, what are we to make from all that has been revealed?

With the benefit of hindsight, and never having been a footballer, I am struck by the deference expressed by the players of the 1940–60 generations. Judged by today's standards, such players were far too reverential in what they considered their Blade duties. But I suspect many a reader will lament the loss to the game which was their dignity and decency. Playing as they did, in an archaic system, the wage freedom that came their way in 1961 did not benefit them so much as their successors of 30 years later.

Those who wore the United kit between the late 1960s and the late 1980s displayed different attitudes. Frequently opinionated and idiosyncratic, they belonged to the time when the game became estranged, to a large degree, from its spectators. High wages and the accompanying consumerist lifestyle meant that the young footballers migrated to the new suburbs and competed with pop stars in the new media's fascination with trivia and controversy. Surprisingly few of this era, however, made enough money in football to retire young. Many blew much of what they earned, possibly believing that their football days would never end. Many suffered a degree of personal crisis when the game no longer needed them.

From the late 1980s, a new techno-rational professionalism has affected everybody employed in the club, regardless of their capacity. Whether this has produced a more entertaining or capable footballing spectacle is debatable. All the dieticians and head doctors in the world cannot produce the 'heart' that makes for the good professional footballer. This indefinable asset comes, instead, from the social milieu into which the boy is born where he grows, and which he later takes with him onto the pitch. Playing for the local team was all that many thousands of young men have ever aspired to do. Whether local teams will exist in the next millennium is difficult to predict. Whether local clubs will bother to nurture local talent is even harder to guess at.

What is revealing to me is the number of people who left Bramall Lane angry or disillusioned. The joyous spectacle most evident in the scoring of a goal and shared in the camaraderie of social occasions seem such fleeting moments amid the daily grind of training, which culminates in either first-team football and precarious glory, or non-selection and disillusionment. Sandwiched between these weekly events is the endless repetition that is a prerequisite of keeping fit. But such hard work frequently comes to nothing when injuries are sustained and enforced layoffs require a player to start all over again.

Many players seem to possess a remarkable level of courage. Few readers will ever have to endure catcalls and abuse from thousands of strangers. Few readers need fear, on a weekly basis, that what they are about to become involved in could become, as a result of a vindictive action, a career-ending injury and lifelong disability. The inevitability of being dropped requires an inner strength to continue, and the ever-present threat of transfer to places and to people you know little about makes for an uncertain, and often unwelcoming, future. The arrival of the newcomer is the death-knell for someone else's career.

Who would ever want to be a football manager? For such men, whose main role lies in their ability to motivate and arbitrate, their task is becoming harder and the day of their dismissal more inevitable. While fans always want team victories, the manager now has to contend with impatient directors, whose concerns lie more in stock market prices than League position.

This is because the professional game in Britain over the last 15 years has become an uncomfortable mix of business and sport and, for its followers, an increasingly expensive leisure-time pursuit. In many cases, football clubs have ceased to be the hobbies of local rich men and are now vehicles for investment, wherein the football club becomes subordinate to the PLC, which seeks the finance available from sponsorship and TV coverage and cares little about fans.

But, although the British game has never been richer, the money has never been more unevenly distributed. Those that have it care little for those who do not. This devil-take-the-hindmost attitude could have huge implications for the have-nots, which may well include Sheffield

United. The money-men connected to the club over the past few years have not had the financial payday they hoped their investments would deliver. Defeat in the First Division play-off at Wembley in 1996 saw the share price in the club fall by 30%, and £9 million was wiped off the stock market listing.

The seemingly endless Bramall Lane boardroom saga looks likely to run and run. Rumour of a top-level power struggle circulates as I write. At the last match I attended before completing this book in May 1998, I witnessed the somewhat incongruous situation of the PLC chairman watching the game as, only eight rows behind him, sat the former director and vice-chairman, who that same week had notified him of his intention to sue him for £½ million over what he considered deceit in the sale of his shares during the takeover that turned United into a publicly quoted company.

Money is certainly not the root of happiness at this football club. Fans were informed in May 1997 that the reverse takeover share flotation of Sheffield United had brought into the club's coffers around £12½ million. Furthermore, reports stated the club was in the black for the first time in years and £4 million was available for the manager to spend on players (*Green 'Un*, 27 May 1997). The manager, Howard Kendall, was not impressed: he departed a month after this announcement and was succeeded by one of his playing squad, Nigel Spackman, who took the managerial reins without a contract. Problems soon surfaced when it became evident that the new manager was not permitted full control in the buying or selling of players.

The club's annual general meeting, held in December 1997, proved a hostile occasion for the new board. Holders of original shares were furious at what they considered to be unreasonable behaviour following the club's takeover. Questions were asked as to who was in control of team matters and what role the PLC played in the affairs of the FC.

Two months earlier, plans were revealed by members of the PLC to build a £25-million leisure park at Bramall Lane that would include a housing development, hotel, nursing home and shops. Where the money was to come from to fund this scheme was the subject of much debate. Argument then turned to hostility when, in December, the proposed sale of a centre-forward was put on hold when fans sang his name throughout what was thought to be his final game in a United kit. The prospective Dutch buyers returned home days later without their target, while the United chairman went public to explain that players had to be sold to stave off 'financial suicide', before criticising the attendance of 19,000 as insufficient to sustain the club and pay players' wages (*The Star*, 29 December 1997). The player spoke of his predicament in not wanting to leave United and how, refusing to join an English team a month earlier, had been told, upon his return, to train with the juniors. Not revealing who instructed him to do this, the article significantly told of how the manager did not want him to leave. The public statements of other departing players hinted of an unhappy dressing-room atmosphere and the belief in the words of one that they were mere tools to be used for financial gain.

The chairman and chief executive forced the sale of five first-team players in late 1997 and early 1998 in return for a total of £3.2 million. Matters came to a head in March 1998 when Spackman, having lost his two leading goalscorers eight weeks earlier in deals that were not of his making, was instructed by the chief executive to raise another £1½ million from transfer sales within a week. He resigned, as the club stood third in the League and faced an FA Cup semi-final fixture days later. The chairman told journalists the manager had put his self-interest ahead of the club and, furthermore, had no 'bottle'. He then threatened to resign if he faced any fan protest at the next home match.

Facing taunts from around 100 in the car park, he resigned days later as club chairman and director, but remained involved with the PLC. The following week, interim accounts of the PLC revealed a £3.1 million loss. His successor as chairman told reporters that the chief executive would, from now on, take on tasks 'away from football and team management affairs' (*Green 'Un*, 7 March 1998). Then, in June, a tiny article in *The Star* informed fans that the same man had severed all connections with Sheffield United, both FC and PLC (17 July 1998). Losing the Cup semi-final, United also lost out in the promotion play-offs. In July, the club dismissed the commercial manager and the acting chief executive gave notification of his intention to quit two months later.

Thus, in August 1998, the fans of Sheffield United faced a future in a game almost bereft of sentiment, supporting a club with currently little local identity and apparently obsessed with commerce. The new season opens with supporters following a directionless club, out of touch with the very people who remain the guarantors of its existence.

★   ★   ★

Not every enquiry has to have a teaching purpose. I do not have any moral to pass on, nor do I wish to suggest that this book teaches a reader anything about the game. Suffice to say that football has a future and footballers will still have tales to tell to later generations. Because, as one South American novelist has written:

> Cultured or uncultured, rich or poor, capitalist or socialist, every society feels this irrational need to enhance idols of flesh and blood, and burn incense to them . . . Footballers are the most inoffensive people on which one can confer this idolatrous function.
>
> (M. Vargas Llosa, *Making Waves* [London: Faber & Faber, 1996])